The Egypt of the Pharaohs

Dans les musées ... la nuit emplit les salles où sont les chefs-d'oeuvre ... blocs de marbre soumis aux grandes lois générales qui régissent l'équilibre, le poids, la densité, la dilatation et la contraction des pierres, ignorants à jamais du fait que des artisans morts depuis des millénaires ont façonné leur surface à l'image de créatures d'un autre règne.

MARGARET YOURCENAR, *Le denier du rêve*

Jacket illustration: funerary mask of Psusennes I

Jean-Pierre Corteggiani

The Egypt of the Pharaohs

at the Cairo Museum

Photographs by Jean-François Gout
Preface by Jean Leclant

Translated by Anthony Roberts

Scala Books

© 1986 Hachette Guides Bleus, Paris

First published in English in 1987 by
Scala Publications Ltd
26 Litchfield Street, London WC2H 9NJ

Distributed in the USA by
Harper & Row, Publishers
10 East 53rd Street
New York, NY 10022

Distributed in Egypt by
Les Livres de France
Immobilia
Kasr el Nil Street
Cairo

ISBN 1 870248 10 4 (UK hardback)
ISBN 0 935748 88 1 (US hardback)
LC 87 061730

Filmset by August Filmsetting, England
Printed and bound in France by Aubin Imprimeur, Poitiers

Contents

Preface by Jean Leclant   6

Introduction   7

The Museum and its Collections   9

Map of archaeological sites in Egypt   17

Plan of the Museum   20

Commentaries   21

Chronology   180

Glossary   181

Table of concordance
between various object numbers   184

Index   187

Preface

Can you think of a more exciting prospect than that of a visit to the Cairo Museum; to survey, through a collection of masterpieces and extremely diverse documents, three thousand years of one of the most fascinating civilizations in the world? This is what we are invited to do in this book, under the guidance of Jean-Pierre Corteggiani – and the experience is not a disappointing one. Through a choice of 120 ancient monuments and artefacts which, in itself, is that of an informed connoisseur, the author appears, through his restrained and precise commentary, both a man of taste and a great scholar. Having lived for a long time in a country that he loves, and possessing a deep knowledge of its treasures and its history, Jean-Pierre Corteggiani, Librarian at the Institut Français d'Archéologie Orientale du Caire, communicates his enthusiasm to those who choose to follow him through the galleries of such a huge repository of historical treasures as the Cairo Museum. However this book is not a guide and it does not try in any way to be exhaustive, which would be delusory. It provides, in an effective and elegant manner, a sort of initiation to Egyptian archaeology. In a simple style, Corteggiani gives us first of all a concise history of the collection, then, having outlined the powerful figure of its founder, Auguste Mariette, he describes the stages of its development at Bulaq and later at Giza (on the site of the present zoo), and finally in the important building of Qasr el Nil. With many anecdotes about one piece or another, we are given a glimpse into the great days of archaeological discovery in Egypt.

Some of the pieces are very well known, others totally ignored; although the Sheikh el-Beled and the treasures of Tutankhamun had to find their place in such a book, it also contains accessories and tools used by scribes, carpenters and masons; statues of gods and kings (one gallery contains a wealth of portraits of the Pharaohs), but also simple objects used in everyday life. From the earliest prehistoric times to the Graeco-Roman period, 120 well-documented and concise explanatory notes provide a detailed description and the identification and catalogue number of each artefact; suggestions are made as to their origin and their cultural or historical meaning; Corteggiani expresses his opinion as to their aesthetic value and urges a reaction on our part. Nothing

commonplace: as we progress historical problems are posed and solutions suggested; although the book is not, in theory, aimed at specialists, they are sometimes uppermost in his mind: the period of the Middle Empire is suggested for the famous gold falconhead of Hierakonpolis; in front of the sarcophagus of a she-cat, we are invited to meditate on the fate of Prince Tuthmosis, eldest son of Amenophis III; if he had survived, what would have happened to the 'Amarna revolution'?

A first edition of this book was published in 1979 but now the author has updated it to take into account the most recent studies. He has reviewed his interpretation of the Ezbet el-Walda stelae. But he refuses to attribute to the 26th dynasty the small ivory statuette once found by Flinders Petrie; according to him it belongs to Cheops, the only one incidentally – which seems an astonishing paradox – to have been executed by the great builder. He relates the recent rediscovery of the tomb of Maya at Saqqara, and the evidence confirming the importance of the 18th dynasty; the Bubasteion cliff also reveals the existence of another of Tutankhamun's viziers and of great dignitaries of Semitic origin. It can also be noted that a 'portrait of the Faiyum' has been replaced by one more typical.

A well-documented work – each explanatory note is usefully accompanied by a photograph, and sometimes by references – it is complemented by several indexes and a concordance table. Corteggiani's attractive work will no doubt induce people to reflect on the art of ancient Egypt. Even with surprisingly limited means – the palette remains restricted and the sculptors make up for the lack of abrasives with their patience – the results are perfect: this civilization of stone achieved excellence in the representation of animals; an extraordinary vividness animates statuettes such as that of Rahotep and Nofret, the famous couple of Maidum or the famous wooden *ka* image of the mysterious King Hor. Contrary to common prejudices, they are neither boring nor rigid. In a few pages Jean-Pierre Corteggiani has managed to show in depth the astonishing variety of a civilization which was dominated by the eminent dignity of the Pharaohs for more than thirty centuries.

Paris, August 1986
JEAN LECLANT
Professor at the Collège de France
Permanent Secretary
to the Académie des Inscriptions et Belles-Lettres

Introduction

From colossus to amulet, the collection of Egyptian antiquities at the Cairo museum is, as one might expect, by far the world's richest, containing over 100,000 objects.

This book, which offers a selection of 120 pieces, is not intended as a catalogue, nor as a guide to the Museum. The concept behind it is different; in no way does it pretend to replace the *Guide du visiteur au Musée du Caire*, Sir Gaston Maspero's seminal work, which went into several editions between 1902 and 1915 and upon which the present *Description Sommaire des Principaux Monuments* is largely based.

The purpose of this volume is quite simply to suggest one way of viewing the Museum, among the many that could be proposed in theory. Rather than giving brief descriptions of large numbers of objects, I have chosen to linger over a few which, taken as a whole, may be considered as an introduction to Egyptian civilization and as a fitting representation of the Museum's greatest treasures. I think the reader will readily understand the difficulty involved in picking out a few dozen 'treasures' in a museum which possesses so many. Although I feel no compunction to justify the choices I have made (since these are obviously personal and might just as easily have been totally different), nonetheless, it may be useful here to outline the reasoning that has governed my selections.

If this book had been intended for a mass readership, it would have been perfectly possible to confine it to descriptions of objects which are 'treasures' in the ordinary sense, by reason of the sheer value of the materials from which they are made. The Cairo Museum is stuffed with objects of this type, dating from every period of Egyptian history. But if one is trying to find out about a vanished civilization, the word 'treasure' can also describe an adze, a painted shell, a lamp or a mason's level. Objects like this are just as readily available as golden vessels or precious stones.

The more books on Egyptian art one reads, the more one realizes that the famous masterpieces they describe are nearly always the same. Yet many other masterpieces exist, and it would be a simple matter to assemble several volumes illustrating the unknown treasures of the Cairo Museum. Although this is not the main purpose here, an attempt has nevertheless been made to feature certain lesser-known treasures alongside the great works of pharaonic art which cannot be ignored, such as the statue of Chephren or the portrait of Nefertiti. After all, the Mona Lisa is perhaps not Leonardo's greatest picture, but it is unquestionably his best known and people would be most surprised if it received no mention in a book about the paintings in the Louvre.

The system of classification used here is necessarily chronological, with objects numbered from 1 to 120. This method has the advantage of demonstrating the evolution of a form of art which has all too often been accused of resisting progress. With about ten objects representing protohistory and the Thinite era, twenty for the Old Kingdom, fifteen for the Middle Kingdom, nearly fifty for the New Kingdom and thirty for the Late Period (from the Third Intermediate Period to the Meroitic era), the number of objects representing each one of the great periods in Egyptian history are roughly equivalent to their respective time spans. Any apparent bias in favour of the New Kingdom is illusory, since several of the pieces dating from that time, which have been included because of their great beauty (shabtis, tools, toilet articles...) are uncharacteristic and might just as well have been replaced by other, similar objects, dating from earlier or later periods. Moreover, no less than nine objects from the treasure of Tutankhamun have been included. In one sense this is too much, since Tutankhamun only reigned for ten years and was in no way predestined by history for his subsequent fame; and in another sense, it is too little, given the astonishing ensemble of the pharaoh's funeral trappings, which numbered over 2000 individual objects. The part of the Tutankhamun treasure on exhibiton in Cairo fills twelve rooms of the Museum's first floor.

The lesser arts, which are sometimes unfairly disregarded, are brought into relief by the priority given to items of furniture, which anyway tend to constitute the bulk of each collection. While these testify to the skills of their authors in bas-relief and mural painting, clearly the visitor would be well-advised to view such things *in situ*. The sculpted walls of the Saqqara mastabas, the reliefs in the temple of Seti I at Abydos, and the painted tombs of the necropolis of Thebes, are obvious examples.

With the exception of the 'Israel Stela' and of a few pieces which were on loan for an exhibition in Japan at the time when the photographs were being taken (Nos. 39, 49 and 64), all the pictures in this volume are original. Given the book's format, and the likelihood that many people will not have the good fortune to read it *and* visit the Museum, we have chosen to illustrate details from the larger objects, rather than show them in their entirety. Hence the statuary we have included constitutes a kind of portrait gallery of the principal pharaohs and other important individuals.

Prior to the commentary, which attempts to situate each object in its historical, artistic or archaeological context, a few brief facts are supplied: the material from which the object is made; its dimensions; date; exhibition number (if any) and present position in the Museum (Ground floor and First floor). Also included are the room number and exhibit location.

Finally, in order that this book should not be entirely useless to specialists (for whom it is not, of course, primarily intended), we have included at the end a concordance table of the principal numbers attached to the objects.

I would like to express my gratitude to all those who have made this book possible. My most particular thanks go to Dr Dia Abu Ghazi, Director of Egyptian Museums, whose competence and inexhaustible kindness have facilitated many aspects of my task, and who has most generously supplied some of the photographs which follow. I would also like to thank Dr H. el Achirie, the previous Director of the Cairo Museum, and its conservators, Mrs Saneya Abd el-Al and Messrs Ibrahim el Nawawi, Mohamed Mohsen and Mohamed Saleh, the present Director of the Cairo Museum. Finally, I wish to acknowledge a considerable debt of gratitude to Professor Jean Vercoutter, Directeur de l'Institut Français d'Archéologie Orientale du Caire, who was kind enough to allow my friend Jean-François Gout to use some of the Institute's photographic equipment.

Cairo, December 1978

The Museum and its Collections

Because it was not entirely military, Bonaparte's expedition at the close of the eighteenth century marked the beginning of the modern era in Egypt. The future emperor took great trouble to bring a battalion of scholars along with his troops, and these men subsequently drew up the first complete scientific survey of the Nile Valley. Nothing escaped their notice, as the monumental *Description de l'Egypte* testifies. Fauna, antique objects, local technology, minerals, flora, the flow of the Nile when swollen with floodwater – all were meticulously described, recorded and measured.

One of the consequences of this French rediscovery of a country which was then little more than a province of the Ottoman Empire, was a vogue for Egyptian antiquity.

Until that time, no collection exclusively devoted to Egyptian art had yet been assembled, though some collectors had managed to acquire a few objects. This situation suddenly changed when Europeans assigned to official positions in Egypt began to collect with a vengeance, on the strength of 'firmans' (permits) which could easily be obtained from Mohammed Ali. Within a few years the agents employed by the Consuls Salt, Drovetti and Anastasi, among others, succeeded in building up magnificent private collections, which today form the cores of Europe's principal museums of Egyptology. Unfortunately, their sole preoccupation was to find the rarest objects, and archaeological sites were consequently ransacked without the slightest regard for scientific method. At the same time, Egypt was in the first throes of industrialization. Antique structures were disappearing stone by stone into the limekilns; and it is no surprise that Jean François Champollion, during his remarkable Egyptian travels between 1828 and 1830, became alarmed about the situation. Having found only a few blocks of stone where entire temples had stood only thirty years before, Champollion (whom we know today as the founder of

Egyptology) drew the attention of Mohammed Ali to the imminent danger threatening Egypt's monuments. Before his departure for France, Champollion presented a memorandum to the viceroy recommending the establishment of a service for the conservation of antiquities. The recommendation was not at first implemented for the good reason that it was obstructed by those who stood to lose by the creation of such a service.

Nonetheless, the idea had been launched and after five years the first concrete initiatives were taken. In 1835 Mohammed Ali passed a series of conservation measures, but his purpose in doing so was more to make trouble for the French Consul-General, Jean François Mimaut, who wished to export his private collection, than to protect the ancient monuments of Egypt.

The text of the decree published in the *Journal Officiel* on 15 August 1835, was highly significant:

'Foreigners are destroying ancient edifices, by removing stones and other carved objects, which they export to countries overseas. If this conduct continues, there is no doubt whatever that in a very short time there will be no ancient monuments left in Egypt and that all will have been transported abroad.

'It is also a known fact that the Europeans have buildings which they devote exclusively to the upkeep of antiquities; stones covered with paintings or inscriptions and other objects of a similar nature are carefully kept within these buildings, and shown to those inhabitants of the country, or foreign travellers, who desire to see and know them; establishments of this kind confer great honour upon the countries that possess them.

'In consideration of these facts, the government has deemed it right to prohibit the exportation abroad of the antique objects which may be found in the ancient buildings of Egypt, which are very precious; and to designate a place within the

Auguste Mariette

capital to serve as a repository for all objects which have been, or will be, found in the course of excavations. It has also been deemed that these objects should be exhibited to travellers visiting Egypt; that the destruction of ancient buildings in Upper Egypt should be prohibited; and that all possible care should be taken to keep such buildings in good repair.'

This at least led to the creation of a Cairo Museum, if not an Antiquities Conservation Service. The embryonic Museum was housed in an annexe of the Ecole Civile then being constructed on the site of a former palace beside the lake of Ezbekiyya. Nonetheless, despite the inventory of sites carried out by Louis Linants de Bellefonds, who was instructed to bring all transportable objects back to the Museum, and despite the efficiency with which Youssef Zia Effendi carried out his task as chief administrator, the Museum quickly became a kind of reserve into which the viceroy was prone to dip when he wished to please his important visitors. He did this so often that after several years the collection was reduced to no more than a single room of the Ministry of Public Education at the Citadel. In 1855, Abbas Pasha abolished this first Cairo Museum altogether by the

expedient of giving everything in it to Archduke Maxmillian of Austria, who happened to be visiting Egypt.

For the next 25 years, the history of what eventually became the Museum we know today was interwoven with the life and work of Auguste Mariette, whose tenacity alone made it possible.

Mariette arrived at Alexandria on October 1850, having obtained French support for an official mission to purchase Syriac and Coptic manuscripts in the libraries of Egyptian convents, as several other European governments had already done. It had taken him several years to obtain this support, which had required the intervention of Charles Lenormant of the Académie des Inscriptions et Belles Lettres to become a reality. But the Coptic patriarchs wished to put a stop to these practices, and Mariette immediately came up against a host of obstacles placed in his way by the religious authorities, despite the fact that they dared not meet him with a categoric refusal because his mission was officially backed.

To escape the enforced idleness of his predicament, Mariette toured the ancient sites near Cairo, dreaming that he would discover some priceless object himself. Finally, at Saqqara, he discovered a sphinx buried in the sand, resembling others which he had already noticed in Alexandria and Cairo. Mariette was convinced that these sphinxes originally came from the 'dromos' leading to the Serapeum described by Strabo (XVII, 1, 14). He therefore decided to drop his earlier mission which seemed fruitless, and to begin a search for this monument. Using the money which had originally been intended for the manuscripts, he began excavating, but without any 'firman' authorizing him to do so. In spite of the jealousy of rivals who managed to have his site closed down for several weeks, Mariette's intuition was borne out and on 12 November 1851, he entered the Serapeum.

By this time, his initial funds were exhausted; he petitioned for more, and the Chamber of Deputies voted an exceptional credit of thirty thousand francs in recognition of Egyptology's first great discovery. This credit was to apply to 'the excavation of a temple dedicated to Serapis, discovered among the ruins of Memphis, and the transport to France of the art objects within it'. This was somewhat jumping the gun as far as the viceroy's government was concerned; the latter, though quite willing to cede to France the monuments already unearthed, would only permit the excavation to continue on condition that any future discoveries would remain in Egypt. This was bound to happen, but nonetheless Mariette succeeded in shipping more than seven thousand objects to the Louvre. This accomplishment earned him the title of assistant conservator of the Egyptian Antiquities Department a few months after his return to Paris in the autumn of 1854.

Neither his new functions, nor the honours showered on him, would deter Mariette from dreaming of a return to Egypt.

He was soon presented with an opportunity, when friends introduced him to Ferdinand de Lesseps. He managed to convince the great engineer of the need to act quickly to save the Egyptian monuments, at a moment when Prince Napoleon, a cousin of the Emperor, was planning a visit to Egypt. Lesseps, who was securely in the favour of Said Pasha because of his planned canal project, offered to submit a report by Mariette to the viceroy. This Lesseps duly did, and so successful was he in tying the problem of the monuments to the preparations for Napoleon's visit that Said Pasha immediately had him engage Mariette to excavate and assemble a collection of antiquities for the prince. There was no question here of protecting ancient monuments or founding a museum, but Mariette accepted the mission. Prince Napoleon arranged ministerial backing for an eight month period, and Mariette left for Egypt at the end of October 1857.

As soon as he arrived in Cairo, he was given money, a steam boat and mission directives. Several excavations were begun, but again Mariette had to cope with the jealousy and intrigues of rivals, who attempted to persuade the viceroy that France had other, more sinister motives which had little to do with antiquities. This suggestion was quashed by the French Consul-General, Raymond Sabatier, but soon after it was learned that the prince's visit was likely to be cancelled. When the latter, as a courtesy to the viceroy, asked if he might buy the collection, Mariette presented his case so well that Said Pasha refused to hear of any financial transaction and presented Prince Napoleon with all the objects he wanted, as a gift.

As a mark of gratitude to Mariette, who had been ordered to return to his post at the Louvre, the cousin of Napoleon III offered to recommend him to the viceroy 'should his Royal Highness request of France the assistance of a scholar in establishing an Egyptian museum'. This suggestion was conveyed to Said, who despite opposition nominated Mariette 'mamour', or Director of Egyptian Antiquities, on 1 June 1858.

Thus Mariette found himself directly responsible to the viceroy, in an administrative position which was by no means clear. However, he did have a specific mission to uncover and preserve monuments, and to collect antique objects with a view to constituting a new museum. His immediate concern was to acquire a depot, since Said persisted in treating the collections brought to Cairo as a repository of gifts; in addition, certain parties in France were by no means favourable to the creation of a Cairo museum which might one day rival the Louvre.

Mariette was eventually authorized to install his museum at Bulaq, beside the Nile, in rundown premises that had formerly belonged to the Compagnie Fluviale. Prior to the advent of the railway, this company had provided the riverboat link between Cairo and Alexandria. Mariette moved in with his family and set about organizing four exhibition rooms, aided by his faithful assistants Bonnefoy and Matteo Floris.

The first year of the Service des Antiquités was marked by the important discovery of Queen Ahhotep's jewellery. This business nearly had very serious consequences for Mariette, but he contrived to turn the situation to his advantage, obtained a promise from the viceroy to build a new museum, and acquired the title of 'Director of Egyptian Historic Monuments and the Cairo Museum' on his return from Paris in autumn 1859.

In 1861, Mariette was obliged to return home to France for health reasons. Napoleon III took this opportunity to entrust him with a diplomatic mission aimed at detaching the viceroy from British influences, by persuading the potentate to visit France. As an Egyptologist, Mariette had every interest in turning his hand to diplomacy, specifically because the construction of his museum was being drastically delayed by Said Pasha's financial problems; problems which could be remedied by the attribution of loans in Paris. When the emperor's invitation reached Cairo, Said was overjoyed and his gratitude knew no bounds, but Mariette was content to request funds for the construction of the museum, and these were not refused. At the same time, in 1862, he was nominated commissioner general to the Universal Exhibition in London, and given the title of Bey, first class.

In January 1863, the sudden death of Said Pasha seemed likely to call the entire museum project into question, but Ismaïl Pasha, his successor, hastened to reassure Mariette, promising

The museum at Bulaq, exterior view

The museum at Giza, exterior view

immediate help with the enlargement of the old museum whilst awaiting funds for a brand new one that would be truly worthy of Egypt. The enlarged premises were opened in October 1863.

In 1864, the slanders put about by his rivals, which hitherto had failed to trouble him, at last placed Mariette in difficulty. For a short period he found himself in semi-disgrace; this ended in 1865, when he was once again nominated general commissioner to a Universal Exhibition, that of Paris, to take place in 1867. To this exhibition Mariette

The museum at Bulaq, the treasure of Ahhotep

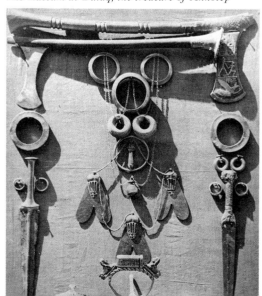

The museum at Bulaq, interior view

sent some of his museum's greatest masterpieces, among them the magnificent statue of Chephren, the Sheikh el-Beled, and the jewellery of Queen Ahhotep, which were displayed in an Egyptian 'temple' reconstructed according to plans drawn by the Commissioner. Ironically, the immense success of this endeavour caused Mariette very serious problems, because nobody wanted to see the pieces return to Cairo, and the Empress Eugénie herself did not hesitate to apply directly to the viceroy for a gift of some of the jewellery. Ismaïl dared not refuse and referred the decision to Mariette who, despite the precariousness of his position, formally and flatly refused. It would have been so much simpler and more comfortable to accept; he would thereby have avoided the ill-will of both the French Court and of Ismaïl, who was angry with him for irritating the French

sovereigns. But Mariette had learnt his lesson. He declined afterwards to send any important pieces to subsequent exhibitions in Vienna (1873), Philadelphia (1875) and Paris (1878).

Ismaïl's displeasure vanished as the official 1869 inauguration of the Suez Canal drew closer. Mariette's services were once again required, this time to write the plot for the libretto of *Aida*, and to receive the guests of Ismaïl, who had now become 'khedive'.

The last years of Mariette's life were clouded by trouble and grief, which obliged him to make several voyages to France. In May 1878, he was elected a member of the Académie des Incriptions et Belles Lettres, although he was not a resident of Paris; but in the same year, floods from the Nile virtually devastated the entire Museum. Khedive Ismaïl, in serious financial trouble, was on the

The museum at Giza as it appeared in an old photograph

point of being deposed and replaced by his son Tewfik. Mariette could scarcely hope to acquire new premises in the immediate future, since all public funds had been cut back. In June 1879, he was invested with the title of pasha, but the Museum was merely raised in height.

At the beginnng of 1880, funds began to flow again, due to a grant from the Académie des Inscriptions et Belles Lettres; but that year Mariette was forced to travel to France for health reasons. Against the advice of his doctors, he returned to Egypt, only to die on 18 January 1881, shortly after the reopening of the museum, in whose gardens he was buried. His tomb has since followed the Museum in all its subsequent moves – to Giza, and then to Qasr el-Nil. The exhedra, marble sarcophagus and bronze statue by Puech may now be seen in the grounds of the present Museum, to the left of the façade.

At Mariette's death, the Antiquities Service no longer depended on the khedive. It was now integrated into the administrative framework, and Mariette's successors Sir Gaston Maspero (1881–86), E. Grébaut (1886–92), Jacques de Morgan (1892–97), V. Loret (1897–99), and then Maspero again (1899–1914), to speak only of the period immediately prior to the First World War, were spared the difficulties which had afflicted the Museum's founder.

In 1891, the collections were moved from Bulaq to Giza, to one of the former private residences of Khedive Ismaïl which stood on the site of the present zoo and botanical gardens. Here they remained until 1902, when they were installed in the present Museum building. The first stone of this edifice had been laid by Abbas Hilmi II on 1 April 1897; it was constructed to plans by the French architect Marcel Dourgnon, after an international competition. The Museum comprises a basement area where reserves are stored, two exhibition

The main façade of the Cairo Museum

floors, and a smaller upper floor which is not open to the public. More than a hundred display rooms fan out from a central atrium. The ground floor houses the conservator's offices and the library, along with the heavier monuments (statues, sarcophagi and stelae). These are chronologically classified, clockwise from the entrance. On the first floor, the remainder of the collection is exhibited according to types of object (papyri, Middle Kingdom reliefs, jewellery, funerary masks), or by collective find (eg Tutankhamun, Hetepheres, the Royal Necropolis of Tanis, Hemaka).

The visitor will perhaps be surprised to discover that a single statue can carry several numbers, either on the object itself or on its labels. This is, however, the case at Cairo; and according to one of the greatest authorities on the Museum it has been the source of many a headache for specialists trying to establish concordances between the number in the *Journal d'Entrée*, (which fails to record such famous works as the statues of Rahotep and Nofret); the *Catalogue Général* (written in red, but also in white and black on the exhibits); the exhibition numbers (in black on white labels); or those of the temporary register (on the pieces, in the angles of a cross). To these must be added the numbers of the curator's special inventory, (in white on black labels) and, when they exist, the numbers of the excavators (beginning with 'K' for statues from the Karnak trove, or with 'T' for the Tutankhamun treasure).

In its present form, the Museum has a number of problems. The most obvious of these is overcrowding, which detracts from the quality of presentation. Individual objects suffer from the sheer abundance of the Museum as a whole. Many fine pieces, which would be the pride and joy of any European or American curator, are relegated to the shadows or to the top shelves of display cabinets.

Here the difficulty is not to add to the collections (the Museum no longer has a purchasing budget, as it once did), but to find space for the monuments turned up by each fresh excavation. For example, if another tombful of objects like Tutankhamun's were ever to be discovered – and this is always a possibility – the present system of exhibition rooms would have to be completely altered.

There has been talk for a long time of building a new museum which would exhibit only the greatest works of art in the most favourable circumstances; the present Museum would be kept as a reserve and as a place for specialists to pursue their studies. For the moment, the cost of such an operation is too high for it to be seriously considered, but with financial cooperation to the tune of several million dollars, plus a portion of the profits realized by exhibitions abroad, the present building is about to be renovated. This involves the installation of air-conditioning throughout the building; a reduction of overcrowding by the use of the ground floor and second floor reserve rooms as display areas; the introduction of proper lighting; and the installation of fire and theft prevention systems.

Air conditioning is absolutely essential. A new bridge was completed opposite the Museum in 1978, reducing the size of the Museum gardens, and open windows now expose the pieces to intense traffic vibrations and polluted air from the immense Midan el-Tahrir bus terminal (soon to be relocated).

At the same time, the policies of the Antiquities Service tend to give priority to provincial museums, in which Cairo might deposit some of its pieces. Luxor has had an ultra-modern museum ever since 1975; Aswan is scheduled to receive a similar facility, devoted to Nubian antiquities, in a few years; and other towns like Mallawi, Zagazig or Isma'iliya have collections worthy of interest. There is also, of course, the great Graeco-Roman museum at Alexandria.

Mariette's tomb

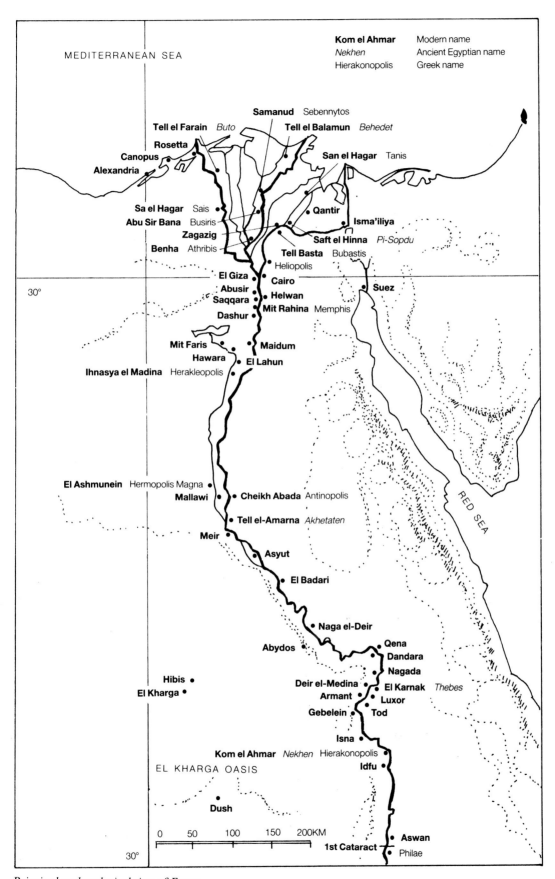

MEDITERRANEAN SEA

Kom el Ahmar   Modern name
Nekhen   Ancient Egyptian name
Hierakonopolis   Greek name

Samanud   Sebennytos
Tell el Farain *Buto*
Tell el Balamun *Behedet*
Rosetta
Canopus
Alexandria
San el Hagar   Tanis

Sa el Hagar   Sais
Abu Sir Bana   Busiris
Qantir
Zagazig
Isma'iliya
Benha   Athribis
Saft el Hinna   *Pi-Sopdu*
Tell Basta   Bubastis
Heliopolis
El Giza
Cairo
Abusir
Suez
Saqqara
Helwan
Dashur
Mit Rahina   Memphis

Mit Faris
Maidum
Hawara
El Lahun
Ihnasya el Madina   Herakleopolis

El Ashmunein   Hermopolis Magna
Mallawi
Cheikh Abada   Antinopolis
Tell el-Amarna   *Akhetaten*
Meir
Asyut
El Badari

Naga el-Deir
Qena
Abydos
Dandara
Nagada
Hibis
Deir el-Medina
El Karnak   *Thebes*
El Kharga
Armant
Luxor
Gebelein
Tod
Isna
Kom el Ahmar   *Nekhen*   Hierakonopolis
EL KHARGA OASIS
Idfu

RED SEA

Dush

0   50   100   150   200KM

30°

Aswan
1st Cataract
Philae

Principal archaeological sites of Egypt

17

The Museum around 1930

48

Plan of the Museum

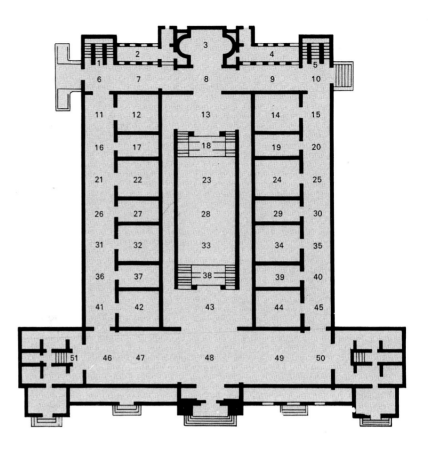

Ground Floor

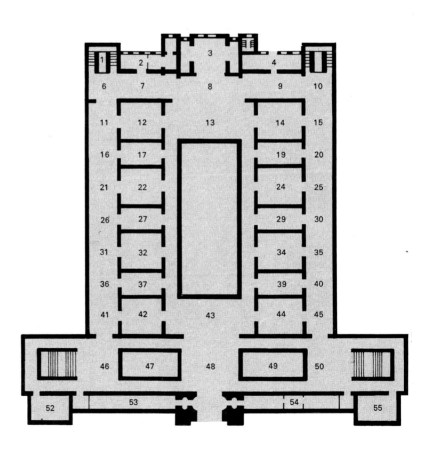

First Floor

1 | Protohistoric ceremonial knife

Silex, plaster and gold; H. 30.2 cm; Gerzean (?) Period; P53, centre

In order to reach the first floor galleries containing the Museum's prehistoric and protohistoric objects, the visitor must cross several other exhibition rooms. A cursory inspection here of the statues dating from the eras of recorded history will have impressed on him how Egyptian civilization was principally based on the use of stone; thus he will scarcely be surprised to discover that prehistoric Egypt had already brought the quality of stone tools to a pitch of perfection that was never surpassed elsewhere.

Certain flint and obsidian blades from the Protodynastic period may fairly be described as works of art, by reason of their purity of form and perfect execution. One is lost in admiration for the disconcerting ease with which the flakes of stone seem to have been removed, in order to achieve the regular patterning of flint surfaces or cutting edges.

Some of the knives are beautifully finished, with ivory or gold handles; these were probably not in ordinary daily use, but were kept for special religious rites. This probably applies to the astonishing knife discovered in a tomb at Gebelein, which was bought at Qena in 1900 by James Edward Quibell, along with other pieces presumed to have been found in the same cache.

The fact that this object was not produced by a scientifically-controlled excavation caused earlier experts to doubt its authenticity, on the specific

Flaked obsidian blades and flint knife

grounds that the gold handle was held in place by rivets piercing the flint blade – which itself was undoubtedly of ancient origin. Apparently, modern specialists no longer worry about this; the Museum owns another, similar knife whose rivets do not pass clean through the flint, but simply support the gold leaf on the plaster which partially covers the blade, thereby lending a form to the handle which is warrantably genuine. In addition, the two-pronged blade of the knife is without

question contemporary to the handle's engraved decoration; on one side, it consists of a barque with two cabins and pennants, and on the other, of three female figures, one of whom carries a kind of fan. This motif may be found on a number of vases from the Naqada II period, which Egyptian prehistorians also refer to as the Gerzean period, placing it somewhere between 3700 (or 3500) and 3200 (or 3000) BC.

2 | Antelope vase

Pink limestone; H. 9 cm; Protodynastic period; No.5517; P54, central display case

As a pastoral people, the Egyptians have always known how to observe nature, especially animals, with precision and sympathy. Hence from time immemorial Egyptian artists have understood how to paint animals, whether their goal in doing so was to represent a creature straightforwardly and realistically, to confer a stylized outline on a utensil, or to express the mystery and power of some divine being through a conventionalized image.

From the very first manifestations of artistic activity in Egypt, animal art is present. Examples are palettes in the form of fishes or antelopes, and combs of bone or ivory shaped like birds and ibexes.

Along with pottery carrying painted motifs of wild creatures, the use of animal-shaped vessels prevailed from the earliest prehistoric times right up to the Roman era. Many survive in both stone and porcelain: frogs, hippopotamuses, turtles, elephants and hedgehogs.

This piece, bought by the Museum in 1936, is one of the loveliest. It is carved in compact pink limestone, with the stylized but completely recognizable form of an antelope, the eye being inlaid with a round piece of bone. The body of the bowl is polished smooth, with four holes close to the lip. It is difficult to say whether these holes were intended to accommodate a lid, or to allow the jar to be hung up. The same four holes, and the same mystery, apply to a pair of similar jars in the British Museum, dating from the same Protodynastic period, when these objects were much in favour.

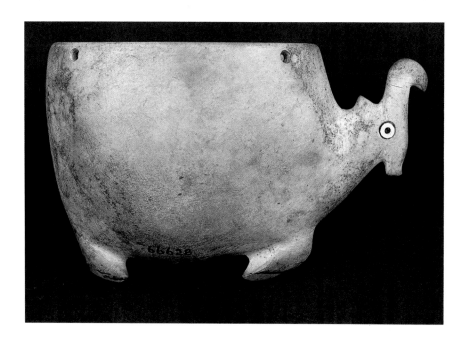

3 | The 'Libyan' palette

Grey schist; H. 19 cm; beginning of the 1st Dynasty;
G43, east side

To be precise, this piece is the lower section of a palette which must have had the same form, and perhaps the same proportions (60 cm high) as the famous Narmer palette, which is on display in the same room.

The fragment shown here comes from Abydos and belongs to the series of large illustrated palettes which characterize the beginning of the historical period. These ceremonial pieces are rarer and simpler than their forerunners, the animal-shaped palettes of prehistoric times used for grinding malachite or galena (lead sulphide) eyeliner. Although they are undoubtedly votive in nature, they remain palettes and as such incorporate a bowl in which the cosmetic was presumably crushed to powder. In this case, the bowl has vanished, along with most of the rest of the object, and it is thus impossible to distinguish which is the obverse and which is the reverse.

One side of the fragment is divided into four panels. The first three show animals, grouped according to species, as on various knife handles from the Naqada II period: bulls, donkeys and sheep with horizontal twisted horns. The fourth panel is filled by eight trees which some experts have suggested may be olives, though there is little to support this theory. Everything which later characterized the Egyptian style is already present here. In spite of the archaic nature of the relief, we can perceive the skill of the Egyptian artist, who from beginning to end was always a precise imitator of animals and nature. These creatures seem to be rough casts of the mastaba bas-reliefs, with their long files of beasts in which, from time to time, one turns its head in a different direction, thus happily breaking a pattern which might otherwise have become monotonous.

To the right of the trees are two hieroglyphs,

(a throwing stick placed vertically above the oval earth symbol), which combine to form the name Tjehenu, designating Libya and the regions east of the Nile Delta. Hence the object as a whole is known as the 'Libyan Palette'.

The other side of it consists of a single panel, but above a separating line one can decipher the remains of another panel, with the feet of two figures turned to the right.

On two levels, seven fortified towns are depicted by their bastions. Within each of these are a few buildings, roughly rendered alongside the hieroglyphs which name the towns: an owl, a crested bird, a pair of wrestlers, a scarab, two raised arms, a reed hut and a bush.

These towns were all originally crowned by symbolic animal figures, grasping hoes embedded in the walls. Only four of these survive, and they probably represent different aspects of the same royal or divine power: a falcon, a lion, a scorpion and two smaller falcons perched on banners. Since 1879, when the German scholar Georg Steindorff published the first description of this palette, it has been generally agreed that the symbolic animals are in the act of destroying the towns, assumed to be in Libya by reason of the name included in the decoration on the reverse side. Hence the object as a whole may be interpreted as a commemoration of military victories and conquests, and the exaction of tributes from the vanquished. While it is true that certain later texts, dating from the early 4th Dynasty to the end of the 5th Dynasty, mention the arrival of large quantities of livestock, there is

nothing to prove with any certainty that this interpretation is the correct one: indeed there is another, equally well-grounded, which will be seen to be preferable.

According to customary symbolism, the pharaoh wielding a hoe is carrying out some constructive act, such as digging and filling an irrigation canal, like the King Scorpion on the mace found at Hierakonpolis, now at the Ashmolean Museum at Oxford. Another example (3000 years later) would be the founding of a temple, like one of the Ptolemies on the bas-reliefs of Idfu or Philae. On the other hand when King Narmer, depicted on his palette in the form of a bull, tramples some enemy people, the destructiveness of his act is emphasized by the representation of an open city wall broken down by the creature's massive horns. The impression of power in movement is very well rendered, while the figures which dominate each city that remains intact are fixed and immobile, more akin to written characters.

The decoration of the larger, well-known palettes has obviously been inspired by contemporary events, and often constitutes evidence of the armed struggles which wracked Egypt during the period of unification. Nonetheless, it seems reasonable to postulate that the 'Libyan Palette' may refer to struggles of a different kind: peaceful ones, waged with nature to open up the Libyan markets of the Delta, and to found new cities in areas which had to be reclaimed from marshland. This is a theory which deserves serious consideration.

4 | Bracelets from the Tomb of King Djer

Gold, semi-precious stones, pâte de verre; L. 10.2 cm to 15.6 cm; 1st Dynasty; Nos.4000–4003; G43, north side

These four bracelets, which are among the oldest pieces of jewellery in recorded history, were found at Abydos in 1901 by the workers of Sir W. M. Flinders Petrie. They were discovered under the linen bandages encasing a mummified arm, which had been long ago concealed in the cavity of the

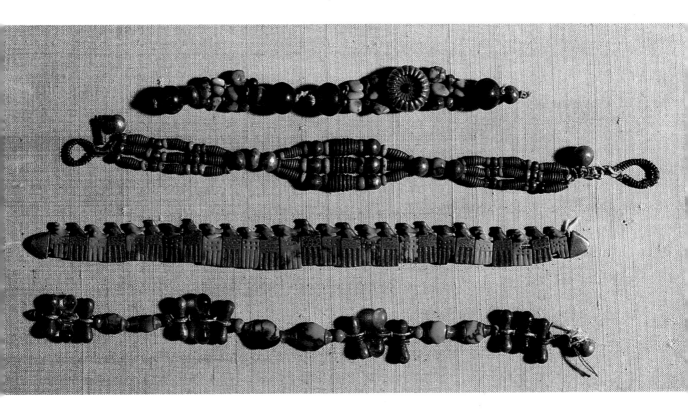

brick wall of a tomb or cenotaph during some grave-robbing episode. The tomb was that of King Djer, the third Pharaoh of the 1st Dynasty; hence the bracelets must have belonged to the king himself, to the queen, to some secondary wife, or at least to someone in the king's entourage.

Each bracelet demonstrates a perfect mastery of techniques which had already been brought to a high pitch of accomplishment: gold work, cutting and polishing of semi-precious stones and even the manufacture of thick pâte de verre.

The smallest piece, which was worn closest to the wrist, is composed of two distinct ensembles that were still linked at the moment of its discovery by a cord of twisted gold and hair (perhaps from the tail of a giraffe). Each includes two spherical amethysts, some irregular-shaped turquoises, and gold beads, but the right hand section is also adorned with a kind of golden rosette, in the form of the dried fruit of a lotus-flower. The second piece includes beads made of rolled up golden thread, lapis lazuli cut to the same shape, and round discs or beads of turquoise and gold. The third is made up of 29 elements, 27 of which (alternately in gold and turquoise) represent the 'serekh', or stylized façade and plan of a royal palace surmounted by the silhouette of a falcon signifying 'Horus', the first and the oldest of the five names in the royal protocol. The blue elements on which the heads of the falcons are lower are perhaps not all cut from stones: it would be interesting to find out if some are of pâte de verre, but this would entail analysis and the sacrifice of one or several of the pieces. The fourth bracelet consists of four groups of curious, unpierced, hour-glass-shaped beads, as well as three intermediary groups of gold beads and two cut from turquoise in the form of lozenges. The unpierced beads, a series of two gold elements framing a third in amethyst on brown stone, are held in place by a double knot adjusted to fit the 'waist' of each stone.

These pieces of jewellery, simple yet original, employ the principal semi-precious stones which the Egyptian artist found readily at hand. What we call precious stones were unknown to him. The various reddish tones of carnelian, milky green felspar, certain forms of jasper, faience, along with the turquoise and lapis lazuli which blend so well with gold, or with amethyst, constitute the entire range of pharaonic jewellery.

5 | Funerary stela of Irni

Limestone; H. 19 cm; 2nd Dynasty; First floor, case H

This modest little stela was donated to the Museum in 1947 by King Farouk. Along with about twenty other pieces of the same type, it emerged from excavations funded by the king and directed by Zaki Saad at Ezbet el-Walda (Helwan) in 1940, in a necropolis of the 1st and 2nd Dynasties.

These monuments are the most ancient inscribed elements from private tombs that are known to us. They resemble paving stones, much longer than they are wide; only the central area is decorated, with a depiction of a funeral repast approximately framed within a square.

Not one of these lintels was actually discovered in its original position; those which were seemed to have been were found face downwards covering (often inadequately) the entry shafts to the catacombs. They were probably placed there by thieves since the shafts in question were frequently no more than grave-robbers' caves. Saad, who found similar objects at Saqqara, was wrong to qualify these curious stelae as 'ceiling stelae'; they

were really lintels of false doors, whose brick tiles served to mask the unsculpted parts framing the central tableau.

This tableau (see illustration) represents the dead man facing a heap of offerings, like thousands of subsequent Egyptians on their funerary stelae, up till the period of Roman domination.

The deceased is seated on a backless chair; only the rear leg of this chair, sculpted in the form of an ox's foot, is visible. He wears a round wig, with ringlets indicated as little squares, and he wears a long, narrow robe which is attached at the left shoulder. The right shoulder is bare, and the left hand rests upon it. The right hand is stretched out towards an offering table, on which are standing four tall pieces of bread.

The rest of the space is filled with representations or allusions to offerings. Immediately in front of the dead man's face are his name and title: he was a carpenter named Irni. The hieroglyphs are rough and not always legible, but just above the right hand, however, we may discern the outline of a trussed goose, an allusion to wine, and immediately above the table, a kind of garment, some bread and a piece of meat.

The area to the right, which is divided into compartments wherein the offerings are inventoried, with details of quantities (ten loaves of such and such a kind, ten jars of ointment), foreshadows the offering lists of Old Kingdom tombs, where dozens of funerary offerings are carefully listed in regular columns. Finally, in the lower right hand corner, the heads of an ox and a goose symbolize offerings of red meat and poultry.

6 | Stone vases

Schist(greywacke) and amethyst; H. 16.5 cm and 4.7 cm; 2nd–3rd Dynasties; Nos.6255–6256; First floor 42; cases I and J

The number, perfection and magnificence of the stone vases bequeathed to us by the artisans of the earliest Dynasties is nothing less than breathtaking. These jars were hewn, sometimes from the hardest materials, using a rudimentary drill with a

hard stone bit. The shaft of the drill was weighted with two sacks of pebbles and manoeuvred with a crank handle. The vase-driller, as depicted in bas-reliefs, would work away tirelessly with this tool at a block of alabaster; he knew how to use the veins in the stone to cut out corollas not only in tender limestone, but in granites, diorites, breccia, schist and quartzite, which are infinitely harder.

This obviously presupposes an entirely different notion of time to our own, since it could take a very long time to cut certain pieces. The vases shown here are among the thousands that testify to an art which the Egyptians completely mastered; indeed the image of the vase driller's tool came to symbolize the word 'artisan' in general, and even the word 'artist'.

These two vases have been chosen for the beauty of the materials from which they are made (speckled light grey schist and amethyst), and for the simplicity of their forms. They were found in one of the deep galleries 33 metres below the Step Pyramid. During the winter of 1934–35, Quibell

and Jean-Philippe Lauer unearthed thousands of vases here; many had been smashed by collapsing ceilings, some had perhaps been ritually broken. Debris from the excavation of these subterranean passages had to be carried out in boxes, in order to avoid mixing fragments of different vases. The clearing of a mere 12 metres in Gallery VI required no less than 1400 boxes; in all, nearly 40,000 vases were removed in a total of 6000 boxes.

Not all of these vases belonged to Djoser, and many date from the 1st and 2nd Dynasties. This is proved by several dozen engraved inscriptions, and more than a thousand inscriptions painted on the vases in black ink. The fact that the builder of the Step Pyramid neither added his name, nor substituted it for those of his predecessors, would seem to prove that it was not his intention to appropriate these items of royal crockery but that he had simply re-interred them as an act of piety after they had been excavated from tombs which had already been ransacked in his own time.

7 | Stone basin, imitation of basketwork

Schist (greywacke); L. 22.5 cm; 2nd Dynasty; No.6281; Ground floor 43, north-east hexagonal case

At the beginning of the Historical period, the art of the stonecarver attained heights which still amaze us. It seems that the tastes of certain artisans led them to create objects of extraordinary technical quality that were functionally useless, alongside their vases, whose simple shapes were

directly inherited from the arts of pottery and ceramics. Thus a number of stone pieces have been unearthed, which are bizarre rather than beautiful or useful, and which date from the first Dynasties. They tend to be objects imitating, either stylistically or realistically, things like broad-ribbed leaves with several lobes; schist ewers, in the form of two arms holding a looped cross (ankh); dishes, whose folded edges are so skilfully fashioned that they seem to have been shaped with soft paste; and various basketwork imitations, perhaps less astonishing in their conception.

The dark grey stone basin in the illustration belongs to the latter category. It was discovered by W. B. Emery in a 2nd Dynasty tomb at North Saqqara in 1937–38. A similar piece was found by Quibell and Lauer under the Step Pyramid; both copy every detail of a kind of small, cleverly woven rectangular basket.

In one corner of the piece, on the upper edge, the symbol for 'gold' is carved. From this we may deduce that the real basket must have been used as a temporary repository for jewellery or small ingots of metal, and that the funerary stone version was intended to fulfil this same function for all eternity.

8 | Statue of Khasekhem

Schist (greywacke); H. 54.5 cm; 2nd Dynasty; No.3056; Ground floor 43, east side

In a museum which possesses such a plethora of miraculously undamaged statues, one is liable to overlook this one, which has lost over half of its face. But the piece should not be ignored, because, in spite of its almost classical pose, this is the most ancient royal statue known to man – a portrait of Khasekhem, one of the last kings of the 2nd Dynasty. A limestone duplicate also survives (whose body is in much worse condition but whose face is undamaged), in the Ashmolean Museum, Oxford. Both statues come from Hierakonpolis, where they were discovered by Quibell during the highly fruitful excavations of 1897–98. Also unearthed at the same dig were such famous objects as the Mace of the King Scorpion, the Narmer Palette, the copper statue of Pepy I (No.26 in this book), and the falcon's head in gold (No.34).

The Oxford statue was found in what the excavators called the 'main deposit'. By contrast, the Cairo version had been buried in the floor of a room on the east side of the temple, where it lay jumbled up with a massive terracotta lion and assorted elements of the great metal portrait of Pepy.

Khasekhem is seated 'in majesty' on a low-backed throne much like those found in the succeeding dynasty with the statue of King Djoser (No.10). He is wrapped in the cloak usually reserved for jubilee celebrations, and he wears the white crown of Upper Egypt. The right hand, which must have originally grasped a removable sceptre (or mace), rests on the thigh, whilst the left hand is somewhat stiffly pressed against the torso in a pose which imparts a rigid aspect to the whole figure. In front of the feet, which are close together, the king's Horus name has been carved, and it is under this name that we know him. The missing part of the head has never been recovered, but what is left of it shows careful modelling, especially in the face, which may be favourably compared to that of the ear or the hands. In general, it closely resembles the face of the limestone statue – apart from the paint-free eyes.

Little is known of Khasekhem, and we cannot even say for certain if he should be identified with his near-namesake, King Khasekhemwy. He seems to have been exceedingly warlike and apparently concentrated on the reconquest of the Delta, which had perhaps wished to escape southern domination. This is confirmed by inscriptions on an alabaster ewer and a granite vase, also found at Hierakonpolis, and by the rough figures scratched on the sides of the king's monument. The latter represent the crumpled corpses of the king's northern enemies. The inscription on the front of the plinth gives their number as 47209, a figure which is exactly corroborated by the Oxford statue!

Statue of Khasekhem

9 | Statue of a kneeling priest

Pink granite; H. 39 cm; end of 2nd, beginning of 3rd Dynasty; No.3072; Ground floor 43; west side

This massive statue, discovered by Grébaut in 1888 on the site of Memphis, at Mit Rahina, has not been registered in the Museum's *Journal d'Entrée*, but it is marked No.1 in the first volume of the *Catalogue Général* by L. Borchardt, devoted to statues and statuettes of kings and other individuals. Its thickset aspect, a characteristic of archaic sculptures, is emphasized by the position of the body, which is unusual for the period. The figure is that of a man kneeling in an attitude of prayer. He sits on his heels, not on a chair. He is

dressed in a simple, barely distinguishable loincloth, and he wears a short, rounded wig with regular rows of ringlets.

The head, the size of which is accentuated by the wig, cranes forward and seems hunched into the shoulders; the arms and legs are nowhere detached from the body, and the modelling of the whole is stiff and crude.

A rough inscription, gouged into the right shoulder, gives some indication of the date of this exceedingly archaic statue, with the Horus names of the first three kings of the 2nd Dynasty set out in their exact order of succession: Hetepsekhemwy, Raneb and Ninetjer. The piece thus belongs at least to the second half of that dynasty, and perhaps to the beginning of the next. A clumsy outline of a bird on what appears to be a pyramidion, which precedes the first of these names, is difficult to interpret. Some have identified this as a falcon, but it may just as easily be a 'benu', the grey heron from which the phoenix form was later taken.

On the upper part of the base, just in front of the figure's knees, a short inscription is sculpted in relief. The signs, which are very worn, stand out so little from the granite that their full meaning is not altogether certain, but the word Hetepdif can be discerned following what was probably a title. This then was the name of the man portrayed; his attitude, if later examples are anything to go by suggests that he was a funerary priest of the cults of several 2nd Dynasty kings.

10 | Statue of Djoser *detail*

Limestone, with remains of paint; H. 1.44 m; 3rd Dynasty; No.6008; Ground floor 43, in mid-entrance

This life-size statue of the king was discovered during the excavations of 1924–25 conducted by the English archaeologist Cecil Mallaby Firth, who in the same year tackled the excavation of Djoser's immense tomb complex at Saqqara.

The figure was still in its original position, immured in its 'serdab', a small chamber just beneath the casing of the north face of the Step Pyramid, a few meters from its north-east corner. Two round holes in the wall at head-height kept the statue in contact with the world of the living, from which it continued to receive offerings. Today, a cast has replaced the original, and the two spy-holes enable visitors to view the king's impressive countenance looming out of the shadows.

The original statue at the Museum is of siliceous grey limestone. It represents Djoser seated 'in majesty' on a low-backed chair. He wears a very tight garment from which only the shoulders, the hands and the feet emerge. This robe which is still partially painted white, is one of those worn by the pharaoh during the great jubilee of Heb-sed. The king's beard, part of which is broken off, is unusually long; his head-dress is curious, consisting of a 'nemes' clearly revealing a voluminous black wig, instead of hiding it. The face has been badly damaged; the nose is smashed; the eyes and the encrusted eyebrows have been chiselled out; and the ochre colouring has practically vanished. Nonetheless, in spite of these mutilations, the general, very strong impression is one of raw power.

Like other contemporary inscriptions, the one carved on the front of the plinth identifies the builder of the Step Pyramid by his Horus name, Netjerikhet; only later did he become known as Djoser.

The Museum contains several finely wrought fragments from other portraits of the king (First floor 42). Of these, the base of one statue (no.6009, on the right in the same room) is perhaps the most historically important. This limestone plinth, which was unearthed not far from the entrance colonnade of the funerary monument, originally supported an erect statue of Djoser. Only the feet remain, and under these are depicted the 'Nine Bows', or the nine peoples which were the traditional enemies of Egypt; here shown, with magical aptness, under the complete domination of Djoser. In the same almost simple manner, heavy with meaning, three 'rekhyt' birds (crested plover) are immobilized on the ground with their wings intersecting; they symbolize the pharaoh's subjects stretched submissively at his feet. Later iconography has them with arms raised in token of adoration. But, more interesting than this decoration, which is conventionally repeated over the centuries on a number of plinths of royal statues, is the inscription carved on the front. This inscription has served to preserve the name of Imhotep, the king's great minister, from oblivion. In the midst of alternating 'djed columns' and 'Isis knots', and beside Djoser's Horus name, we read: 'The chancellor of the king of Lower Egypt, first in the nation under the king, administrator of the great palace, hereditary noble and high priest of Heliopolis, Imhotep, carpenter, sculptor and maker of stone vessels.'

Tradition was to add many other titles to the chancellor's name, such as vizir and chief ritualist. After being acknowledged as a great scholar, then

Base of a statue of Djoser, no. 6009

as a patron and protector of scribes during the New Kingdom, Imhotep became venerated as a god, one of the sons of Ptah, in the Saite era. Thus he tends to be represented as a seated figure, reading a papyrus spread out on his knees. The Greeks, who knew him as Imouthes, identified him with Aesculapius, god of medicine. Finally, although stone had been sporadically used before his time, Manetho's *Aegyptiaca*, written at the beginning of the Ptolemiaic period, attributes the invention of the art of construction in dressed stone to the genius of Imhotep.

11 | Blue faience panel from the Step Pyramid

Tiles of faience on limestone, plaster; H. 1.84 cm;
3rd Dynasty; First floor 42, corridor

Thanks to the patient and scholarly work carried out by Jean-Philippe Lauer over the last 60 years, the astonishing funerary complex built by Djoser at Saqqara may now be visited by the general public. So skilful and understated is the restoration work that in many cases it is confined to the merest suggestion; and because of it we are able to understand how the elements of this immense 15 hectare ensemble were organized, and how the genius of its architect, Imhotep, could totally transpose into stone a type of architecture which until then had been limited to perishable materials.

Once past the entrance colonnade, onto which the single gate of the great fortified perimeter opens, all the surface buildings are readily accessible, from the courtyard of the Heb-sed to the temple on the north side. But few visitors are allowed the privilege of descending over 30 metres underground to the two burial apartments reserved for the king's 'ka'. The one built to the east of the granite vault beneath the pyramid itself has been closed for many years; as for the other, which adjoins a smaller vault under the southern precinct, its cramped area and the fragility of its ancient faience wall facings have kept it out of bounds to the general public.

Yet here is a prodigious example of architectural décor, which is not only unique of its kind, but one of the most successful *tours de force* in the whole of Egyptian art. We are fortunate that Lauer was able to transport to the Museum a wall panel from these wonderful 'blue chambers', in the form

of excess blocks out of the unfinished rooms discovered by Firth ten years earlier, along with a few elements of original mounting torn out of the tomb on the south side by grave robbers in antiquity, and new blocks specially cut for the purpose.

The walls of the decorated chambers were covered with a preparation of fine limestone, with specially dressed stone designed to receive a covering of built-in faience tiles. These were originally of an intense blue, though in some cases the colour has faded considerably. The rows of faience imitate wickerwork, around 'blind-door' stelae representing the Horus Netjerikhet carrying out various rituals, and on panels surmounted by arcatures of 'djed columns', the Osirian amulets which symbolize stability.

The reconstruction at the Museum belongs to the latter category, and enables us to form some idea of what the ensemble looks like. The faience plaquettes, which are held in place by plaster, were not only built into the limestone, but also literally 'sewn' into the support with a plant-fibre cord which passed alternately through several plaquettes and then into the stone. This was clearly a pre-Imhotep technique, and it may be seen on the ancient block, stripped of its blue covering, which is exhibited alongside. Eighteen of the thirty faience blocks are original, and the faience itself is completely so, with the exception of one or two plaquettes which have been reconstructed in coloured plaster.

12 | Wooden panel of Hesyre

Wood; H. 1.15 m 3rd Dynasty; No.88; Ground floor, west side

Like five others of the same type displayed alongside it, this carved wooden panel comes from a large mastaba built with sun-dried bricks discovered by Mariette in the northern zone of the Saqqara necropolis, then re-excavated and studied by Quibell at the end of 1911. This re-excavation, conducted with the aid of a worker who as a boy

had been present at Mariette's dig, proved very fruitful, because the founder of the Cairo Museum had apparently been content to bring back five wooden panels without completely clearing the monument of debris. Its architecture was nonetheless worthy of interest, with a number of entirely original elements – especially the vault, which consisted of a 36 metre-long corridor scarcely more than 1 metre wide. One wall contained eleven geometrically decorated niches; the wooden panels were built into the backs of these niches, presumably because the brick could not be sculpted satisfactorily. Quibell discovered the remains of a sixth panel still in place, but the five others had completely disappeared. The other wall, whose surface was carefully plastered, carried an unusual painted scene apparently overlooked by Mariette. After recording this, Quibell had to rebury it in the sand because the paint could not stand up to the humidity and variations of temperature. It included pictures of tools, vases, furniture, games and chests, lined up almost geometrically on trays, where one might have expected to find the traditional bringers of offerings, or scenes from the life of the tomb's occupant. The burial chamber, which was very deep, had long since been violated. But, in addition to a knife handle bearing the name of Hesyre, Quibell found (in one of the last baskets of debris) the pieces of a clay seal with the Horus name Netjerikhet, which confirmed the dates suggested for the panels by several specialists.

Hesyre was thus a high official during the reign of Djoser. Among his many other titles, that of royal scribe seems to have been the most prestigious, because on each one of the remaining five panels, which are in fact the main elements of so many 'false doors' (*cf.* No.25) he is represented, seated or standing, with the emblems of this function. These are the palette with two cakes of ink, one red and one black; the reed pen; and the leather pouch which probably contained a reserve of powdered ink and which was later reinterpreted as a small jar of water.

The scene is superbly executed in shallow relief, standing out against a background which is slightly lower. Hesyre is portrayed in a sitting position, stretching out his right hand towards a simple table which carries pieces of bread. Above it are

mentions of traditional offerings: wine, incense,
meat. A long, tight garment knotted at the left
shoulder leaves free only the upper chest, with its
clearly defined bone-structure; the right arm held
out towards the offerings; and the left hand slant-
ing across the chest, grasping a cane and a 'sekhem' sceptre indicating his authority.

Hesyre wears a short wig with tight, regularly-
spaced curls, in contrast with the ringlets or long
tresses of the other panels, which faithfully repro-
duce the same aquiline profile, well-defined mouth
and moustache.

The hieroglyphs, each of which is a minor
masterpiece, are not arranged in clearly defined
columns, but nevertheless produce a superbly
ornamental effect. They should be scrutinized at
close range for a full appreciation of their
workmanship.

13 | Statues of Rahotep and Nofret

Painted limestone; H. 1.20 m and 1.18 m; 4th Dynasty; No.223; Ground floor 32, case E, opposite entrance

By reason of their extraordinary state of preservation, the famous statues of Prince Rahotep and his wife Nofret are justly counted among the most astonishing works of art in the Museum.

In 1871, a dealer from Alexandria who had requested a permit to search for bones, discovered a large mastaba of sun-dried brick a few dozen metres to the north of the pyramid of Snofru at Maidum. He reported his discovery to the authorities, but Mariette, who was busy with the preparations for the première of *Aida*, was unable to leave Cairo. Daninos was sent in his stead, with orders to reconnoitre the monument, date it if

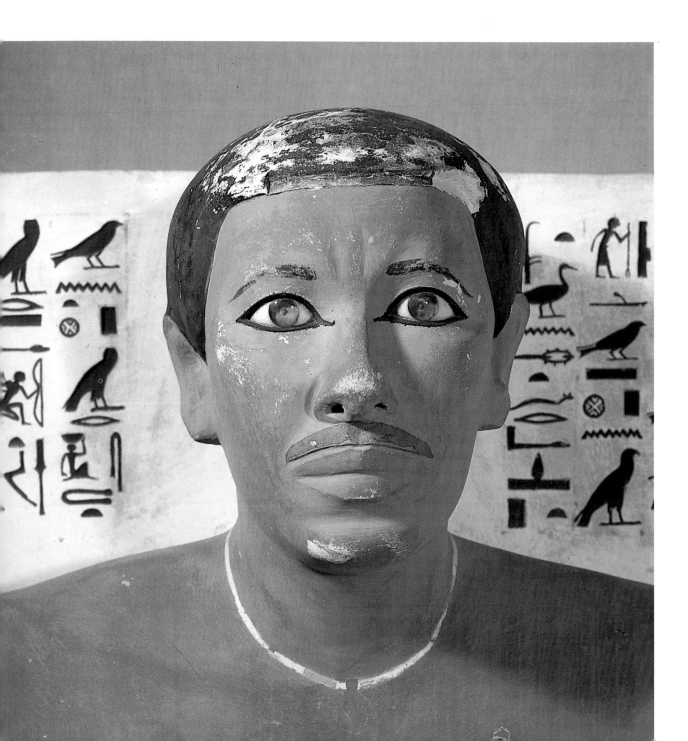

possible, and to carry out the necessary measures for its protection.

In his instructions, Mariette specified that 'if by chance any statues are found, they should be scrupulously left in place!'

For the time, this demonstrated a thoroughly praiseworthy degree of scientific rigour, and Mariette was quite right to make the stipulation, for the dig (which employed about a thousand workers) revealed that there were several thicknesses of carefully-laid stone in the limestone casing of the monument's east side. These stones had served to close the entrance to a vault which no human being can have entered since the most distant antiquity. What followed is perhaps best described by Daninos himself, in a letter written 15 years later to Maspero, Director General of the Antiquities Service. In it, Daninos gives an emotional account of the moment of discovery.

'... When the last two blocks of stone had been shattered and, fortunately as it turned out, removed from the excavation on my orders, the stonemason informed me that he had felt gusts of unbearably hot air escaping from a space behind them. He requested a candle, whch we handed to

him, and once again vanished into the tunnel. When he reappeared a few minutes later, he was in great haste and obviously in a state of terror. He told me that when he reached the end of the tunnel, he found himself confronted by the faces of two living beings with their eyes fixed upon him; which had scared him so thoroughly that for a moment he thought he would never find the exit. Wishing to see for myself whatever it was that could have made so strong an impression upon him, I climbed the ladder and entered the passage myself. What was my stupefaction to find myself in the presence of two wonderfully fashioned heads, whose eyes, reflecting the light I held in my hand, seemed so alive that they were in truth thoroughly disturbing. A covering of bronze, representing the eyelids, encased the eyeballs which were made of fragments of white quartz, skilfully veined with pink; in their centres, pieces of rock crystal, slightly convex, imitated the pupils of the human eye. Below this crystal was fixed a shining nailhead, which defined the point of vision and produced the glistening effect that created so lifelike an impression and fully explained the fear of my stonemason. I peered into the gloom and to my immense satisfaction discovered that the heads belonged to two almost life-size statues in painted limestone, and that they were completely intact.'

The statues were subsequently wrapped in hundreds of metres of cloth and carried by porters to Cairo, where the general public can now contemplate the extraordinary skill with which the artist contrived to imprison life in these blocks of limestone, as images of eternity. The fright of the worker who was the first to clap eyes on them is understandable, and when one considers that for the Egyptians a sculptor was (among other things) 'he who makes to live', his reaction seems a fitting homage to the absolute mastery of the artist who created these superb objects.

It is clear that the statues were made in a royal workshop. While Nofret is described simply as having belonged to the Pharaoh's entourage, the fine black hieroglyphs on the head of Rahotep indicate that he was a high priest of Heliopolis, a general and the son of a king, who, given the siting of the mastaba, must have been Snofru, father of Cheops.

The pair were thus important people at court; their sculptor has managed to surpass simple portraiture by expressing the essence of their personalities. The attentive, slightly anxious expression of Rahotep, and the slightly flaccid gentleness of Nofret's pudding face are the very image of powerful courtiers under the Old Kingdom.

14 | Fragment of stucco painting

Mineral colours on plaster; H. 27 cm; early 4th Dynasty; Ground floor 32, south side

Like the famous 'Maidum Geese' displayed beside it, this fragment of mural painting, which carries only two hieroglyphs, comes from the vault built by the noble Nefermaat in his immense mastaba for the funerary cult of his wife Itet.

When these pieces of wall were removed and taken to the Bulaq museum, shortly after the discovery of the statues of Rahotep and Nofret in a neighbouring mastaba, L. Vassali was obliged to take infinite care because of the thinness of the stucco supporting the colours. A few years later, when he reopened the excavations at the point where Mariette's workers had abandoned them,

Petrie discovered other painted fragments from the same wall. These are now divided up among several museums in London, Manchester and Boston, as well as Cairo; but the American William Stevenson Smith has been able nonetheless to reconstruct the scene of the single wall to which they all originally belonged. The wall was that of the north side of the tunnel leading through to the vault, and the décor consisted of an upper and lower register. The lower register showed scenes of ploughing and sowing, and the upper one was devoted to pictures of hunting with nets. The frieze formed by the three pairs of geese constituted a sub-register, above which the four sons of Itet were seen engaged in spreading nets to catch birds. They were identified by their names, and the two painted hieroglyphs which concern us represent one of these names.

The wicker basket has a handle which reads 'k', and the Egyptian vulture corresponds to the semitic 'aleph'. These probably represent the end of

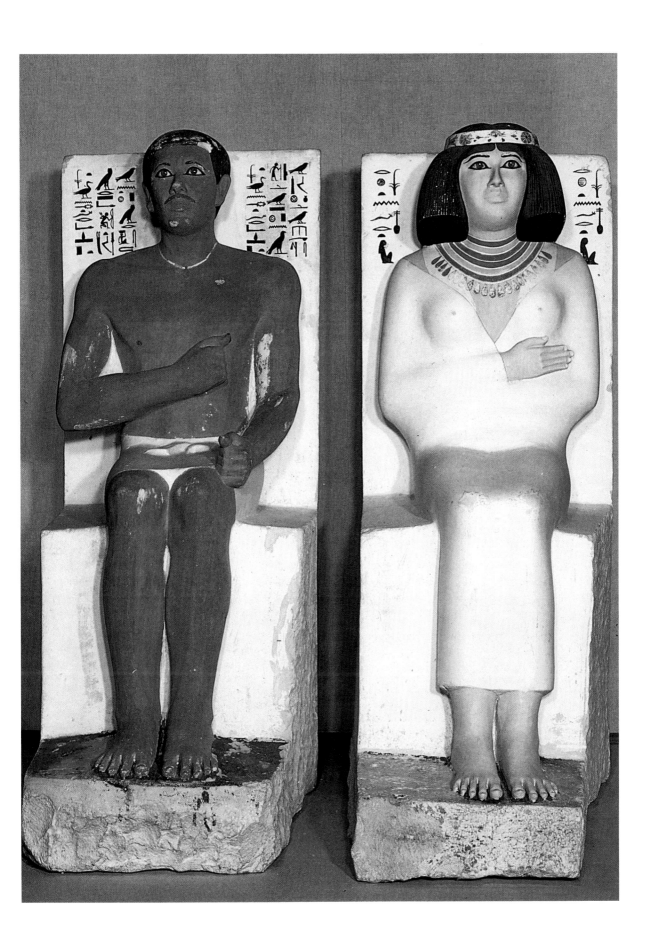

The 'Maidum Geese' (detail)

the name 'Serefka', which occurs (without an 'aleph') in several places on the tomb's façade, curiously decorated with grooved forms filled with coloured paste.

Like the geese, or the third fragment set beneath them, these simple but detailed hieroglyphs offer an insight into the techniques and materials used by Egyptian painters, the colours, applied in distemper to a clay or whitewashed surface, were made from powdered mineral pigments and held together with a fixative (vegetable gum, egg-white) added to the water. Ochres provided the full range of yellows, reds and browns, while greens and blues were derived from powdered azurite or calcinated copper salts. White and black came from limestone and wood charcoal, and completed a palette which may seem limited to us, but which served the Egyptian artist well enough for over three thousand years.

15 | Statuette of Cheops

Ivory; H. 9 cm; 4th Dynasty; No.4244; First floor 43, one of the two central display cases

This little figurine, which was found by Petrie at Abydos in 1903, has an interesting story attached to it. Along with a number of fragments of wooden

statues from the same period, it was found during the excavation of a storeroom in the northern part of the temple of Osiris, not far from Kom es-Sultan. At the moment of discovery the head was struck off by an unlucky blow from a pickaxe, the ivory from which it was carved having been rendered extremely fragile by a sojourn of over four thousand five hundred years in the humid earth. In this state, it would scarcely have attracted much attention, had there not been a 'Horus' name – the most ancient of the five names borne by royalty – carved beside the figure's right leg, which identified it as a likeness of Cheops. Aware that no statue had ever been found that could be attributed with certainty to Cheops, the great English Egyptologist was ready to do anything to recover the head.

After three weeks of incessant sifting of debris, Petrie's efforts were at last successful and the first portrait of Cheops was complete. It has been dated recently as 26th Dynasty (though the arguments in favour of this are not very convincing). Today, by an ironic twist of fate, this minute figurine remains the only image left to mankind of the builder of Egypt's most gigantic monument.

The king is dressed in a simple loincloth – the shendyt – and he wears the red crown of Lower Egypt, the back of which is missing. He is seated on a low-backed chair. His pose is similar to that

of Djoser, described above: the left hand lies flat on the thigh and the right hand, which holds the 'flabellum', is placed on the breast.

Small as it is, and despite the lamentable state of the ivory, the statuette is by no means devoid of majesty. However, even if the head (which is disproportionately large) is a realistic portrait of the king, it is hard to recognize here the impious, cruel tyrant, the oppressor of the people, whom the over-credulous Herodotus describes.

The overall impression is rather one of severity, accentuated by the vague smile which lingers on the face. Petrie exaggerated when, in the first flush of his discovery, he described the statuette's 'commanding air', and its reflection of 'the energy and indomitable willpower... of the man who marked the character of the Egyptian monarchy for all time'.

16 | Statue of Chephren

Diorite-gneiss; H. 1.68 m; 4th Dynasty; No.138;
Ground floor, opposite entrance

This famous statue is often deemed the greatest masterpiece in the Cairo Museum; indeed it may be justly called one of the key sculptural works in mankind's history. It was discovered by Mariette's excavators in 1860. Along with other statues of the builder of the second pyramid of Giza, it had been hurled down a shaft in the vestibule of the temple of reception fronting his funerary complex. This was the 'granite temple' which Mariette had almost finished excavating six years earlier, when, at the request of the Duc de Luynes, he had surveyed the site to see if there were any truth in

Pliny's assertion that the Sphinx had been built of elements from the tomb of a certain king Armais.

Matter, composition, relief, expression or finish, it is hard to choose which is the most admirable in this monument of Chephren. The king 'in majesty' is sculpted from a superb block of dark diorite, veined with white. He is seated on a throne with feet in the form of lion's paws, which on either side frame the symbol of the union of the two nations: the heraldic plant of Upper Egypt and the papryus of Lower Egypt, knotted on a sign which reads 'sma' (lungs and trachea) and signifies 'uniting'.

This kind of chair is usually backless, but here the high, thick back seems to have been introduced to support the image of a falcon, whose outstretched wings envelop the nape of the king's neck, and are exactly moulded to the shape of his headdress. The falcon is Horus, the god of monarchy, who seems at once to protect and to present the pharaoh, reminding the onlooker that the latter is a living Horus, his heir and successor on 'the throne of Horus'.

Chephren, whose name is carved on the plinth of the statue, is dressed in a shendyt only, and he wears a beard (broken) and a 'nemes' from which the 'uraeus' barely emerges. His eyes stare into the distance, he sits very straight, the left hand laid flat on the knee and the right grasping a case containing the document which makes him master of Egypt. Nothing else testifies to his rank, but Chephren's expression of serene strength can only belong to a man invested with the calm power of a god. Never, perhaps, has royal majesty been so simply and forcefully expressed; and we may easily imagine the effect that such a statue must have produced in the light that fell from the high apertures in the walls of the granite temple.

17 | Mycerinus triad

Schist (greywacke); H. 93 cm; 4th Dynasty; No.149; Ground floor 47, north side

The Museum possesses three of the four complete Mycerinus triads that G. Reisner brought to light in 1908, in the Valley Temple, at the smallest of the Giza pyramids. The fourth triad, differing from the others in that Hathor is positioned seated in the centre of the group along with the magnificent dyad of the King and Queen Khamerernebty, has gone to the Museum of Fine Arts in Boston, which carried out the excavations in a joint effort with Harvard University.

Like the others, this group, which represents Mycerinus between Hathor (right) and the personification of the nome of the dog (17th nome of Upper Egypt) is sculpted from a dark green stone commonly referred to by Egyptologists as 'schist'. It is not in fact schist, but greywacke, a crystalline, fine-grained sedimentary rock which looks like schist but which is not metamorphic.

Mycerinus stands upright, with his left foot forward as if walking. His arms are pressed to his sides and his hands grasp little scrolls. He wears a pleated shendyt with a long front piece, a beard and the white crown of Upper Egypt, without uraeus.

Hathor, like the king, is walking forward, while the secondary goddess is standing still, with her feet together. They stand slightly behind him and both wear long, clinging robes which reveal more of their bodies than they hide. Both goddesses have the features of the queen; they each pass one arm behind the king's back and in their other hand they bear the sign 'shen', a round cartouche symbolizing everything encircled by the sun in its daily course.

Above her long, striated wig, Hathor wears the traditional cow's horns enclosing the solar disc; whilst the head of the other female figure, who personifies the 17th province of Upper Egypt, is surmounted by its emblem (the black dog Anubis with an ostrich feather fixed in his back to indicate his sacred chamber). The emblem is carved in low relief on the stone from which the group is emerging.

The fine grain of the stone has allowed the sculptor to give special attention to the modelling of the bodies – the king's physique is strongly muscled, while the female bodies have softer curves – and to the idealized faces, which seem

18 | Statue of 'Sheikh el-Beled' *detail*

*Wood, copper and stone; H. 1.10 m; late 4th-early
5th Dynasty; No.140; Ground floor 42, north side*

This statue, which is rightly famous, scarcely
needs any introduction. The humblest school
manual, if it does not include the 'seated scribe' at
the Louvre, will at least have a photograph of this
figure to illustrate the great private statuary of the
Old Kingdom. When it was found at Saqqara
(probably in 1860) Mariette's workers were so
struck by its resemblance to the mayor of their
village that they gave it the name of 'Sheikh el-
Beled', which has stuck ever since. In fact, the
features are those of a chief ritualist named
Kaaper, who lived either at the end of the 4th
Dynasty, as evidenced by the architecture of the
great mastaba of air-dried brick in which the
statue was found, still upright in the sand; or else
at the beginning of the 5th Dynasty, if the crite-
rion for dating is confined to the extraordinary
realism of the portrait. There is no reason why we
should rule out the possibility that Kaaper's life
began at the close of one dynasty and ended at the
opening of the next; we already have the example
of an official who spent his early years at the court
of Mycerinus and terminated his career during the
reign of Niuserre.

The man portrayed so realistically in this
sculpture stands with his right foot forward in the
eternal attitude of gods and kings. The left arm is
bent and the left hand carries a long cane (modern)
while the right hand and arm are held to the side
of the body and must originally have held a 'sekhem' sceptre, a symbol of authority. Kaaper wears
a simple straight loincloth, which emphasizes the
corpulence resulting from his (clearly considerable) social success. The whole body is modelled with remarkable realism, though the feet and
the lower legs have been restored. The extraordinary art of the sculptor is chiefly evident in his
treatment of the head, which is enlivened by its
eyes of alabaster, rock crystal and black stone.

The neck is thickset, and the round head with
its shadow of a smile expresses both the dignity
and the self-satisfaction of a man who has 'arrived'
and who is now important, whilst the balding scalp
attests to the fact that he is no longer young.

utterly confident of their divine nobility. To the
balanced composition of the whole, which is already quite extraordinary, the artist has been able
to add a kind of breadth, expressed in the king's
forward movement, which accentuates the slightly
different directions in which the figures are
looking.

The texts carved on the flat part of the base
make clear that Mycerinus is 'beloved of Hathor,
the lady of the Sycamore', and the goddess of the
nome perpetually brings him all kinds of 'perfect
things' from her province. This last point prompts
the thought that there must have been as many
triads like this as there were provinces during the
4th Dynasty – about forty. The other triads which
have been found, whether complete or fragmen-
tary, would seem to offer the same conclusion.

19 | Birds in a papyrus swamp

*Limestone with paint traces; H. 1.02 m; 5th
Dynasty; Ground floor 47, north side*

So little remains of the mural decoration of the 4th
Dynasty funerary temple, that it was thought to be
non-existent, prior to the excavation of the lower
temple of the rhomboid complex of Snofru at
Dashur, where a number of very beautiful reliefs
were discovered. During the 5th Dynasty, however, all royal temples, whether their purpose was
solar or funerary, contained bas-reliefs which were
often of exceptional quality. Examples are the all-
too-rare fragments unearthed at Saqqara during
the excavations carried out by Firth in 1928–29 in
the upper temple of the funerary complex of Userkaf, the dynasty's first king.

This temple, with its unusual site on the
southern side of the pyramid, had been almost
completely ruined ever since the Saite era.
However, new excavations begun in 1948 enabled
Lauer to reconstruct its ground plan. Among other
important elements, it included a large courtyard
with porticos on three sides, which was ornamented by several statues of the king. One of these,
colossal in size, sat with its back to the south wall.
The head of this statue has been recovered
(no.6051, Ground floor 48, south side), along with
a few sculpted blocks from the walls which are
noteworthy not only for the quality of their reliefs
which demonstrate the surprising skill of their
authors in representing movement, but also for
their subject matter, which one would normally
expect to find only in private tombs. The scenes

include hunting birds in orchards, fishing with harpoons, boating and (see above) birds in a marsh.

The remarkable delicacy of the sculpture, the freedom of the composition and the breathtaking precision of the observation lead us to regret the loss of the remainder of the scene. But enough of it survives to astonish ornithologists, who have no difficulty whatever in recognizing each species of bird. At the centre is a black-and-white pied kingfisher (*Ceryle rudis*) caught in the moment of immobility in his flight which occurs just before he darts like an arrow on his prey. Elsewhere, from right to left, we identify the purple gallinule (*Horphyrio porphyrio*) with its strong feet and huge toes; the striped hoopoe (*Upupa epops*) with its fan-shaped crest; the sacred ibis (*Threskiornis aethiopicus*) with beak long and bent; the bittern (*Botaurus stellaris*) which loves aquatic vegetation; the night heron (*Nycticorax nycticorax*) which fishes in the dark; and finally the European kingfisher (*Alcedo atthis ispida*) which waits on a perch for its prey to appear.

20 | Procession of the Domains of Sahure *detail*

Limestone; H. 1.10 m; 5th Dynasty; Ground floor 36, south east corner

The Deutschen Orient-Gesellschaft excavations organized at Abusir by Ludwig Borchardt were highly successful in widening our knowledge of how a royal funerary complex of the Old Kingdom was organized. From 1902 to 1908, the progressive unearthing of the buildings adjoining three 5th Dynasty royal pyramids established the fact that each one had its own reception temple – or 'lower' temple – beside a canal running along the edges of cultivated fields; its own paved road leading towards the plateau; and its own cult temple – the 'upper' one – with its back to the pyramid itself. The best preserved ensemble of this type is that of Sahure, the dynasty's second king, which has yielded a number of very beautiful reliefs, now displayed in Cairo and Berlin.

This relief comes from the vestibule of the smaller, eastern entrance of the upper temple, where it was originally placed on the north wall. It represents a procession of some of the 'nomes' of Lower Egypt and its domains. The south wall was adorned with a similar procession relative to Upper Egypt. For each 'nome' mentioned, whether it belonged to the Delta or the valley, a masculine personification of the province is followed by a varying number of feminine personifications of domains founded by the king. These foundations, whose size might vary considerably, were of two types: they could be enclosures dominated by a manorial dwelling, with one or several cultivable fields; or they could be village-based, perhaps organized around newly-granted lands. In either case, their revenues were used to fund the royal funerary establishments.

In the above illustration, the masculine figure, wearing a loincloth, wig, gorget and godlike beard, represents the nome of Lower Egypt, the emblem of which is placed over his head. Behind this personification of the nome of the Black Bull (of which Athribis, now Benha, was capital) come two female figures each representing a domain which is mentioned by name. The first of these (the only one visible in the photograph), comes forward proclaiming 'I bring you all the offerings of the estate of Sahure (named), the abundance of Sahure' and she carries a 'was' sceptre, which is the most prized of all offerings – a loaf of bread placed on a mat, a libation jug, 'ankh' signs, and a young bull. Grid markings are still visible on these finely-sculpted reliefs. To the left, a column of text which was at least as high as two registers, gives the name of the royal pyramid: Kha-ba-Sahure ('The soul of Sahure appearing').

21 | Statuette of seated man

Yellow limestone; H. 61 cm; 5th Dynasty; Ground floor 42, south west corner

De Morgan discovered this statuette in an anonymous tomb at Saqqara. The same tomb, which was first excavated in 1893, also contained the celebrated 'Seated Scribe of Cairo' (same room, south east corner) which, despite its different treatment, would seem to be a portrait of the same individual. Instead of squatting cross-legged on the ground, the man sits on a backless chair, wearing a simple pleated loincloth, in the so-called 'classic' pose which appeared in the 4th Dynasty and which is probably inspired by some royal model. He sits stiffly, the eyes stare straight in front of him, and the right hand is held vertically on the right thigh and grasps a scroll. The other hand lies flat on the left knee. The face, framed by a short wig with tight curls rendered by small rectangles in relief, has a calm, smiling expression. The eyes are inlaid, according to the early 4th Dynasty technique, and have a curiously lifelike effect conferred by the contrast of alabaster and rock crystal set into a copper which has been thickened by oxydation. The statue is sculpted in fine yellow limestone with a very smooth finish; the modelling is precise if somewhat angular. The sculptor has taken the trouble to detach the arms from the body – a rare feature – and has given much attention to the musculature of both arms and legs. Odd details are the two copper ornaments which once decorated each side of the wig next to the ears; of these, only two hooks remain.

22 | Panel of Rawer

Alabaster, with traces of paint; H. 85 cm; 5th Dynasty; Ground floor 47, right of entrance

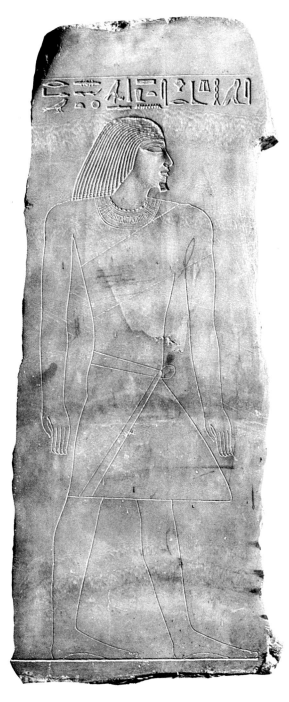

This magnificent alabaster panel emerged during the Egyptian University excavations conducted by Selim Hassan at Giza in the 1928–29 season. It was discovered in the tomb of a great personage named Rawer immediately to the south west of the Great Sphinx. This tomb is not, strictly speaking, a mastaba, *ie*, one of those massive edifices whose regular groupings at the foot of the royal pyramid offer an image, forever fixed in stone, of the hierarchical society which dominated the pharaonic system. Rather, it is a far wider and more complex construction, containing as it does no less than twenty alcoves and twenty-five walled corridors – serdabs – in which over a hundred statues once stood. Of these, only ten were eventually found intact.

The panel was still in place, built vertically into the wall at the back of one of the niches, at the top of three steps. It consists of a roughly rectangular slab of yellow alabaster, perfectly smooth, which bears nothing more than the portrait of the tomb's occupant, below a single line of hieroglyphs. These give the name of Rawer, as well as four of his titles, all of them religious: 'sem' priest, ritualist, initiate of the secret words of the gods (*ie*, hieroglyphs) and 'khet' priest of Min.

The portrait is very striking because only the head emerges in bas-relief; great feeling is shown by the accentuation of the face in profile, which is the most characterisitc feature of the individual. The rest of the body is simply carved in outline. Rawer wears a necklace, a wig and a little square beard. He is garbed in a simple short loincloth with a triangular apron. A piece of cloth stretches diagonally across his chest and over his left shoulder.

A short inscription discovered in the main 'serdab' of the tomb tells us that Rawer lived during the reign of Neferirkare, third pharaoh of the 5th Dynasty; but even more interesting than this chronological precision is the content of the biographical text. Usually, such texts are confined to recitals of the individual's high achievements which, in the case of Rawer, is confined to a single incident, one so important that it was deemed the only occurrence worthy of mentioning to posterity. It is this: during a ceremony in which a god's barque is hauled up from the water, Rawer, who was carrying out his office of 'sem' priest, was about to hand the king some kind of ritual garment and was accidentally struck a blow by the king's staff. The latter, for the sake of the affection he bore for the priest, whom 'he loved above all others', immediately commanded that no man should lay hands on him, and that a stela should be placed in his tomb to preserve the memory of this event, which was duly done in the royal presence.

This anecdote shows very clearly how great was the taboo on the king's person. The Egyptians who built the pyramids were utterly convinced that their pharaoh was a living god, which partly explains the gigantic scale of their buildings. This sacred character of the king and the fact that no-one was allowed to touch him physically, also explains why an important individual like Rawer carried other titles, in addition to his religious and civil ones, like 'coiffeur' or 'supervisor of the royal ornaments'. Duties like these would obviously oblige him to practise on the pharaoh's person the same gestures as the priest would carry out on the statue of the god, while performing the daily mysteries of the divine cult.

23 | Reliefs from the mastaba of Kaemrehu
details

Limestone; H. (from the register) 24 cm; 5th Dynasty; No.79; Ground floor 41, west side

The weighing of gold and the modelling of a statue

The almost obsessive desire of the Egyptian to find beyond the grave everything he had previously known on earth, has produced the strange paradox that nothing in Egypt is so descriptive of life as the houses of the dead.

The painted and carved scenes which decorate Egyptian burial vaults were intended, by the magical properties of the image, to restore to the dead man in the next world what had been his way of life in this. Hence these tombs have become for us marvellous open books of images, as well as precious sources of information. We need only consult them to find forceful descriptions of how carpenters, fishermen, brewers, butchers, bakers, goldsmiths and labourers went about their business, or of how the leisured classes amused themselves by listening to musicians, hunting, fishing, or visiting their domains.

This wall-facing, which comes from the mastaba of a priest of the pyramid of Niuserre named Kaemrehu, contains four registers of highly varied activites, such as grain harvesting, the fabrication of vases and statues, brewing, pouring beer into pitchers, metalworking, and the keeping of accounts. In scenes of this sort, a few hieroglyphs above the figures define the act in question (shaking or sifting wheat, filtering beer, etc), or indicate what they are saying to one another ('Will you take some beer, in honour of Sokaris?' 'Hey, you dirty swine, move that herd along!' 'Hurry up, friend!' etc).

The details in the lower register show two stages in the fashioning of a statue, and the weighing of gold ingots prior to the goldsmith's work.

The forms of the statue are first roughed out with dolerite pebbles and then entrusted to two sculptors who do the finer work with chisels. The weighing of the precious metal, which is recorded by a scribe, takes place as soon as the ingots are brought from the mine. The scribe uses scales which hang from a hook held by another man.

The reliefs are meticulous in character, but they do not match the subtle modelling of the great Saqqara mastabas, which no visitor should miss. For illustrations of the working life of ancient Egypt, perhaps the best mastabas are those of Ti, Ptahhotep and Mereruka.

24 | Family of Kaemhesit

Painted limestone; H. 52 cm; 5th Dynasty; Ground floor 42, south side, case D

This painted limestone group, with colours partially lost, is a portrait of the overseer of sculptors and royal carpenter, Kaemhesit, with his wife and son. It was found by Quibell in 1913, in a small room within a mastaba dating from the end of the 5th Dynasty. The mastaba is sited to the west of Mereruka's tomb, not far from the pyramid of Teti at Saqqara.

The couple are seated on a simple, high-backed, cube-shaped chair. The wife's right arm lies affectionately over her husband's shoulders; Kaemhesit's hands rest on his knees. He is dressed in a pleated loincloth and he wears a broad necklace and thick wig with serried curls. His wife's body fits tightly into a long, clinging dress and her neck is adorned with a collar which was originally painted. On her head, she wears a wig parted into two equal masses of hair which frame a rather simpering face.

The couple's son is portrayed between them; he is small and naked and he leans against the seat, which is exactly his height. He stands with his left arm pressed against his body, the right bent with a finger to the mouth in the traditional gesture of childhood.

Although it is scarcely exceptional, this group is nonetheless of good quality and represents a typical portrait of a bourgeois couple, petrified for all time in the fullness of their own self-satisfaction. It is rather like one of our modern family photographs.

25 | 'False door' stela of Hesesi

Limestone; H. 2.35 m; 6th Dynasty; No.175; Ground floor 42, north side

Of all the architectural elements comprised in a mastaba, the type of stela known to archaeologists as a 'false door' was undoubtedly the most important. The stela was commonly placed at the far end

of the tomb, and functioned magically just like a
real door; in other words, the dead man's soul
could make use of it to collect the offerings left for
him by the living people who remained faithful to
his cult, and otherwise to come and go. To this
purpose, the stela bears a representation of a door
with panels perpetually ajar; it is topped by a kind
of roller-blind, raised to allow the spirit of the
departed to pass through; and the spirit himself is
sometimes depicted about to emerge, either in bas-
relief or sculpted in the round.

But in the eyes of the Egyptian, even this was
not enough, because he felt that his survival after
death still depended over-much on the good will of
those in the land of the living. So he resorted to
magic, combining the creative power of the image
with that of the word; and the representation of
the door was reinforced by that of the dead man,
seated in his burial vault before a heap of offerings.
The remaining space around him was covered in
funerary formulae containing his name and titles
and enumerating everything he hoped to receive in
the next world. Once the necessary offerings had
been depicted in stone, the occupant of the tomb
could be sure that he would be nourished for ever
in his eternal habitation, however seldom some
living person came by to read aloud the texts engraved on the stela. For this reason the text of an
'injunction to the living' would feature on the stela
itself, or at the entry to the burial vault. By this,
the owner of the mastaba, far from placing a curse
on those who entered, (whether they were scribes,
priests or anyone else) would beg them 'to give
force to the (funerary) formulae' by reading them
aloud.

The 'false door' stela of Hesesi was found north
of the Step Pyramid of Saqqara. Hesesi's main
title seems to have been that of 'scribe of the royal
archives', and it was bought in 1887 by Grébaut.

Beneath a high Egyptian moulding, whose
colours have almost completely vanished, a torus
defines the decorated area with hieroglyphs cut
into the stone; these were once painted blue. In
the upper area, next to a standing figure of the
deceased, are three lines of text which express the
hope that, because of the offering made 'by the
king and by Anubis, foremost in the Divine Booth,
invocation offerings might be made for him' during various important feasts whose names are
invoked. Under this first formula, on either side of
the dead man depicted in his vault, are figures
representing his son Sheshi sprinkling Hesesi's 'ka'
with incense and offering him cooked fowl. In

another two-line, horizontal inscription, just below the 'door' itself, Hesesi voices the desire 'to be buried in his tomb in the necropolis as a revered one whom the god loves'. Finally, over eight symmetrically-placed columns on either side of the door opening, all Hesesi's titles are listed: 'first after the king, overseer of all the king's works, overseer of the two granaries and the two treasuries, initiate of the secret of all the royal

ordinances', along with various formulae by which he again asks that 'invocation offerings' be made.

Further on, he expresses a wish 'to travel the roads that are passable (in the West) which are commonly travelled by those who are honoured (next to the Great God)'. The decoration of the stela is completed below those columns of text by a double portrayal of Hesesi's two sons, Sheshi and Itji, bearing incense-burners and offerings.

26 | Statue of Pepy I *detail*

Copper, obsidian and limestone; full height 1.77 m; 6th Dynasty; No.230; Ground floor, north west corner

The seven known fragments of the 'Palermo Stone' preserve the royal annals which, up till the 5th Dynasty, recorded at least one important event and the height of the Nile flood waters for every year. The same stone informs us that a large cop-

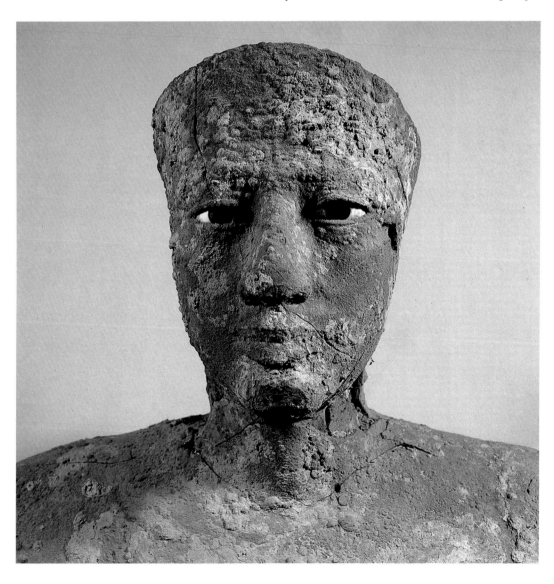

per statue of Khasekhemwy was made at the end
of the 2nd Dynasty and that Neferirkare, third
king of the 5th Dynasty, used this material to
execute two model boats for his solar temple. Thus
the manufacture of very large copper objects must
have been something very much out of the ordinary in the Old Kingdom.

Today, the largest and most ancient metal statue
that has been brought to light in Egypt remains
that of Pepy I, which was discovered at Hierakonpolis by Quibell and Green at the same time as the
statue of Khasakhem (No.7). There was, in fact, a
second statue, much smaller, which was discovered
soldered by oxidation inside the other's torso.

The two statues originally stood side by side on
the Nine Bows of the same plinth. They were
made in the same way, with bodies and limbs
fashioned from hammered copper plates, which
were subsequently assembled and nailed to a
wooden support. In spite of restoration work by
Barsanti, corrosion of the metal has been so extensive that it is impossible to say if certain areas,
such as the heads and hands, were cast or
hammered.

The lifesize statue is that of Pepy I, advancing
at a walk. The hands, with fingernails which were
originally gilded, once carried a mace or sceptre,
and a long staff. The king was certainly dressed in
a loincloth, and must have had a crown denoting
his royalty; but since the hips and the back of the
head have disappeared, there is no way of knowing
what kind of clothing or headdress the statue wore.
All the same, certain traces allow one to suppose
that both these elements were in moulded and
gilded plaster. The modelling of the body is indif-
ferent, but the mysterious, smiling face offers a
powerful portrait of its owner. The intense expression in the long eyes, inlaid with limestone and
obsidian, serves to accentuate the contrast between
the shiny stones and the almost powdery effect of
the oxidized copper.

The smaller statue, whose left leg is larger than
its right, is of a child. It has been suggested that
this also is Pepy I, but logic, and the clearly different facial traits, compel the conclusion that the
statue portrays Merenre, Pepy's son and successor.
Merenre was perhaps already associated with the
throne at the time of the first royal jubilee mentioned next to the king's cartouche on a fragment
of the metal plinth, which was found soldered by
time to the king's chest.

Statue of Merenre

27 | Statue of Niankhpepy-the-Black

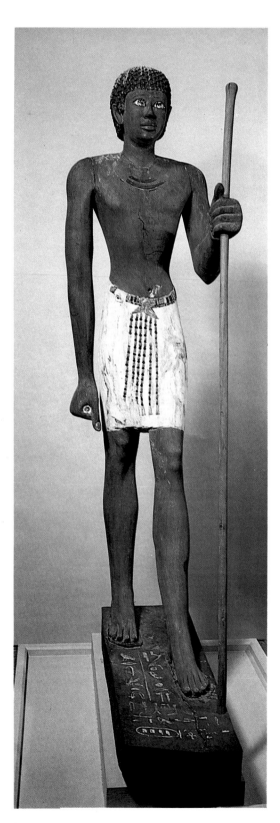

*Painted wood; H. 1.05 m; 6th Dynasty; No.161;
First floor 32, south west corner*

This statue, which is certainly more remarkable
for its excellent state of preservation than for the
quality of its sculpture, is a fine example of the
kind of statuary which was being produced in
provincial workshops towards the end of the Old
Kingdom. It was found at Meir, the necropolis of
the capital of the xivth nome of Upper Egypt, in
1894, and represents the 'Governor of Upper
Egypt, Chancellor and unique, honoured friend of
the great god, ritualist and overseer of prophets,
Niankhpepy-the-Black', according to the inscription on the stand.

This important personage is depicted advancing
at a walk, leaning with his left hand on a long staff,
and probably carrying some symbol of authority,
now lost, in his right (a sekhem, perhaps). He
wears a one-piece loincloth with a belt and apron
of richly-coloured stones, along with a short wig.
The curls are rendered by small rectangles in
relief. The details of the woodwork are finely
executed, but the proportions of the figure are
bizarre, with curiously elongated torso and limbs,
hands too big and head too small.

The tomb contained a large number of other
statuettes, which are displayed in another case
nearby (no.6133, collective display case K). These
represent male and female servants carrying out
various tasks – preparing flour, baking bread,
roasting fowls or brewing beer. The most original
of these, which is now exhibited on the ground
floor, case B, is known as the 'Cairo Porter'; it
portrays a servant carrying his master's baggage.

There was also another statue of Niankhpepy,
smaller than the first, with head unadorned and a
long white loincloth. It seems – as Capart has
suggested – that the presence of these two statues
corresponds to an inexplicable custom of the era,
whereby the deceased was given two different
effigies of himself, one bare-headed, in a long
garment, the other bewigged, in a short loincloth.

28 | The Noble Ipi in his sedan chair

Limestone; H. 1.12 m; 6th Dynasty; No.61; Ground floor, south side

The reconstructed wall to which this scene belongs is all that remains of a 6th Dynasty mastaba which was discovered (according to Maspero) south of Saqqara in 1883; the site was the levelling course of a similar, 4th Dynasty tomb. Borchardt, on the other hand, gives the date of discovery as 1886,

either at Saqqara or at Dashur. In any case, the tomb belonged to Ipi, who is depicted supervising harvesting and the slaughtering of livestock, while inspecting his lands from a sedan chair carried by fourteen porters in two rows.

This form of vehicle was habitually used by great lords whenever they travelled any distance, prior to the appearance of the horse and the chariot at the close of the 'domination of the Hyksos'. It appears frequently in 4th and 6th Dynasty mastabas and there seem to have been two distinct types. In one case, the shafts supported a kind of box, in which the passenger crouched with his knees drawn up to his chest (see the Hetepheres palanquin, no.6041, First floor, west). The other consisted of a chair with a back of varying height, and a stool for the feet.

Ipi's contraption is of the latter type, but it includes a palanquin with a canopy supported by elegant narrow columns. The top of the canopy is decorated with 'djed' pillars and bound papyrus plants two by two.

The seated Ipi is twice the size of the figures standing either side of him. He wears a loincloth with a triangular, starched apron; a panther skin, with one foot and claws visible on his left shoulder; a broad necklace; and a ringletted wig swept back over his shoulders. He carries what appears to be a reed pen and a fly whisk made of three small animal skins. In the customary fashion, his name and titles are exactly listed. The secondary figures are on three different principal levels, with a fourth which includes only one individual: they are all servants carrying items of their master's property, parasol-bearers running along beside the palanquin, or various other members of the household.

The bas-relief technique is characteristic of the 6th Dynasty; the surface is worked much more deeply than is usual for the 5th Dynasty and the figures stand out more clearly from the background. However, this greater thickness is not used to accentuate the modelling, which thus lacks the subtle nuances afforded in the 5th Dynasty by the play of tiny surface differences.

29 | The Noble Meketre inspecting his livestock

Painted wood; H. 55 cm; 11th Dynasty; No.6080; First floor 27, west side

Under the Old Kingdom, people of quality were not satisfied merely to secure eternal life by covering the walls of their tombs with bas-reliefs; little by little, they began to acquire the habit of arranging statuettes of servants perpetually carrying out their daily duties, all around the statue of the dead man himself. These smaller figures were generally carved from limestone and in earlier cases there would be only one or two at a time. Later, during the 6th Dynasty, they proliferated, becoming much smaller and switching from stone to wood. Finally, by the First Intermediate Period and the Middle Kingdom, they ceased to be isolated effigies and became complete scenes, real maquettes of the daily lives of peasants and artisans which were buried along with the deceased.

The 11th Dynasty was the golden age for these painted wooden figures, which subsequently disappeared during the dynasty that followed. The most beautiful of all were found in March 1920, by Herbert E. Winlock and the excavations of the Metropolitan Museum of Art, New York, in the double tomb of Meketre, a chancellor and steward in the reign of Mentuhotep I. This important figure had built the tomb for himself and his son Inyotef, in a rocky outcrop south of the temples of

◁ *Weaver's workroom*

Carpenter's workshop ▷

Deir el-Bahri. Nearly thirty exceptionally detailed models were piled up in a roughly-hewn hiding place, whose walled-up entrance was so cunningly concealed in the floor of the main tunnel leading to the tomb that it had escaped the notice of Daressy in 1895 and Mond in 1902.

The find consisted of models of a garden with a veranda, stable, butchery, granary, bakery, brewery, spinning and weaving shops, carpenter's shop, carriers of offerings, fishing and pleasure boats: everything, in fact, which could assure Meketre of the same comfortable existence after death that he had known in his lifetime. Some details were even provided in duplicate.

The largest models represent the counting and recording of livestock, in the presence of Meketre himself. This operation played so important a part in Egyptian life that it was used as a reference for reckoning years at the end of the Old Kingdom. Meketre, with his son beside him, is portrayed sitting on a dais in the shade of a colonnaded pavilion. To his right, four scribes are carrying out their function; the chief herdsman stands in front of his master, paying his respects, while other herdsmen drive nineteen head of mottled cattle past the dais.

Obviously, not many of the other models of this kind found in Egypt are of a quality to match those of Meketre – though they are often very touching in their clumsy workmanship.

Nonetheless we are able to piece together the daily life of ordinary people, with a wealth of technical and picturesque detail, in a way that no historian would have dared hope for, even in his wildest dreams.

30 | Bas-relief of Mentuhotep I

Limestone; H. 1.40 m; 11th Dynasty; Ground floor (atrium), east side

This beautiful bas-relief came to the Museum in 1936, the same year that it was discovered by the excavators of the Cairo Institut Français d'Archéologie Orientale. It was found at Tod, a small town about 20 miles south of Luxor on the right bank of the Nile. Tod was the ancient shrine of Montu, the warlike divinity of the Thebes nomos, from whom the obscure Amun later wrested the primacy of the dynastic gods.

The temple, which was dedicated to Montu from the time of the 5th Dynasty, was reconstructed by Sesostris I during the 12th Dynasty. Today it is almost entirely overwhelmed by modern housing, some of which had to be expropriated in order to uncover the ancient remains.

Several decorated stone blocks were found, which attest that the kings of the 11th Dynasty kept the temple under their protection prior to its complete rebuilding by Sesostris I. The one illustrated here is in the finely-carved intaglio (incised) manner; it depicts king Nebhepetre Mentuhotep making a ritual offering to Montu, with the goddess Neith behind him.

The god is represented with the head of a bird and the body of a human being; he carries a 'was' sceptre in one hand, and the 'ankh' in the other. He wears a kind of corselet, along with a loincloth to which is attached the tail of a bull. His head-dress is composed of two falcon's tailfeathers projecting from a wig, a solar disc, and two uraei which alone would identify him as Montu.

The king wears a loincloth with a triangular apron, a beard denoting divinity, bracelets and a broad necklace. On his brow sits the white crown of Upper Egypt. Of Neith, who stands behind him, only the upper torso remains; but she is recognizable by the red crown of Lower Egypt, which had become her traditional feature because of her title of 'lady of Sais'. It is noteworthy that this ancient archer-goddess, who in some folklore was worshipped as a creative and androgynous figure, carries the 'was' sceptre of the male gods rather than the 'wadj' sceptre which was usually reserved for goddesses.

A text, obviously decorative in conception, frames the scene described above. The hieroglyphs here are particularly refined. They are divided into columns and specifically describe what is going on in the picture. In exchange for the worship he enjoys Montu of Djerti (Tod) bestows 'all life and power' and 'places all foreign nations under the domination (literally, under the sandals) of the king of Upper and Lower Egypt, Nebhepetre... the son of Re Mentuhotep, the perfect god, lord of ritual'.

This is the pharaoh whom most Egyptologists have now come to recognize, after years of debate, as Mentuhotep I, the most important monarch of the 11th Dynasty. It was Mentuhotep who brought an end to the feudal system of the First Intermediate Period, at the beginning of the Middle Kingdom, thereby restoring the unity of

Egypt. This king did not facilitate the task of later historians – during his long reign, which spanned half a century, he seems to have changed his title twice and the writing of his first name once. Hence some scholars have been led to believe that three distinct kings ruled in the time spanned by his reign.

Some reliefs found at Gebelein proffer the information that Mentuhotep was not content merely to annex Lower Egypt, but also made war on the Asiatics, the Libyans and the Nubians. Hence it is no surprise to find him here making offerings to a war god, in company with one of the principal goddesses of the Delta, whose Greek equivalent was Athena.

31 | Figurine of a woman

Wood, Nile mud; H. 23 cm; 11th Dynasty; First floor 34, case I

Several dozen figurines of this type are known to exist; the majority come from tombs which can be reliably dated in the second half of the 11th Dynasty, and which were discovered near Deir el-Bahri by the mission organized by the Metropolitan Museum of Art, New York. The one shown here is perhaps one of the most complete, and was found in 1930–31 in a tomb of the Asasif.

The body lacks limbs, apart from two stumps of arms. It is reduced to a stark silhouette, more concise than stylized, and it is cut out of a small wooden plank. The head, which is roughly made from a ball of alluvium, is very small in proportion to the rest of the body. This smallness is accentuated by the abundant hair, which is curiously arranged in a style which was common in Nubia until recent times, according to Winlock: *ie*, in rosaries of clay beads with larger, conical pieces at the ends. The eyes are made of two round pieces of bone or shell and have the naïve look of children's drawings. Likewise, the simplistic way of suggesting a short, indefinable garment by cross-hatching and coloured squares offers the same childish note. The garment covers neither the torso, which is tatooed around the breasts and the wide necklace, nor the belly, which is wholly occupied by a deliberately emphasized female sex.

This magnified sex, as in many prehistoric statuettes, is in fact the sole *raison d'être* of this kind of figurine. While some of them may have been ordinary dolls, or even fertility charms for the little girls to whom they belonged, all the rest were frank representations of the principle of femininity itself. They were placed at the dead man's disposal, along with the food offerings, on the assumption that he would recover all his virile potency along with all the other attributes of a living being – and hence his needs would not be confined to eating and drinking.

Similar figurines in faience, ivory, wood, stone and clay have been found in 12th Dynasty tombs, and are perhaps more realistic and more pleasing to the eye. Some experts have postulated that they are effigies of the soul, or even (despite the absence of legs) of dancing girls. However, the description of 'dead men's concubines', though scarcely perfect, at least seems apt.

32 | Sarcophagus of Princess Kawit *detail*

Smooth limestone; total H. 1.05 m; 11th Dynasty; No.623; First floor, north side

This well-known scene forms part of the décor of a limestone sarcophagus discovered in 1904–05 by Naville and Hall, in the course of excavations conducted by the Egypt Exploration Fund at Deir el-Bahri.

The coffin, made of six stone slabs tied together with ropes, bears the name of the lady Kawit, a priestess of Hathor, who belonged to the family (or the harem) of Mentuhotep I. She shared this distinction with five other queens or princesses, buried, as she was, in a row of six vaults within the royal funerary complex.

Kawit is seated on a chair with elbow-rests. She holds to her lips a cup which has just been filled by a servant, and a woman is arranging her coiffure. The princess wears a long, sheathlike dress and a short rounded wig which encases her head. Her neck is adorned with necklaces, her right wrist with a bracelet, and both legs with anklets. In her left hand she holds a mirror to watch the work of the coiffeuse, who is delicately plaiting a strand of hair under others which she has drawn apart and is holding in place with a hairpin.

The other servant is in all likelihood pouring into a cup the result of the milking depicted farther on. He exhorts Kawit to drink: 'For the sake of your ka, Mistress! drink what I offer you!'

While the elongated bodies of the figures are a heritage of the First Intermediate Period, the pronounced features of the faces, the style inherent in the clear contours, and a certain overall rigidity, testify to the art of Thebes in the early Middle Kingdom.

It will be noted that in the funerary inscription above this scene, the two horned vipers corresponding to the letter 'f' are shown with severed heads. This was a magical defensive measure designed to destroy their power to hurt the spirit of the princess in the afterlife.

33 | Sesostris I embraced by the god Ptah

Limestone; H. 3.35 cm; 12th Dynasty; No.265; Ground floor, west side

Legrain cannot have suspected what awaited him when, at the request of Maspero, he began excavating the courtyard between the constructions along the east-west axis of the temple of Karnak and the seventh pylon raised by Tuthmosis III. At the end of December 1901, he discovered this beautiful limestone pillar beneath the ancient paving. It had once been part of a jubilee building constructed by Sesostris I, the foundations of which seemed to be almost exactly in place. Legrain therefore made experimental digs to a lower level, in an attempt to find the floor plan of a building which must have been two metres below the surface. Practically nothing remained, but in 1903, statues began to be unearthed beneath a layer of stone blocks dating from the beginning of the 18th Dynasty. Thenceforward, for three seasons, Legrain found himself down in the mud, engrossed in a veritable 'pêche aux statues', to use

Maspero's phrase. Legrain had discovered not treasure, as he first thought, but a cache, or favissa. Quantities of ex-voto effigies had been buried there, probably under the last Ptolemies because they were encumbering the rooms and courtyards of the temple of Amun. In 1905, having reached a depth of 14 metres in water, the excavators finally gave up the attempt to complete their work; but in three years they had extracted no fewer than 751 statues and stelae (see Nos. 54, 57, 77, 81, 85, 89, 96, 97, 98, 99, 101 and 103 in this book), and about 17,000 bronzes!

At the time of its discovery, the pillar of Sesostris I had retained its bright colours, despite the water and the years. These faded quickly in contact with the air and eventually vanished completely, perhaps allowing us a better appreciation of the very fine reliefs on all four sides of the block. On each facing, the second sovereign of the 12th Dynasty is seen with a different headdress and different clothes, accompanied by a different god. These are, in succession, Amun, Atum, Horus and Ptah. In the illustration, the latter is portrayed in the traditional way, as a man wearing a skullcap and tightly fitting, mummylike robe, with only the arms emerging. Ptah, the demiurge of Memphis, stands on a dais to welcome the king into his pavilion; 'the perfect god Sesostris', whom Ptah grasps around the waist, wears a simple 'shendyt' adorned with a bull's tail (the end of which is visible), a necklace, and the 'nemes'. The god Ptah is denoted as 'he who is to the south of his wall', an epithet probably alluding to the White Wall(s), the ancient name for one of the oldest quarters of Memphis. He proclaims that he 'bestows all life, stability and dominion, all health and all joy to the king of Upper and Lower Egypt, Kheperkare, endowed with life, stability and authority as Re'.

Around the two figures, the hieroglyphs of these stereotyped formulae admirably fill the decorative rôle assigned to monumental calligraphy. Their perfection, which is close to that attained by the 'White Chapel', also built under Sesostris, combines with the beauty of the relief itself to make us regret that so few Middle Kingdom buildings have survived.

34 | Head of a falcon

Gold and obsidian; H. 35.3 cm (with feathers); 12th Dynasty; No.4010; First floor, case 3, left of windows

This glorious masterpiece of the goldsmith's craft was discovered by Quibell under the paving stones of a room in the temple of Kom el-Ahmar, the present name for the site on the left bank of the Nile, about 20 kilometres north of Edfu, which was once Nekhen, prehistoric capital of Upper Egypt, known to the Greeks as Hierakonpolis.

It is the head of a composite statue of a mummified falcon, the falcon being the special form taken by the Horus of Nekhen. At the moment of discovery, at the beginning of the excavation of the 1897–98 season, the head was still in place atop a wooden body, plated with copper, which had been nailed in place with copper nails. The ensemble, which did not survive, was perched on a long, hollow, bronze stem, which in turn was buried in a cylindrical clay support with a vase at its end. This was complemented by a bronze statuette of a king, about 20 centimetres tall, which was placed in front of the divine bird.

The head was hammered out, then chiselled from a single sheet of metal – with the exception of the beak, which must have been fitted and very skilfully soldered – since gold cannot be indefinitely manipulated and deformed. The eyes are not, as one might imagine, two stones set in the gold. They are formed by a single stick of obsidian which passes right through the head. Both ends are so polished and rounded as to suggest with astonishing realism the mesmeric stare of a living bird of prey.

The crown, along with the uraeus riveted to it and the tall feathers simply cut from a metal sheet, is made according to a technique which is infinitely less complex than that of the head. It is even possible that these ornaments may be the work of a later craftsman. It would seem, in fact, that the cult statue of the Horus of Nekhen possessed several interchangeable crowns, and might, according to the ceremony to be performed, wear the solar disc, the white crown of Upper Egypt, the 'pschent', or feathers. At all events, there is no reason why all these things should be the work of one and the same artist.

The archaeological context of the discovery leaves room for doubt as to the exact date of the statue. It is usually attributed to the 6th Dynasty, because the statue of Pepy I (No.26), whose body was fashioned with the same technique of copper plaques nailed to a wooden support, was found in a room nearby. Is this a good enough reason? Probably not, since the statue of Pepy is not contemporary with the rest of the objects with which it was unearthed, which included a terracotta lion which was more ancient, and a statue of Khasekhem, a pharaoh of the 2nd Dynasty (No.7). On the other hand, the excavators state clearly in their publication that the falcon was discovered under a basalt paving stone in a well carefully sunk in the middle of the central room of a building which they dated in the 12th Dynasty. So one is entitled to think that it was perhaps in its original place, a cult object which had been ritually buried rather than thrown away pell mell with a lot of other statues which were considered no longer useful – like those of Pepy and Khasekhem.

Thus it is fair to postulate that the famous 'Hierakonpolis falcon' belongs to the 12th Dynasty, which was the great period of Egyptian goldworking.

The text of a small funerary stela, now at the New York Metropolitan Museum of Art, would seem to confirm this dating. This stela is from the 13th Dynasty; its owner, a certain Horemkhauf, who was a high priest of Horus of Nekhen, relates how he was commanded to bring the statues of his god and of Isis, his mother, to the Residence; ie, the capital, which at that time was Itjtawy (now called Licht). Does this mean he had been told that other cult statues had been finished? Was he supposed to bring back to the temple of Nekhen statues which had been sent to the capital for special festivities such as those involved in a royal jubilee?

Whatever the answers to these questions, this expedition, for which he used a cargo boat, was the most important event of Horemkhauf's life; and it has been suggested that the 'divine image' to which he refers was the one discovered by Quibell.

35 | Funerary stela of the steward Inyotef

Painted limestone; H. 62.5 cm; 12th Dynasty;
Ground floor, east window

The Abydos site has yielded hundreds of stelae of this kind. They are not strictly speaking, funerary stelae, in that they were not placed in tombs but in ex-voto commemorative monuments; these monuments were indispensable to anyone of means in the holy city of Osiris, whither the living and the dead desired to come as pilgrims. It was in this place that the most important part of the god's dismembered body, his head, was supposed to be buried.

Most of the stelae date from the Middle Kingdom. They belonged to burial vaults in which they were left along with offerings and statues. The tomb-chambers in question, raised by one or several individuals, were equivalent to the great royal cenotaphs of Sesostris III, Sethos I, and Ramesses II, and their function was the same: namely, to associate their builders for all eternity with the mysteries of Osiris, and to allow them to benefit from offerings and rituals in honour of the god.

The stela of Inyotef, son of the (deceased) lady Sitamun, was discovered by Mariette in the northern necropolis. Three others are known to exist for the same individual, which must have come from the same votive chamber; one of these, dated in

Gold and gemstones: H. of front section, 5 cm; 12th Dynasty; No.6116; First floor, case 8 to the right of the windows

the 24th year of the reign of Sesostris I, is also at the Cairo Museum, and the other two (probably done by the same remarkable artist) belong to the Louvre collection.

The stela consists of a limestone slab, slightly taller than it is wide; extremely well-preserved, apart from the lower left hand corner, which has been broken away. The entire surface is surrounded with the usual frieze of small coloured rectangles, and has in one way or another been decorated or carved.

The upper area consists of the traditional funerary formula in three incised lines. The king makes his offering to Osiris, lord of Busiris and Abydos, in the hope that the god will permit further offerings to be made on his behalf during various festivals, and that, among other things, he should be welcomed into the Neshmet barque (the ship of Osiris) when he takes the way westward.

Beneath this slightly banal text is a unique, almost square picture, decorated with finely-rendered bas-reliefs which still retain much of their original colouring.

The left side is occupied by the two figures of Inyotef and Sithathor, who was probably the steward's favourite spouse since another stela portrays her accompanied by a second wife named Meryt. The man wears a starched loincloth, a short, curly wig and a broad throat-piece. In one hand he carries a staff and in the other a sceptre of authority. The woman wears a long black wig and her body is tightly confined in a dress which leaves her breasts uncovered. Her left hand rests on her husband's left shoulder and in her right she carries a lotus flower.

The right section of the stela is subdivided into three smaller registers. At the top, three figures (one man, two women) approach the dead pair with flowers, a pitcher, a looking-glass, a piece of fabric, a casket and a bowl of milk dangling in a mesh bag. Between the two women is a wide-mouthed vase on a stand, filled with lotus flowers. The two lower registers each contain a single person, Sesostris, Inyotef's son, who presents offerings, and a woman carrying a bowl on her head and a lotus flower in her left hand. In front of these figures, offerings are piled on a dresser and on two low tables – loaves, pieces of meat, onions, trussed fowl, vases and flowers.

Legends of great antiquity explain why a hooded cobra goddess, rearing and ready to strike, is placed on the crowns of the gods, the kings and even the queens of Egypt. There is not sufficient space here to recount the full story in detail; in any case, the motivations of the Egyptian gods tend to be confusing to the modern mind. All we really need to know is that the Sun god, Ra, in order to allay the fury of one of his eyes at being supplanted, gave it the form of a serpent which he placed upon his brow. Henceforth, the serpent's allotted task was to defend Ra and to be a symbol of his power.

Thus, the rôle fulfilled by the uraeus (the Latin form of a Greek word derived from the original Egyptian) is that of the burning eye of Ra, with which the royal crowns were always identified during the Lower Epoch. In addition, it symbolizes the tutelary goddess of Lower Egypt who annihilates the pharaoh's enemies by spitting forth the flame of her venom.

The uraeus, like the sceptre, the crown and the false beard, was part of the royal insignia. Hence this superb example is far more than an ordinary piece of jewellery. It was undoubtedly worn by Sesostris II, because it was found lying in the dust

and debris of a votive chamber not far from the sarcophagus vault of his pyramid at El-Lahun. It was probably dropped centuries ago by the grave robbers who pillaged the king's tomb, where it was discovered by Guy Brunton in 1920, during the excavations conducted by Petrie. For two years thereafter, until the discovery of the treasury of Tutankhamun, it was the only piece of royal insignia known to Egyptology.

The piece is made up of several pieces of gold, soldered together to form a thick sheet, which was then hammered out and richly inlaid with other elements. The finely-modelled head is in lapis lazuli, and the one remaining eye is made of obsidian bordered by gold thread. Under the head, a ribbed gold band (the ribbing was originally emphasized by flakes of precious stones), divides the hood in two; the stylized lines around the snake's distended throat are rendered with coloured stones: amazonite (or enamel imitating the tones of amazonite), edged by crescents of lapis lazuli. The remainder of the hood is made of carnelian. Behind, the shining coils and undulations of the body are hollow, not solid. Two rings are included here, for attaching the uraeus to the royal headdress, which must have been made of cloth or leather.

37 | Hippopotamus figurine

Faience; H. 10 cm; 12th Dynasty; No.4221; First floor, in one of the two central display cases

No one knows exactly why the Egyptians of the Middle Kingdom placed hippopotamus statuettes in their sepulchres, but whether they were figured standing up (as in this example), or with half the body raised and jaws wide open, facing backward, hippopotamuses are by far the most common animal figurines in tombs of that era. Some museums possess literally dozens.

Several reasons may be given as to why these slightly heavy objects should have accompanied the dead to their graves. If we are to understand those reasons, we must forget our preconceptions about the creature, *ie* that it is large, placid and docile, and may be seen at zoos rolling around in blue-green water. For the Egyptian, particularly at the beginning of his history, the hippopotamus took on a very different guise: in those days the waters of the Nile, which are now innocent of pachyderms, were filled with these enormous and terrifying beasts. A herd of them could devastate crops and endanger human lives and in consequence they were viewed as the personification of evil. Hippopotamus hunting began as a vital necessity and developed into the preferred sport of kings and nobles, who gave it the extra dimension of a magic ritual aimed at destroying harmful forces.

Wall depictions of hippo hunts are very common in mastabas, but became rare in the Middle Kingdom period. In all likelihood they were replaced by figurines arranged around the corpse, both to protect from evil and to provide the pleasures of the chase. Most hippopotamus statuettes are in faience, but they also exist in alabaster, limestone (painted and unpainted) and wood.

This one is intended to portray the animal in its natural, aquatic surroundings. Lotus plants and pondweed are shown as if stuck to the hippo's body, which is blue like the water from which it has just emerged.

Here we should perhaps recall that Egyptian 'faience', a noble substance known to the ancients as 'brilliant', is not tin-bearing enamel on a clay support, but calcined ore covered with a form of glazing which the Egyptians had known how to apply to steatitic beads ever since the Badarian period.

38 | Statue of the steward Sikaherka

Quartzite; H. 62 cm; end of 12th–beginning of 13th Dynasty; Ground floor 22, east side, case C

If the private statuary of the Middle Kingdom is compared to that of the Old Kingdom, two facts become apparent: first, that the works that have come down to us from the Middle Kingdom are far less numerous; and second that they are much smaller (with a few exceptions) under the kings Ammenemes and Sesostris than under the kings of the 4th, 5th and 6th Dynasties. The relative scarcity of non-royal statues from the Middle Kingdom is largely due to the fact that, apart from the great sepulchres of the nomarchs, the tombs of administrators and dignitaries from this epoch were less grandiose than the mastabas of the Old Kingdom and thus could not contain so many funeral effigies. Their more modest scale is explained by the fact that ever since the close of the 6th Dynasty, private individuals could receive the royal permission to place votive statues in temples, thereby taking part in the cult and receiving their share of 'all the good things on which a god subsists'.

This lovely statue belongs to the latter category, and is a little-known masterpiece carved in yellow quartzite, which unquestionably deserves better than the ill-lit display case to which it has been consigned. It was discovered in the temple of Karnak; according to the short inscription clumsily carved on the front of the loincloth and the base, it represents a steward by the name of Sikaherka.

Sikaherka wears a long robe knotted under his arms and the flared wig is characteristic of his time. He is seated on a low-backed chair, in a passive, somewhat fixed attitude with his hands flat on his thighs and his eyes staring straight ahead. The modelling of the body is conventional and not especially noteworthy; unlike the face, which is highly individual, carefully sculpted by the artist in the realistic style adopted by the kings

of the later 12th Dynasty. The result is a beautiful portrait of man marked by age, a tormented mask that expresses pathos or sadness according to the light in which it is viewed. As such, it is in vivid contrast to the serene, idealized heads from the beginning of the dynasty.

39 | Head of Sesostris III

Black granite; H. 28 cm; 12th Dynasty; No.340; Ground floor 22, east side, case C

In the long gallery of royal portraits of Ancient Egypt, few faces are so immediately recognizable which was originally adorned by a uraeus, now almost completely gone. The eyes are set well back beneath heavy lids, with prominent bone structure accentuated by hollow cheeks and a turned-down mouth. These features combine to give the king a serious, disillusioned expression, in which are

as that of Sesostris III. Despite the disappearance of the rest of the statue and the inscriptions identifying it, this isolated head found at Madamud in 1896 unquestionably represents the great warrior monarch under whose reign the 12th Dynasty attained its apogee.

The king's chiselled features, made familiar to us by so many other statues which portray him at various times of life, are here those of a man at the crossroads between maturity and old age. His face is haughty and majestic, slightly prognathous; its powerful bone structure is framed by a nemes

mingled the lassitude and bitterness of a man much tried by life.

This effect is precisely what is original about the royal statuary of the period. After the decline of the monarchy, the political and social troubles of the later Old Kingdom and the First Intermediate Period, and the rise of a form of bourgeoisie, kings are no longer represented as serene, impassive divinities. On the contrary, they appear as men who seem to assume their heavy burden of responsibility with wisdom and experience.

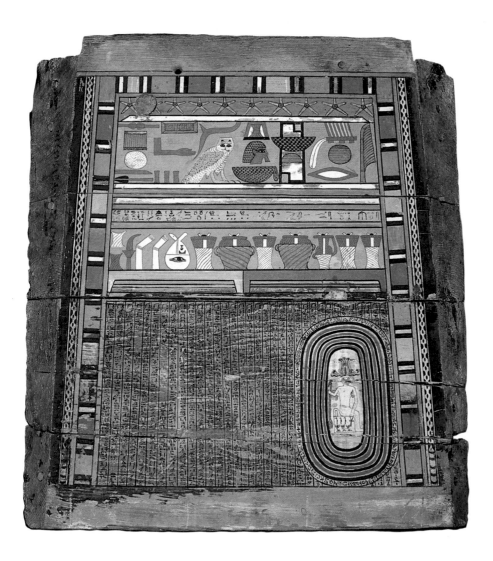

40 | Sarcophagus of the general Sepi *detail*

Painted wood; H. 60 cm; 12th Dynasty; No.3104;
First floor, north west corner

This wooden panel constitutes one of the two ends of a rectangular sarcophagus case, whose other elements are exhibited in the same room. When it was discovered at the end of 1897 at El-Bersha (the necropolis of the fifteenth nome of Upper Egypt) it still contained the very beautiful anthropoid coffin of a general named Sepi.

These cases were conceived as 'houses' for the dead. Similar examples from the same epoch display a stereotyped décor oriented to the position of the mummy. Outside the strips of text, two eyes were painted at head height; these were supposed

to allow the dead man to enjoy the spectacle of the outside world. There was also a painted door through which he could pass, and, on the inside, a long band of text, pictures of funerary furnishings and chapters from the *Sarcophagus Texts*. The bottom of the case was inscribed with the 'Book of the Two Ways', illustrated with a map of the next world.

The orientation and content of the line of large hieroglyphs painted under a band of starry sky indicated that this is the inside of the case end against which rested the head of Sepi, 'honoured by Nephthys'.

Under these carefully painted signs is a second register of the same height, which in fact extends round the other three sides of the case. This part of the frieze is filled with pictures of the objects considered necessary for the dead man's survival in the other world, such as food, weapons, jewellery, clothing, sceptres and toilet articles. These are represented by seven jars containing oils and unguents ('Festival perfume', 'Pine Essence', 'Essence of Libya'), a bag of green cosmetic powder (probably malachite), two pieces of cloth, an incense burner and two bedheads. The objects are carefully laid out on two low tables and identified by a line of text.

Like other, similar sarcophagi of the same era, the lower half of the panel is inscribed with chapters from the *Coffin Texts*. These texts are written in columns of cursive hieroglyphs and they constitute the great funerary bible of the Middle Kingdom, the same way as the *Pyramid Texts* (from which they are derived) served the Old Kingdom, and the *Book of the Dead* served the New Kingdom and the Late Period. Knowledge of these formulae ensured the survival of the dead man in the next world; by this time, they were no longer the exclusive preserve of the pharaoh alone. Here, five different formulae, accompanied by a curious vignette of Osiris wearing an 'atef', are written over thirty-four columns.

41 | Statuette of a harpist

Painted limestone; H. 18.5 cm; 12th Dynasty; First floor 34, north side, small case between cases D and E

This statuette was discovered by Reisner in 1913, during the Harvard–Boston excavations at Sheikh Farag, the northernmost cemetery in the huge necropolis of Naga el-Deir, on the right bank of the Nile between Asyut and Abydos. It was lying in the debris strewing the floor of a small chamber hollowed out of the rock, a modest tomb which had long ago been pillaged and which also harboured an alabaster vase and some pottery. These objects enabled experts to identify the ensemble as belonging to the 12th Dynasty.

Despite the yellow ochre shade of the body, which was customarily reserved for female statuary, the figurine represents a man who is 'striking the harp', to use the Egyptian expression. The musician wears a white loincloth; one of his feet is curled under him and the instrument, whose soundbox is adorned with wedjat eyes, rests against his left shoulder. He is blind; as he plays, he stares sightlessly into the distance. As in many other Middle Kingdom 'models', the quality of the sculpture is mediocre; but it is not quality, but rarity, which is its principal interest. This may be surprising, since from the Old Kingdom to the Late Period, mural representations of harpists are very common. In fact, from its first appearance in the 4th Dynasty, the harp in all its forms was always the favourite musical instrument of the Egyptians.

In several New Kingdom tombs, the text chanted by the blind harpist as he plays is carved beside him. Sometimes, he addresses the dead man who has just been left in his tomb, in tones of comfort and reassurance in regard to his future in the next life.

'Thine appeal is to Ra; Khepri hears thee, and Atum replies. The Lord of the Universe does thy will; he whose name is hidden addresses thee. The solar disc shines upon thy breast and illuminates thy burial vault. The west wind blows upon thee and into thy nose; the south wind swings to the north for thy sake. Thy mouth shall be drawn to the teats of the cow Hesat.'

But elsewhere, the harpist's message is to the living. When he speaks to those participating in the funeral banquet, who have just brought one of

their own to the last resting place, he says something else entirely. This is the famous 'Song of the Harpist', which throughout its many versions renders the same bitter and disillusioned verdict on man's lot and exhorts him to enjoy the fleeting moments of life that are left to him.

'Famous and noble men lie buried in their tombs. They built their houses; houses that stand no more. What has become of them? None comes to tell how it is, to tell what they need, to soothe our troubled hearts, till we ourselves go where they have gone. Therefore, may forgetfulness profit you! follow thine own heart, as long as thou livest... trouble not thy heart, till the day when the funeral lamentations are for thee... make thy days happy, and do not tire of happiness. See, no man has ever taken his belongings with him! See, no man, once gone, has ever returned!'

The pessimism of this text, which probably goes back as far as the Middle Kingdom, was still present when Herodotus visited Egypt. He repeats (II,78) that 'at the banquets of the rich, when the meal is over, a man carries a wooden figurine among the guests which represents a dead man in a coffin, painted and sculpted with great precision, and one or two cubits in size. He shows it to each guest, uttering these words: "Look well, then drink and rejoice; for when thou art dead, thou shalt be as he"'.

42 | Bust of Ammenemes III in his priestly costume

Black granite; H. 100 m; 12th Dynasty; No.506; Ground floor 16, north east corner

This curious monument was brought to light at Mit Faris, on the site of the city of the god Sobek which in former times was the capital of the Faiyum. Its style is akin to that of a group of contemporary statues (a sphinx, offering bearers) which were discovered at Tanis and which the Egyptologists of the last century dated to the 'Hyksos' era because of their oddity, which testified to some foreign influence. However, a comparison with other well-authenticated portraits of Ammenemes III leaves no doubt; beneath the bizarre and heavy accoutrements of his priestly costume we recognize the features of a personage whom we might at first sight take for a simple priest, since the royal uraeus has almost entirely disappeared. Yet this is the king who developed the Faiyum, and whose funerary temple was much admired during the Graeco-Roman era, (when it was known as the Labyrinth). An enormous wig of unique design, with evenly-spaced tresses opening out around the temples and tapering as they hang, frames and accentuates the monarch's highly individual face. His eyes and brows are well-shaped, his cheek-bones prominent, his mouth heavily muscled, his cheeks hollow. An interesting feature

43 | Pectoral with the name of Ammenemes III

Gold cloisonné and semi-precious stones; H. 7.9 cm; 12th Dynasty; No.3970; First floor, case 4

This rich priest's pectoral was found in the second of the two great treasures unearthed by de Morgan on 7 and 8 March 1894, in the 'gallery of the princesses' built by Sesostris III as part of his pyramid complex north of the Dashur site. This fortunate archaeologist, who at the time was director-general of the Antiquities service, later made a number of other comparable discoveries during the 1894–95 season, but it had taken him only two days to bring to light dozens of precious items of jewellery which proved beyond doubt that the art of the Middle Kingdom goldsmiths attained a degree of perfection which was never surpassed.

The pectoral, which is now hung from a collar of gold beads and precious stones from the same cache, has the form of a 'naos', or temple façade, is the natural beard he wears beneath the false one, which is now broken away.

Ammenemes III is bare-chested and his shoulders are covered by a panther skin, with head and one foot showing. The skin is held in place by a double strap which slants across the chest under a 'menat' necklace; on either side, the king presses two insignia against his body; of these, the heads of falcons, in a poor state of preservation are visible half way up the wig. The presence of these sacred batons makes this statue the oldest portrait known to man of a personage bearing insignia of rank. And the fact that the priest's robes easily outweigh the tokens of royalty remind us that, in theory only Pharaoh, the son and heir of the gods, was entitled to conduct the worship of his peers. The priesthood was merely delegated to fulfil this function, as attested by the bas-reliefs of the temples where only the king himself is seen performing the rites.

with the throat above. It is made from a single gold plaque in which each element of the design has been perforated, then edged with a thin cloisonné, which in turn was used as a support for precious stones or carefully calibrated enamel. On the reverse side, two rings are fixed at neck height for hanging the pectoral, and the gold leaf is chiselled in such a way that the details of the scene are as distinct as on the front, where they are vividly coloured.

If the object as a whole resembles a temple façade, the symmetry of the design also has something architectural about it. The motif is very common on the walls of pharaonic temples, from the first dynasties to the Roman era: it consists of the king's ritual killing of the traditional enemies of Egypt.

Under the protecting wings of Nekhbet, the white vulture of Upper Egypt, who holds in his talons the symbols of life and stability, Ammenemes III is portrayed twice, grasping by the hair an armed Asiatic whose brains he is about to beat out with the club he holds in his other hand. Behind the two figures of the king are life signs, with arms brandishing 'flabelli'. The rest of the space is taken up by hieroglyphs distributed

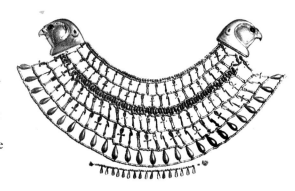

Pectoral of a princess

around the principal personages: Nekhbet is qualified as 'Lady of Heaven, Mistress of the Two Lands', while the king, whose action is described (the expression 'smiting the Asiatics' may be discerned between his feet) is designated by his name alone as 'perfect god, lord of the Two Lands and of all foreign countries, Nimaatre'.

The technique used to make this ornament is breathtaking, but the design is slightly crowded. Although the composition is rigorous the short texts which are meant to provide explanations in fact render it less easy to 'read' at first glance.

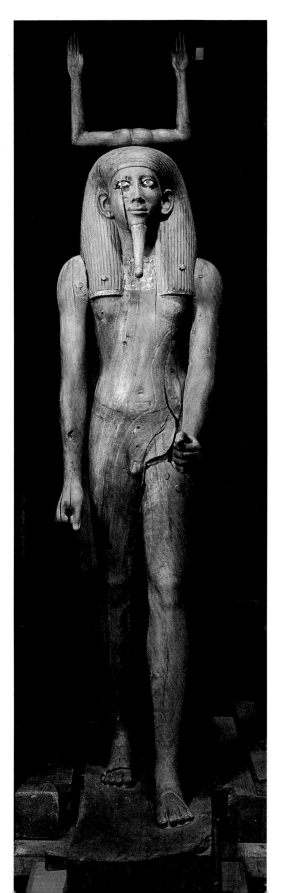

44 | Statue of the ka of King Hor

Wood; total H. 1.75 m; end of 12th Dynasty; No.280; First floor 32, corridor

This statue, which is the only surviving example of a sculpture 'in the round' of a royal 'ka', comes from the tomb of King Hor, discovered intact at Dashur by de Morgan in April 1896. The 'naos' that shelters it was lying in the corner of a narrow chamber, along with the king's sarcophagus and a vase box (for canopics). The statue itself was identified by an inscription on either side of the opening of the 'naos', and was found hidden under a pile of sticks and pottery.

The discovery of this tomb caused considerable problems to Egyptologists, because until that time King Hor had been completely unknown to history, and it was no easy matter to establish his dates. This led to a dispute between de Morgan and Maspero, who disagreed over the reading of the name Hor. De Morgan saw this new pharaoh as the co-regent of Ammenemes III and located him at the end of the 12th Dynasty, citing the archaeological evidence as proof. Maspero's objection to this was that there was no more hope of finding a previously unknown 12th Dynasty king 'than a new Bourbon between Henry IV and Louis XVI'. He placed Hor among the lesser known kings of the 13th Dynasty, because the Royal Canon of Turin mentions a sovereign by this name. In spite of everything that has been written since, the question has still not been satisfactorily settled which would tend to give the edge to Maspero's theory. But in fact the arguments in favour of identifying Hor as a contemporary of Sekhemrekhutawy in the 13th Dynasty do not stand up to close examination. Contemporary scholarship inclines to the view, based on archaeological evidence, that Hor was a younger brother or son of Ammenemes III, with whom he shared the throne and all its titles, but he died before he could reign alone. The evidence is as follows: the tomb's position within the precinct of the pyramid of Ammenemes III, north of Dashur; the vase box with its clay seal bearing the imprint of Nimaatre, the first name of Ammenemes; the neighbouring sepulchre of a princess Nubheteptikhered, whose funerary furnishings, like those of Hor, are in the same style as those of the 12th Dynasty; and, finally, the association of a king Hor and a king Nimaatre on a faience plaque long preserved at the Berlin Museum.

The restored hieroglyph of two raised arms, which is visible on the statue's head, indicates that it represents a royal 'ka', rather than the king himself. The abstract notion of the 'ka' is certainly one of the hardest to define, because despite the 'double' translation adopted during the last century, it does not correspond to any of our conceptions. Let us say that along with the 'ba', the 'akh', the body, the shadow and the name, the 'ka' is to the Egyptian one of the elements which make up an individual's personality. It is also a manifestation of the vital energies, both creative and retentive, which are closely related to sexual potency and the forces which preserve order in the world. The bas-reliefs in which kings are seen accompanied by his 'ka' are evidence that this statue probably carried the ostrich plume of Maat in his right hand, and in his left hand a long staff topped by a king's head wearing the feathered head-dress of Tatenen.

At the moment of its discovery, the body of the statue was still covered in a layer of grey paint, which fell away when touched. The ensemble was sculpted from a single block of wood, with the exception of the left leg, the arms, and the toes, which had been fixed in place with wooden pins. The figure bears no royal insignia, but is treated with the conventions accorded to a divinity. It wears a tripartite wig, framing an idealized face with a long beard curled at the end (restored), and gives the appearance of nudity because the golden belt which once circled the hips and covered the phallus has now disappeared. The eyes are inlaid

according to the Old Kingdom technique, which gives the head an eerie, lifelike expression. Finally, various details were originally covered in gold leaf – the edges of the wig, the eyebrows, the eyelids, the throat-piece, the nipples, the toenails and the fingernails.

45 | Coffin cover of Queen Ahhotep *detail*

Gilded and stuccoed wood; H. 2.12 m; end of 17th Dynasty; No.3888; First floor, south side

Auguste Mariette was not in Upper Egypt when his workers made the great discovery which marked the first year of the existence of the

Antiquities Service, and caused its director such trouble a few years later.

Maunier, the consular agent at Luxor, was told of the find in February 1859 and forwarded a fairly legible copy of the inscription on the 'magnificent mummy-box' which the 'reis' had extracted from a deep well-shaft at Dira abou el-Naga, not far from

the mouth of the Wadi, leading to the Valley of the Kings. Before he even laid eyes on the sarcophagus, which he ordered to be transported immediately to Bulaq by special steamer, Mariette knew that it contained the mummy of the 'great royal wife who assumes the white crown, Ahhotep, living forever'. But he was not to be the first to open the casket, because the provincial government, (out of curiosity or excess of enthusiasm) had already done so and thrown away the royal remains, after first stripping them of the precious objects with which they were laden. These included bracelets, chains, a mirror, an axe, a dagger, and model ships; in all, about forty different pieces, amounting to nearly two kilos of gold.

The sarcophagus box is not exhibited at Cairo. It is painted blue, whilst the broad anthropoidal cover has been entirely stuccoed in white, carved with a feather design and finally gilded. This cover is made from a single block of wood, probably cedar or sycamore. A heavy, rounded wig, whose symmetrical ends curl over the breasts, frames the delicate idealized face of the queen. A smile lingers around the mouth and the inlaid, almond-shaped eyes stare ahead slightly fixedly; the uraeus testifying to her rank has disappeared.

Despite being fashioned in the image of a mummy wrapped in bandages, the coffin of Ahhotep scarcely fits its contours. Though slightly less angular (because of the wig) it bears a curious resemblance, in its massive way, to that of Seqenenre, the husband of the queen. If we compare the two, it would appear that the two sarcophagi were made together; the same feather décor is discernible on both, which Mariette called 'rishi', borrowing the word from his workers. There is also the same pectoral hung across the chest, in which a cobra and vulture stretch out shared wings; the same band of hieroglyphs extending down to the feet; and, finally, the same manner of suggesting the legs by making them stand out rigidly from knee to ankle.

This resemblance is perfectly normal; what was less so according to Mariette (who was not familiar with the Seqenenre sarcophagus, since it was not discovered until 1881 in the royal cachette at Deir el-Bahri), was the similarity he perceived with regard to several other coffins from the same site. The inscriptions on these coffins stated that they belonged to the Inyotef kings, who in Mariette's time were dated in the 11th Dynasty. So, was Ahhotep a Middle Kingdom queen? And what was he to make of the jewellery found on the mummy, which bore the stamps of Kamose and Ahmose, the pharaohs who liberated Egypt from the domination of the Hyksos? Was it possible that too 'long' a chronology had been adopted, since it was beyond doubt that the Inyotef kings had reigned before the 12th Dynasty?

The solution to these problems, which Mariette set before the Egyptian Institute when he displayed his discoveries, was not provided till the end of the century: while there had indeed been Inyotefs at the time of the Middle Kingdom, other kings also bore the name. These kings were the immediate predecessors of Seqenenre in the 17th Theban Dynasty.

46 | Chain and fly-shaped pendants

Gold; height of each fly 9 cm; end of 17th Dynasty; No.4031; First floor, case 10

This chain of plaited gold thread, and the three heavy flies that hang from it, were among the jewels discovered on the mummy of Queen Ahhotep when the governor of Qena had her sarcophagus opened, instead of following Mariette's instructions and expediting it to Bulaq. When Mariette learned that the governor was planning to compound his disobedience by sending the treasure directly to the viceroy Said Pasha, he immediately set off up the Nile to meet the government boat on which it was being transported.

Devéria's colourful account of this episode, which took place at the end of March 1859, when the Nile waters were low, demonstrates that the job of 'mamour' of Egyptian Antiquities was no bed of roses. At that time the essential difficulty was to set authoritative guidelines for scientific archaeology, which would oblige excavators to behave like scholars, and not like common grave-robbers.

'M. Mariette had the happy notion of procuring a ministerial order giving him the right to stop all vessels carrying antiquities, and to take them aboard his own steamer. As soon as this order was delivered, in other words yesterday morning, we set out to get as far up the Nile as the low waters would permit. No sooner had we arrived at a point beyond which we could not progress, than we saw the smoke of the boat that was carrying the remains of the pharaonic mummy.

'Within half an hour, the two steamers were alongside one another. There was intense negotiation; then, seeing that he was getting nowhere, and roused to fury by the obstinacy of his opponent's resistance, M. Mariette resorted to the only method which is recognized as infallible by all here: the "*ultima ratio regum*" . . . he began laying about him with his fists, threatened to throw one man in the water, to burn the brains of another, to send another to the galleys, to hang a fourth . . . and so on. Finally, thanks to this tactic, the said antiquities were surrendered to us and we gave a receipt in return.

'Ten minutes later, we set off for Bulaq, taking with us as a prisoner the overseer who had been

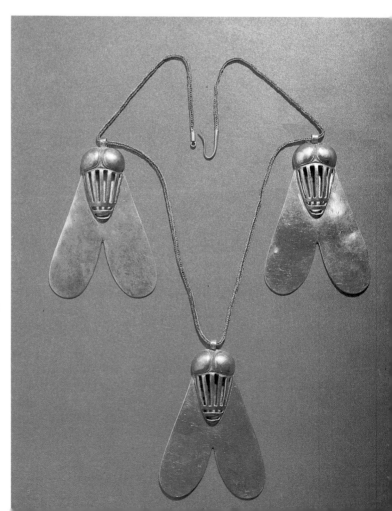

guilty of delivering the mummy into the hands of the governor. He was badly battered, but smoked his chibouq in a philosophical manner. We reached Bulaq just before dinner and only when we arrived were we able to open the box, because of the seals that held it shut. Great was our astonishment when we discovered within a quantity of jewels and royal insignia, nearly all of which bore the names of the first king of the 18th Dynasty (Aahmes or Amosis), while the name of the queen inscribed on the coffin only appeared once.'

A few weeks after this swashbuckling incident, the members of the newly founded Egyptian Institute, at their first session, were able to admire this jewellery, whose '... richness and value were unequalled, both in terms of art, and in terms of antiquity'. Mariette had brought the objects with him for the edification of the learned company, as he was to do in August of the same year when the Académie des Inscriptions et Belles Lettres held their conference.

Other items from the treasure reveal more highly-developed technical ingenuity, but the 'flies of Ahhotep' remain among the queen's most celebrated ornaments. The chain from which they hang is 60 cm long; it is made of simple links, the two ends of which are joined by a hook and ring. The flies are notably stylized, each comprising two elements: a gold plaque in the shape of a rounded A, representing the wings, to which is soldered a smaller plaque; this was heavily pressed, then perforated, to imitate the insect's head, huge eyes and striped thorax. A fixed cylindrical ring for attachment to the chain, projects from the head, in front of the eyes. Altogether, the chain and the pendants weigh about 250 grams.

Other, more modest examples of similar pendants do exist, and various texts and representations lead us to conclude that these were military decorations. They seem to have rewarded the courageous behaviour of soldiers who fought against the enemy on the field of battle with the tirelessness of insects. A different decoration in the form of a jewel, that of the lion, may have been the recompense for valour. One high functionary received six of these from Tuthmosis I; another, a soldier, was awarded two by Tuthmosis III, '... before all the people ... because of his bravery'. A third is depicted on the wall of his tomb standing at the head of the royal troops, with two such decorations around his neck and two lions.

Do flies have some kind of military significance in Ahhotep's case? This is not impossible, in the warlike context of the struggle against the Hyksos and the liberation of Egypt which was set in motion by her husband and completed by his sons Kamose and Ahmose, the latter of whom founded the 18th Dynasty. Whatever the truth may be, what we see is an ornament fit for a queen ... or an empress. This piece, among others, was greatly coveted by the Empress Eugénie at the Paris Universal Exhibition in 1867, and it took all Mariette's force of character to bring it back to the museum at Bulaq.

47 | Stela of King Ahmose *detail*

Limestone; total height 2.25 m; early 18th Dynasty; No.415; Ground floor 12, south side

This stela of the first of the 18th Dynasty kings was found in 1903 at Abydos, by the excavators of the Egypt Exploration Fund. It commemorates the construction of a funerary vault for the king's grandmother, Queen Tetisheri, whom 'he loved more than any other thing.'

Beneath a winged solar disc, which occupies the arch of the upper register, two scenes are depicted which are almost completely symmetrical. Ahmose stands in front of a table loaded with offerings and dedicates them to his grandmother, who is seated on a low-backed throne. On the right hand side the king wears a pschent, and on the left, a white crown. He is wearing a loincloth with an apron, to which the ritual bull's tail is attached; he also bears a throat-piece and carries a long staff and a pear-shaped mace. Tetisheri is sheathed in a long, narrow garment and her head-dress consists of the skin of a vulture topped with two feathers. She grasps the floral sceptre of the queens of Egypt.

Under the winged solar disc, from which two 'uraei' hang, are carved in duplicate the titles and names which identify the personages. There is nothing particularly original about this double scene, whose symmetry, proportions, carefully traced outlines and clear, shallow carving are reminiscent of the Theban reliefs of the early Middle Kingdom. On the other hand, the accom-

panying text is very unusual because of its form and content; without actually giving dates, it consists of an almost direct transcription of a conversation between Ahmose and 'the royal daughter and sister, the spouse of god, the great royal wife, Ahmose-Nofretiri'.

The king and queen are sitting in the audience-chamber of the palace and are discussing how best to honour the dead so that offerings and libations can be made during the main festivals of the year. The queen asks a question; Ahmose seems to listen attentively, then replies that he is preoccupied by the memory of 'his mother's mother and his father's mother, the great spouse and royal mother, Tetisheri', and announces that despite the tomb and cenotaph she already possesses in the Theban 'nome' and the Thinite 'nome', a pyramid

and vault should be constructed to her memory in the necropolis of Abydos. The king makes clear that this memorial will include a pool, plantations of trees, offerings ensured by the nearby presence of lands, domestic animals and all the servants that may be required. The text then adds that 'never had the kings of former times done such a thing for their mothers'.

48 | Sphinx of Queen Hatshepsut

Painted limestone; H. 62 cm; 18th Dynasty; No.6139; Ground floor, west side

This sphinx, discovered in 1928–29, is the best preserved of a pair which stood either side of the first flight of steps leading into the temple of Hatshepsut at Deir el-Bahri. It was found to the north of these steps by the mission organized by the Metropolitan Museum of Art, along with the remains of its counterpart, which was later heavily restored and is now in New York.

While the Cairo piece is by no means perfectly intact, (the uraeus and ears are missing, and the original ochre colouring has faded considerably), its state of conservation is little short of miraculous in view of the systematic destruction of Hatshepsut's temple after her death. The queen – or perhaps one should say the king – had built this monument to ensure the survival of her own funeral cult, as well as to attest the grandeur and glory of 'her father Amun'. It was the priests of Amun who gave Hatshepsut the support she needed to reign as a true pharaoh in the place of her minor half-nephew and second husband, Tuthmosis III, instead of being content with the regency. When the latter finally ascended the throne, he avenged himself for being kept from power so long by having Hatshepsut's titles and portraits obliterated. Nonetheless, patient work by archaeologists has achieved the reconstruction of many effigies of the queen which once decorated the courts and colonnades of the temple. This monument, 'the splendour of splendours', was cleverly blended with the cliffs at Thebes by Hatshepsut's favourite, Senenmut, along lines laid down by Mentuhotep I.

The little sphinx at Cairo and its duplicate in New York are probably the most original works of all the statuary of Deir el-Bahri. They are reminiscent of a sphinx-type that characterized the end of the 12th Dynasty: instead of replacing the lion's head by a human one with a 'nemes' head-dress, the sculptor has simply substituted the royal visage for the animal's muzzle. This has the effect of accentuating the already catlike nature of the queen's delicate face, which is framed by a stylized but realistic mane and prolonged by a huge square beard. The sphinx is above all a portrait: the almond-shaped eyes under arched brows, fine nose and little smiling mouth can be seen in all the statues of Hatshepsut. Below the beard, which was once painted lapis-blue like all the beards of the Egyptian gods, a few beautiful hieroglyphs of the same shade record the sovereign's name: 'Maatkara, beloved of Amun, given life forever'.

49 | Statue of Tuthmosis III

White marble; H. 27.5 cm; 18th Dynasty; No.428;
Ground floor 12, south west corner

Baraize uncovered this pretty statuette, completely intact, during the clearing and restoration of the small Ptolemaic temple of Deir el-Medina in 1912. It had been hidden in debris which had slipped off the mountain into the narrow space separating the hillside from the west wall of the temple precinct. Hence it must have been stolen, perhaps in antiquity, but obviously the theft cannot be dated.

A column of text carved on the back indicates that the statuette represents king Menkheperre Tuthmosis III; he is portrayed on his knees, making a ritual offering of two small globe-shaped vases which according to the bas-reliefs which show kings accomplishing a similar gesture, usually contain wine or milk. Nonetheless, if the inscriptions on certain other monuments are to be believed, this presentation of round vases symbolizes the supreme offering: on the base of two large statues representing Hatshepsut in the same position (which was very common during the 18th Dynasty) it is written that the queen is offering in one case Maat, and in the other, fruit, to the god Amun.

The king's legs seem exaggeratedly long in profile. He wears a pleated 'shendyt' and a 'nemes' with the uraeus. The statuette is carved from white marble slightly veined with grey, which adds the quality and beauty of a material which was rare in Egypt, to the finesse of the sculpture's execution. It seems to inherit a certain residual delicacy from the statuary of Hatshepsut, though it is perhaps a little too 'pretty' to reflect Tuthmosis III's true personality. The sweet, smiling face would tend to make us forget the raw power of the conqueror who was perhaps the greatest pharaoh ever to reign in Egypt, even greater than Ramesses II.

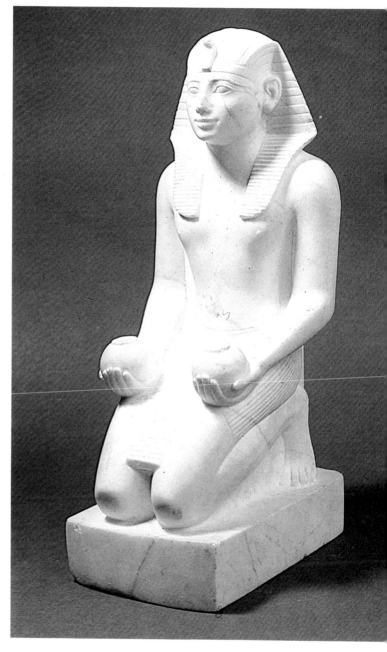

50 | Models of carpenter's tools

Wood, bronze and leather; length of knife, 30 cm;
18th Dynasty; No.6058E; First floor 49, south side

These three tools are in a perfect state of preservation because they have never been used. They are, in fact, votive tools, part of a 'foundation deposit', or group of objects which were buried at various important points around the perimeter of a religious building during the rituals accompanying its foundation. This practice first appears, sporadically, during the Old Kingdom; it became very common during the New Kingdom, particularly under Tuthmosis III, and continued unabated until the Roman era. Foundation ceremonies were usually conducted at night, so that the orientation of the future building could be based on the positions of the stars. Animals would be ritually sacrificed to propitiate the gods; then the objects would be left with them in the sand of a pit or foundation trench whose outline had been marked out on the ground by a cord strung between two stakes.

The number and nature of these votive objects could differ considerably between one foundation cache and the next. Apart from food offerings and crockery, the most complete collections usually contain plaques of gold or faience, scarabs bearing the name of the king responsible for the building, the instruments used during the foundation ceremony (stakes, mallets, and hoes), small samples of construction materials (bricks, metal plaques, blocks of stone), and, lastly, miniature models of the construction tools (sieves, baskets, stone-chisels, hatchets, adzes and wood-saws). These

things, despite their votive character, supply us with valuable information on the equipment used by ancient Egyptian builders.

The models shown here, which are examples of tools going back to the 1st Dynasty, were used for woodworking (see No.30): a saw, a hatchet and an adze. On each blade, which is either driven into its handle, or held in place by a leather thong, a short text is inscribed to record the fact that the tools were buried by the 'perfect god Menkheperre (Tuthmosis III) on the occasion of the foundation of the (building called) Amun-Djoser-Akhet': a completely ruined shrine at Deir el-Bahri which was excavated in early 1966 by the Germans Dieter Arnold and Jürgen Settgast.

51 | Blue faience bowl

Faience; diameter 17 cm; 18th Dynasty; No.6228;
First floor 49, south side, case D

Several archaeological clues serve to place the undecorated Deir el-Medina tomb, (excavated in 1945 by Bruyère), in the 18th Dynasty. It was in this tomb that this beautiful faience bowl was discovered, along with a ring support which seemed to belong to it, despite the difference in glazing. Like many similar bowls dating from the beginning of the same dynasty, it is decorated in a style that evokes the primaeval ocean and water in general. The inside features lotuses, either open or in bud, lilies and two fish, around a rectangular pool filled with water. On the outside, and on the ring support discovered at the same time, the decoration consists of lotus petals only.

These delicate receptacles were probably intended, as their decorative theme suggests, as water vessels. They were used as drinking cups by the living, but were also left to serve the same function for the dead – who, in order to be reborn, could drink from them the creative essences of the 'Nun', as evoked by their aquatic fauna and flora.

They were also used for milk; this fact has been proven by the analysis of solidified elements found on several bowls. According to Bruyère, they may have been used for offerings of milk and white cheese to the goddess Hathor, which would explain the Hathoric elements which sometimes appear in the décors.

There is, perhaps, a more prosaic explanation for these objects. Many have been found with toilet utensils in their vicinity, and thus it seems possible that they might have been used as such, filled with water or milk. This use, at any rate, fits the case of the bowl illustrated here, which was found in a large rush basket with a faience vase, a beautiful mirror of wood and bronze, a comb, two small caskets, alabaster and breccia marble kohl pots and an ebony stick for applying eyeliner.

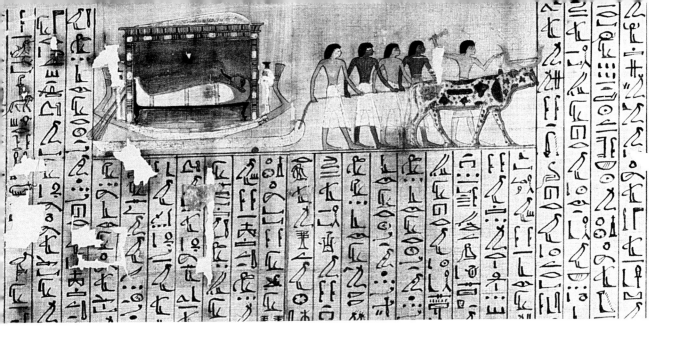

52 | Tuthmosis IV and his mother *detail*

Black granite; total H. 1.10 m; 18th Dynasty;
Ground floor 12, north side, left of entrance

This group in granite, which includes one of the rare portraits of Tuthmosis IV, was discovered in January 1903 during the clearance of the central alleyway of the temple of Amun at Karnak. It was buried almost upright a few centimetres below ground level, in a pillared chamber immediately south of the sanctuary.

The king, who is described in a column of text as the 'perfect god Menkheprure, beloved of Amon-Re, Lord of the Thrones of the Two Lands' is represented, not with a goddess, as one might expect, but with his mother, Queen Tiaa; the pair are seated on a high-backed chair. They embrace each other affectionately, each with an arm across the other's back. Apart from a very few details, they look like a couple of nobles, so simple and unencumbered with royal emblems are their clothes.

The king, who is dressed in an ordinary pleated loincloth held around the waist by a belt and buckle, wears no necklace and no bracelet. His right hand, which holds an ankh, is laid on his

thigh, and his bare feet rest on the Nine Bows carved on the pedestal. On his head is a short, curly, spherical wig, which hides his ears. The uraeus, with head broken off, rears up from the front of this wig, which appears here for the first time. Later, during the Ramessid era, this style was very much favoured.

The queen wears a long tunic with a six-layered throatpiece and rosaceae at the point of each breast. Her head is covered by a broad wig divided into three bunches of fine tresses, which frame her face and fall flat against her shoulders. Only the vulture skin, which was the traditional emblem of Egyptian queens, is there to show her rank, but the vulture's head has almost completely disappeared.

The ensemble is fairly bulky in effect, but the faces, which appear to have received most of the artist's attention, are probably faithful portraits – although the questionable theory has been advanced that the king's features are those of Amenophis II, not of his son. These faces have been described as 'sweetly bourgeois', even 'good-natured', and in fact they do have something of these qualities, which make them resemble many private portraits of the same era.

Tuthmosis IV and his mother No. 52 previous page

53 | The Book of the Dead of Maherpra

Papyrus and mineral colours; H. 35 cm; 18th Dynasty; No.3822AE; First floor 17, hung under glass on the walls of the room, west side

To live after death; to avoid work in the kingdom of the dead; to enter the West and return again; to accomplish transfigurations and glorifications; not to eat excrement or drink urine; to breathe the fresh air and to have water whenever required; to take the guise of a golden falcon or a divine falcon; to acquire the mixing bowl and the palette of the scribe; to know the Souls of Hierakonpolis; to enter Abydos and join the train of Osiris; to have the use of one's eyes; to put the head back in its place, or bring the soul back into the body; these things, among many others, were what an Egyptian might accomplish to ensure his survival by the power of magic, provided he had enough money to take with him to the grave a copy of the *Book of the Dead*.

This work was first published by the German scholar Richard Lepsius in 1842. The heading *Book of the Dead* which is now sanctioned by long use, covers a somewhat incoherent collection of texts of varying lengths. The original title, literally *The Book of Coming forth by Day* is perhaps more apt.

Although the *Book of the Dead* was written on leather, on mummy bandages, or in a fragmented fashion on funeral furnishings or the walls of vaults, it is nearly always found on a scroll of papyrus which bears the name and titles of the dead man. These are followed by the columns of cursive hieroglyphs or lines of hieratic (later demotic), which made up the various chapters of the book.

The beautiful painted vignettes which accompany texts from the New Kingdom make the *Book of the Dead* the world's oldest illustrated book. The choice, number, order and length of the 'formulae' vary substantially from one papyrus to another, and it is only when we reach the Saite epoch that a definitive version appears. Egyptologists divide the almost two hundred known formulae into four broad sections and a kind of appendix.

Maherpra's *Book of the Dead* comes from his tomb, which was discovered intact in the Valley of the Kings by Loret in the winter of 1898–99; the hypogeums of Amenophis II and Tuthmosis III were found at about the same time. Who was this individual, Maherpra, who had received the signal honour of burial among the pharaohs? His titles of 'fan-bearer and child of the nursery' give no clue. Loret suggested that he might have been a son of Tuthmosis IV and one of his black concubines; which is very possible, since Maherpra (who is pictured as a black man) would thus be a half-brother of Amenophis III, whose parents-in-law are the only other personages without royal or princely titles to have been buried in the valley of the kings (see No.56).

The full length of the papyrus is 11.75 metres.

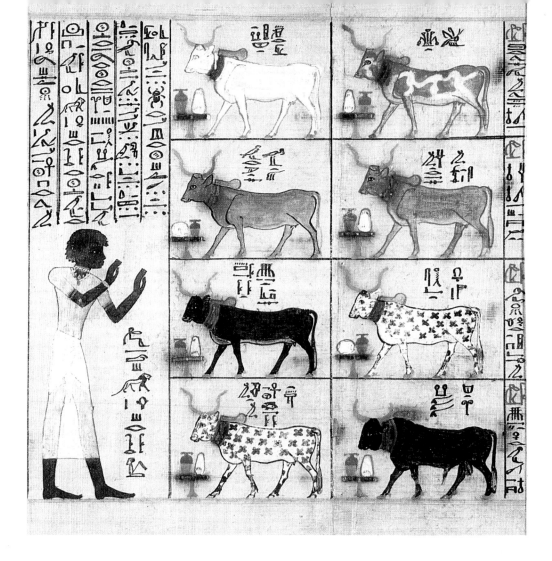

It has been cut into five pieces, glued to a canvas support for exhibition under glass in the Cairo Museum. It includes only 26 chapters, which appear in a different order to that (albeit completely arbitrary) adopted by Egyptologists, and is written in retrograde characters. This means the columns have to be read one after another from left to right, although within each column they must be read from right to left.

An examination of four of these 'formulae' will allow us to gain some idea of the whole.

Chapter 1, which was positioned, not unnaturally, at the beginning of the scroll, was read by the priest on the day of the internment – the 'placing in the tomb'. It consists of Thoth's prayer addressed to the divinities of the other world. The vignette, which is more detailed in some other cases, represents the dead man's catafalque in a boat placed on a sledge, which is being hauled to the necropolis by a team of oxen and four men. Meanwhile, a fifth man is engaged in symbolically 'opening' the road by sprinkling it with milk, and the weeping goddesses Isis and Nephthys carry out their offices beside the coffin.

Chapter 30B, which is sometimes engraved on the belly of a stone scarab, is a 'formula to prevent the heart of the dead man from opposing him in the kingdom of the dead'. Maherpra speaks directly to his own heart, as if this organ had an independent personality which could prove to be an over-critical witness against him before the tribunal of the gods: 'O heart of my mother, heart of my mother, heart of my different ages, do not rise up and accuse me, do not stand against me when I come before the tribunal, show me no enmity in the presence of the keeper of the scales of justice!' This scene is illustrated by the vignette in which the baboon Thoth ascertains that a balance of harmony exists between the individual and his heart, whilst Osiris, the supreme judge, looks on.

The recital aloud of Chapter 92 enables 'the tomb to be opened for the soul and the shade', in order that it may '. . . come out into the daylight and have the use of its legs'. The illustration shows the soul, in the form of a graceful bird with a human face, flying away from the tomb.

Finally, while the text of Chapter 148 aimed at

'provisioning the blessed' is here cut short, the illustration is very carefully executed. It portrays Maherpra wearing a loincloth and a thin linen robe, with his arms raised in adoration before seven cows, a bull and four oars (not visible in the photograph). The text above him reads: 'Hail, thou that shinest in thy disc, living soul that clim- best from the horizon! The Osiris Maherpra knows thee, knows thy name and knows the name of the seven cows and their bull...' And indeed all these beasts, whose rôles are carefully differentiated, are identified by their names: Castle-of-the-ka's, The Khemmite, Great-is-his-love, etc.

54 | Statuette of Amenophis III *detail*

Steatite; H. 28 cm; 18th Dynasty; Ground floor 12, east side, case C

This incomplete figure was discovered in June 1905, one of the eight effigies of Amenophis III found in the cachette of Karnak, and seems to have lost its original glazing. The inscription on its back does not specify that the king portrayed is indeed the 'perfect god, the Lord of the Two Lands, Nebmaatre, son of Re, Amenophis (beloved) of Amun, Lord of the Thrones of the Two Lands...', but the attribution of this little monument to the ostentatious Amenophis III admits of no doubt. The reason lies in the idealized features, which are familiar to us from many other statues of all sizes.

This monarch, whose reign spanned nearly forty years and marked the apogee of the 18th Dynasty after the conquests of his predecessors had endowed Egypt with wealth and political power, is portrayed as a standard bearer. The king's sacred banner was once held rather oddly against his right side by an overlong left arm, now missing. This was very probably the emblem of Amun, with its ram's head; it has now vanished, along with the two hands, but traces of the mounting are still visible on the right shoulder.

Amenophis wears a loincloth with a triangular apron at which level the statue is broken off. He also wears a broad necklace and rings around his arms, while his head-dress consists of a 'nemes', surmounting the 'pschent' – the first time that these two royal emblems appear on one and the same statue. This adds to the originality of the portrait, which, for the New Kingdom, is also one of the most ancient surviving representations 'in the round' of a king carrying a banner; though

Tuthmosis IV is depicted as doing so in certain bas-reliefs.

The juvenile visage is prolonged by a square-cut beard. It is extremely idealized, but nonetheless is fully recognizable as Amenophis III; the same plump cheeks, sensitive mouth, small nose, almond eyes and long eyebrows, so steeply arched that they seem almost frowning, can be seen on a number of other statues. The combination of these features lends the face a harsh expression, barely softened by its hint of a smile.

55 | Head of a statuette of Queen Tiye

Schist (greywacke) with traces of gilding; H. 6.5 cm; 18th Dynasty; No.4527; First floor, one of two central display cases

'The great royal spouse, Tiye, may she live forever! The name of her father is Yuya; the name of her mother is Tjuyu. She is the wife of the powerful king whose southern frontier is at Karoy, and whose northern one is at Naharina'.

This concise inscription was carved after the full protocol of Amenophis III on at least sixty large 'commemorative' scarabs. The custom of issuing these scarabs, like our modern medals, to mark some event, was particularly prevalent during the reign of Amenophis; it had begun a few decades earlier under Hatshepsut. Five series of 'historic' scarabs are known to have been produced in the king's time; they were much larger than those used as seals or amulets, larger even than earlier historic scarabs, with an average length of eight centimetres and brief texts covering several lines. One of these recalls that in the year 2, Amenophis killed 96 wild bulls in a few days; another, that he accounted for no less than 102 lions in ten years. A third scarab states that in the year 10, Gilukhepa, a Mitannian princess came to join the royal harem with a suite of 317 women; and a fourth records that in the year 11, a huge irrigation reservoir was constructed in two weeks at an estate in Middle Egypt owned by the queen. The fifth series, quoted above, is not dated but probably goes back to the very beginning of the reign in the year 2. Perhaps it had been issued to commemorate the marriage of Amenophis and Tiye, as many Egyptologists believe; or perhaps it marks the royal couple's accession to the throne. At all events, even if the purpose was to define the limits of the Empire, from the Euphrates to the far south of today's Sudan, this series is nonetheless marked by a solemn acknowledgement of the importance of the queen, whose humble origins are enumerated. Amenophis III perhaps intended to impose a principal wife who was not of royal blood, and whose lifelong influential position with the king was probably much resented.

This fine dark-green steatite schist statue was found by Petrie in the Sinai in 1904; more exactly in the temple of Hathor of Serabit el-Khadim, near the turquoise mines which had been exploited there since the Old Kingdom. It is definitely one of the best extant portraits of Tiye, along with the equally famous wooden head at the Charlottenburg Museum in West Berlin.

The round-cheeked face with the well-defined jaw appears framed by a wig with regular curls, which leaves the ears uncovered. The queen wears a head-dress, probably a crown of perforated gold, consisting of two winged cobras with bodies coiling symmetrically around the head. From the lower part hang two uraei, whose crowns (now vanished) framed the sovereign's cartouche. The remains of these are sufficient evidence that the white crown of Upper Egypt adorned the uraeus on the right and the red crown of Lower Egypt the one on the left. The unequivocal presence of its name makes this head a precious document for the identification of other realistic portraits of the mother of Akhenaten, when these are unattributed – for instance, the idealized portraits in the colossal group by the Cairo Museum's atrium, or the little glazed stone statuette in the Louvre.

The curved frowning eyebrows and the full mouth turned sulkily down at the corners give the queen a serious expression which is almost hard. There is something haughty, even scornful in this young, energetic face of a woman who seems not only highly aware of her rank, but also intensely proud of having attained it.

56 | Shawabti of the Divine Father, Yuya

*Wood with painted details; H. 27.8 cm; 18th
Dynasty; No.146; First floor 13, case T*

To designate the innumerable funerary effigies
found in the tombs of the Nile Valley, Egyptologists have kept the terms used by the ancient
Egyptians themselves. Depending on the types of
objects, therefore, they call them 'shawabtis'
(liable to forced labours), with reference to their
original purpose; or 'ushabtis' (respondents), a
more recent description deriving from a re-
evaluation of their function. But both words describe the same mummy-shaped statuettes which
are so typical of Egyptian art.

The first isolated examples of these statuettes
appear in tombs of the 12th Dynasty. They are
true substitutes for the deceased person which, as
little stone figurines made in his image, borrow the
features of the osirian mummy. They are thus
unattributed, or else carry no more than the name
and titles of the dead man; who, when his hands
are visible, holds amulets ensuring life, power,
health or stability. Sometimes a single column of
text carved on the front of the body reproduces the
funerary formula which invokes by a magical text
which survived right up to the Ptolemaic era and
which, in its various versions defining the rôle of
the 'shawabti', constitutes the sixth chapter of the
Book of the Dead.

'O, "shawabti"! If I am called, if I am required to
carry out the chores of the necropolis . . . thou shalt
say, here am I!'

Clearly, the dead man is directly addressing the
statuette, which, since it is no longer viewed as a
substitute for the person, but as a servant, must
answer in lieu of its master and assume on his
behalf the tasks imposed on the dead. These tasks
were generally the daily ones of peasant folk, such
as cultivating fields, irrigating meadows, bringing
sand from the east to the west and brickmaking.
This is why the 'shawabtis' carry agricultural tools
in their hands and a sack on their backs. During
the New Kingdom, when these magically obedient
slaves became so numerous that several hundred of
them might be enlisted in a single tomb to carry
out daily chores, they are accompanied by

overseers, dressed in the garb of living people, who 'command' teams of ten.

During the Middle Kingdom, these figurines were made of solid stone, while during the early New Kingdom they were silhouettes of roughly whittled wood. In the portraits of Tutankhamun, they are lavishly gilded; during the reigns of the Ramessid pharaohs, they are made of coloured faience. The treasure of Tanis includes bronze 'shawabtis', while the larger 'ushabtis' of the last dynasties are glazed. The 'shawabtis' of the poor in every epoch are made of more or less crudely-shaped clay. But, whatever the material used, and despite their apparent monotony, these objects vary enormously in terms of detail.

This very beautiful 'shawabti' of Yuya was among the rich funeral furnishings discovered in 1905 by excavators financed by the American, Theodore Davis, in a small side wadi to the left of the entrance to the Valley of the Kings. It was certainly his rank of 'Divine father to the Lord of the Two Lands' (ie, his status as father-in-law of Amenophis III), which brought Yuya the special privilege of burial with Tjuyu, his wife, in the necropolis reserved for the pharaohs. The sepulchre of the parents of the beloved queen Tiye was violated at an early date, and their jewellery had gone; but it was subsequently closed again and sealed by the debris from other tombs, remaining unnoticed until Quibell had the idea of conducting a test excavation between the unfinished vault of Ramesses III and the burial chamber of Ramesses XI, last of the name.

Among the nests of sarcophagi, the chairs, caskets, masses of pottery vessels and various provisions, 'shawabtis' were few and far between, but such as there were had great sculptured beauty, along with their own tall boxes. Yuya was accompanied by 14 figurines (three of which are now at the Metropolitan Museum of Art, New York) and Tjuyu had only four. For most of these refined and delicate statues, the natural colour of the wood had been left untouched, except for the tracing of facial features, wigs or ornaments. In this example, only the eyes are outlined in black and white, while the text of Chapter 6 of the *Book of the Dead* has been carved around the torso, then painted yellow.

The hands are not visible and thus do not carry the tools required for work in the next world. Nonetheless, the precaution was taken of placing scale models of tools in the vicinity of the 'shawabtis', such as hoes, mattocks, straps with baskets attached, and even a little brick-mould, which was something of a rarity.

57 | The Karnak water clock

Alabaster, with remains of pâte de verre and carnelian inlays; H. 35 cm; 18th Dynasty; No.4940; First floor, west side

The ordinary Egyptian of antiquity was not greatly concerned with measuring time, since the daily rhythm of the sun's passage and the annual cycle of the seasons fully sufficed him. Very few historical accounts attempt to give the exact hour that a particular event occurred, and those that do are highly arbitrary, indicating for example the 'moment when the earth was brightening', or 'the time of the evening meal'.

There were, however, certain individuals in ancient Egypt for whom time had great importance: these were known to the Greeks as 'horologues', or that category of astronomer-priests whose job it was to determine the exact timing of both daily worship and important religious festivals. At night, they would observe the phases of the moon and the movements of planets and constellations from the terraces of their temples, and at a very early stage they divided the year into twelve months of thirty days each. In order to make up the count of 365, they added the five extra days traditionally created by Thoth so that Nout could bring her five children, Osiris, Haroeris, Seth, Isis and Nephthys, into the world. Their births had been forbidden throughout the rest of the year by the curse of Ra. With a few minor differences, their calendar is still used today, modified by the reforms of Julius Caesar and Pope Gregory XIII. Another difference is that the Egyptians only recognized three seasons of four months each, as opposed to our four: Akhet (the floods), Peret (the re-emergence of the land from the floodwaters) and Shemu (harvest-time).

While sundials allowed them to determine the passing of the twelve hours of the day, they obviously could not be used at night, hence, in order to measure the passing of every twelve hours, winter and summer, the Egyptians resorted from the beginning of the 18th Dynasty to the use of clepsydras, or water clocks, based on the simple principle of the regular discharge of water from a receptacle.

The Karnak water clock, which goes back to the reign of Amenophis III, was found in pieces in the great trove excavated by Legrain at the turn of the century. It is really a votive clock, since it has the form of a truncated conical basin, in which two identical levels of water could in no way correspond to two equal lapses of time.

Inside, the lower sides are decorated with six alternating 'ankhs' and 'djed' – pillar motifs sculpted in relief. Above each of these signs are carved twelve columns of eleven false holes, more or less close to one another, corresponding to the hours of the night of each month of the year, which are successively indicated on the lip of the bowl.

The water flowed off through a very small hole in the bottom, emerging on the outside under the figure of a seated baboon in relief, which is now missing.

The outside periphery of the water clock is divided into three registers of figures and inscriptions which were originally inlaid with carnelian and coloured pâte de verre.

The upper register is occupied by symbols of certain planets and constellations, and gives a list of the 'decans', or protective spirits of each of the periods of ten days into which the year is divided.

The middle register represents the constellations of the northern hemisphere under the aspects of various gods and animals. In a frame the height of two registers, Amenophis III is pictured making offerings to the sun god Ra-Horakhty, assisted by the moon god, Thoth.

Finally, the lower register is divided into six tableaux (two for each season) in every one of which the king appears between two divinities, corresponding to the twelve months of the year.

58 | Cat sarcophagus

Limestone; H. 64 cm; 18th Dynasty; Ground floor, west side, left of the window

Among the various animal sarcophagi in the Cairo Museum, those of cats mostly tend to take the form of boxes in the shape of the creature itself, seated in the position made familiar to us by the bronze cat-statuettes which are so popular today. Most of the sarcophagi are made of wood and carry no inscriptions.

This example is from Memphis, and is doubly interesting in that it is made of stone and covered with texts and images. The ensemble of box and cover, which Maspero described simply as a 'funerary casket', has the proportions and general appearance of a canopic chest; and it has been several times described as such. It was even included at one time in the *Catalogue Général* of

canopic jars contained in the museum. However, there is absolutely no doubt that this was the coffin of a cat – a she-cat, to be precise – whose name appears no less than eleven times in the texts engraved in the stone, as though the pictures on the coffin's sides were not evidence enough.

The creature was known simply as 'Puss'; in the Egyptian language, the word for this, like the word 'cat' itself, was an onomatopoeia of mewing. She received from her master a sepulchre which many human beings might have envied. Having become an Osiris by virtue of her death, like a man might, the cat's mummy was under the protection of Isis and Nephthys, mourners *par excellence*, since it was they who had watched over the reconstituted corpse of Osiris, first of all mummies. The presence of the two goddesses, who are pictured kneeling on the sign denoting gold, enables us to identify the head and the foot (if it may be so

described) of the sarcophagus; for in the accompanying text, Isis addresses the cat with the words: 'I place my arms beneath thy head'.

Carved on what we must now assume to be the right hand side of the box is a portrait of the cat, complete with collar, beside a table laden with offerings; on the left hand side, a similar image is complemented by that of the mummified animal.

At the corners, four columns of text straddle the box and its lid. These mention Imset, Duamutef, Qebehsenuf and Hapy, the four sons of Horus who traditionally protect the viscera of the dead in their jars. The protection of Nut, the goddess of the celestial firmament, is also invoked; in the inscription on the ridge of the lid, she directly addresses the dead cat. On either side of this ridge, a line of text gives the name and titles of the cat's owner, Prince Tuthmosis, eldest son of a pharaoh, high priest of Ptah at Memphis, 'sem' priest and chief

of the prophets of Upper and Lower Egypt. This prince is little known, but perfectly identifiable as the first son of Amenophis III by a stela at the Serapeum, on which he is seen in the company of his father at the funeral of the first Apis.

This prince Tuthmosis, who was destined by his rank to become the fifth pharaoh of that name, died before succeeding to the throne. His younger brother Amenophis assumed the succession and became the king we know as Akhenaten.

History can seldom be 'rewritten', since it is extraordinarily difficult, if not impossible, to write in the first place. Yet, when one is confronted with this little monument, it is hard to avoid the speculation that had this cat-loving prince lived longer, the Amarna period (a decadent era for some, an astonishing adventure for others), might never have taken place.

59 | Lamp of the overseer Kha

Limestone, painted wood, bronze; H. 1.05 m; 18th Dynasty; First floor 34, case B

The question of how artists, working in the royal tombs sometimes 100 metres from the light of day, were able to see what they were doing, is one of the false mysteries of Ancient Egypt which continues to be mentioned by some guides. In fact, though it is quite surprising that no traces of black smoke remain on the bright colours, it is quite clear that the necropolis artisans used candles and simple oil lamps. This is proven by an overwhelming weight of evidence.

Numerous 'ostraca', and accounts found in the Valley of the Kings itself or at Deir el-Medina, are precise on this point. One is a letter from a foreman requesting pure fat and cloth for wicks from the vizir; another details the number of lamps used in one month; and in another, the scribe assigned to a team of workers specifies the consumption of fifty-eight candles, taking care to distinguish the morning (32) and the afternoon (26) in function of the work on the left and right wall-faces of the hypogeum. Thus we know that the wicks, which might be made from rags of old clothes, were usually bathed in sesame oil or fresh tallow and that their rate of consumption increased in proportion to the depth at which the work was being done.

These 'ostraca' mention no precautions about avoiding the effects of smoke. Perhaps the wicks were previously soaked in salt water, as was the practice in early nineteenth-century France; this would also explain the allusion of Herodotus (II,62) to lamps 'filled with salt and oil'.

Egyptian craftsmen lit their homes in much the same fashion, but used more sophisticated types of lamp, such as multiple candle-holders, torches or hanging lights. Lampstands were also very common and this elegant example was discovered in 1906 by Ernesto Schiaparelli in the intact tomb of a certain Kha, an overseer of works at Deir el-Medina. It was the only object retained from Schiaparelli's find by the Cairo Museum, and the rest of Kha's rich funeral furnishings (including the incomplete parts of a similar, less beautiful stand) are now at the museum in Turin.

The lamp is made up of three distinct parts, made from three different materials. The hemispherical base is roughly fashioned out of limestone. The shaft is of wood, and is cut to look exactly like a small papyrus-shaped column, with a triangular cross-section. The top is composed of a bronze (or copper) bowl, in the approximate form of a fish, supported by three wooden pegs. This bowl is the lamp; it still contains a whitish substance which must be the remains of the fat it once held, and a fragment of what is perhaps solidified perfume.

60 | Ointment jar

Wood with painted bone inlay; H. 14 cm; 18th Dynasty; No.5323; First floor, case F

Scent bottles, decorated combs, looking glasses, kohl pots, stylets, cosmetic spoons, hairpins and ointment jars – these are only a few of the toilet articles we have inherited from Ancient Egypt. They are now found in collections all over the world and perhaps, more than any other category of objects, they testify to the sheer invention and originality of Egyptian craftsmen.

In this minor creative field, which blossomed from the 18th Dynasty onwards, the smallest utilitarian object is to us a work of art, because the artisans' objectives were not primarily functional. Hence they often borrowed shapes from nature, and as such were in no way different from true artists.

In addition to the usual utensils, in the shapes of animals or plants, everyone can recognize the famous 'swimming-girl' variety of spoon – in which the container for the powder is a pool or a water bird, gracefully pushed along by a naked, swimming girl. Indeed, an entire film has been made about one of these objects, which is in the Musée du Petit Palais in Paris.

The kind of ointment or salve jar, in which the jar itself is carried by a man or a young scantily-clad servant girl, is not so common, but examples do exist in museums such as Leyden, Liverpool and Durham.

The piece in the Cairo Museum comes from an undisturbed tomb at the foot of the hill of Sheikh Abd el-Qurna, which was discovered in 1896 by private excavators supervised by Daressy. This was not a painted sepulchre, but a simple chamber rough-cut in the rock. It contained four sarcophagi: the principal one being that of Hatiay, who seems to have been an official at the temple of Aten, probably at the end of the reign of Amenophis III or at the beginning of Akhenaten's time, since the names of other divinities have not entirely disappeared.

The object which concerns us was found in one of the other coffins, belonging to a certain Siamun. It had been left there with a pair of plaited sandals and various toilet articles, namely a finely engraved bronze bowl which contained a cosmetic spoon, a pin and a bone comb decorated with lotus flowers. The object is small and asymmetrical, but remarkably well-constructed. The actual container is a scaled-down model of a vase which rests on the shoulders of a male figurine, half-kneeling on a rectangular pedestal.

The vase is almost as big as the person carrying it and it has retained both its lid and the two buttons which served to open it and (eventually) to seal it with cord. The upper area is decorated with geometrical and floral motifs and the belly of the

Ointment jar in the form of a locust

vase carries a frieze with alternating plants and leaping calves. The latter, which are of inlaid bone, are reminiscent of Cretan motifs and perhaps betray an Aegean influence.

The figure is simply attired in a pleated loincloth. His head leans forward, bowed under the weight of his burden which he holds steady on his shoulders and on the flat of his left hand. His right hand grasps the urn's single handle. The general position of the body is more aesthetic than realistic.

On the other hand, the head is very finely modelled, and the bare, shaven scalp reveals the bone structure of a face that combines delicate treatment with admirable realism.

61 | Statuette of Tjay, the Master of the Horse

Ebony; H. 57 cm; end of 18th Dynasty; No.6257; Ground floor 12, west side, case D

When, in 1899, Loret discovered this statue at Saqqara, it was rolled in a piece of cloth and fragments of the material have remained stuck to the broken-off stump of the left arm. To judge by contemporary statues, the missing arm must have been symmetrically placed in relation to the other, perhaps with the hand open and the palm pressed against the thigh or turned backward. Because of Loret's sudden return to France in the same year, this statuette kept its fragile protective covering for forty years thereafter; and it was only in 1936 that the material was stripped away to reveal one of the finest examples we know of 18th Dynasty private statuary, dating from just before the Amarna interlude.

The person represented, Tjay by name, was a 'royal scribe' and 'overseer of the stables of the Lord of the Two Lands'. These titles are inscribed after the usual funerary formulae, on the topside of the pedestal and on the front of the loincloth. Here

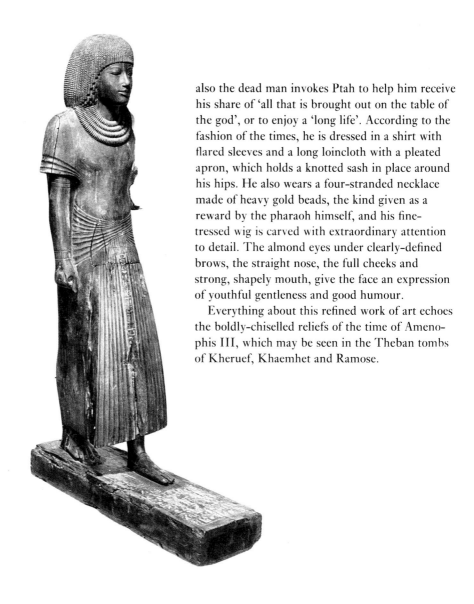

also the dead man invokes Ptah to help him receive his share of 'all that is brought out on the table of the god', or to enjoy a 'long life'. According to the fashion of the times, he is dressed in a shirt with flared sleeves and a long loincloth with a pleated apron, which holds a knotted sash in place around his hips. He also wears a four-stranded necklace made of heavy gold beads, the kind given as a reward by the pharaoh himself, and his fine-tressed wig is carved with extraordinary attention to detail. The almond eyes under clearly-defined brows, the straight nose, the full cheeks and strong, shapely mouth, give the face an expression of youthful gentleness and good humour.

Everything about this refined work of art echoes the boldly-chiselled reliefs of the time of Amenophis III, which may be seen in the Theban tombs of Kheruef, Khaemhet and Ramose.

62 | Head of Amenophis IV – Akhenaten

Indurated limestone; H. 24.5 cm; 18th Dynasty; Ground floor, west side, case F

Akhenaten has been described by some as a mystic, by others as a moron. He has been variously labelled a 'god-crazed king', a 'degenerate', a 'woman-man ... so aberrant and unbalanced that he sought to change his own sex', a 'crank, undermined by sickness', a 'politician of great skill', and a 'weak-willed neurasthenic'.

If an individual's personality may be judged by the passionate reactions he provokes in others, then Akhenaten must have been very much out of the ordinary. The abundant and often fantastical literature that surrounds this 'heretic king' still makes it doubly difficult to speak of him object-

ively, even at a distance of three thousand years. The reasons for this are manifold, but the most obvious is neither political nor religious, but artistic. As such, it is the only reason that can touch us profoundly.

Nor does this refer uniquely to the expressionist art imposed by Akhenaten at the outset of his religious reforms. It must be accepted that the provocative artwork of the period, which was deformed to the point of caricature, can be unsettling and even repellent. One should not view the strange asexual or androgynous colossi which Akhenaten had the audacity to erect at Karnak, as anything other than what they are: symbolic images of the king as the living Aten, mother and father of all creation. If the colossi are taken as realistic portraits of the prophet-pharaoh, they are

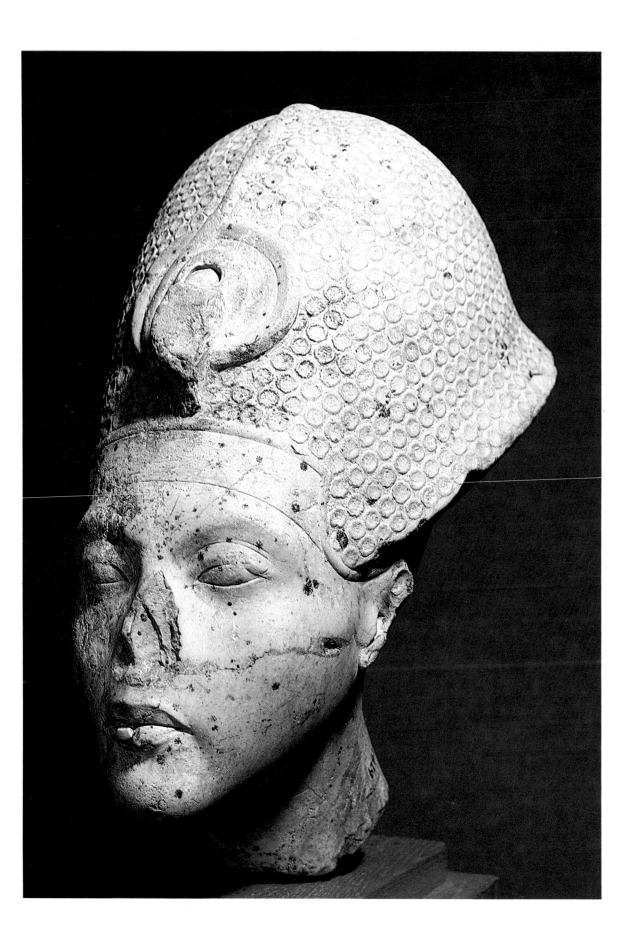

obviously unflattering to the point of repulsion.

This is not true of this fine limestone head, which was discovered by the inhabitants of Tell el-Amarna, during the construction of a road just before a visit by King Fouad. It was subsequently presented to the monarch, who passed it on to the museum just before his death. By contrast with the Karnak statues, which have been condemned as 'abominations', this piece is a faithful (if serious) portrait, closely resembling the fine smiling bust at the Louvre. Akhenaten is portrayed as a young man with an expression of gentleness and gravity. (It is interesting to compare the features with those of his mother, No. 55, which are more severe.) He wears a 'khepresh', for which he seems to have had a clear aesthetic preference: this explains the 'war-helmet' silhouette, which marries perfectly with the strongly prognathous profile.

All that remains of the 'uraeus' which adorned the king's 'blue crown' is the body coiled in a perfect circle; a replacement for the head was in preparation, probably at the same time that the right eyebrow and lower lip were so skilfully restored. The crown is decorated with little rings, save for its back, on the right hand side of the head; here the beginnings of the statue's off-centre supporting pillar may be discerned, and this feature leads one to suppose that the original ensemble consisted not of Akhenaten alone, but of the king and queen standing hand in hand, as in a statue at the Louvre. In the same display case is a head of Nefertiti, acquired by the museum in 1900, which is supposed to have come from the site of one of the boundary stelae set up by the reformer king to delineate the area he had chosen for his new capital. However, to judge by its size and style, the Nefertiti head may well have belonged to the same monument as this sensitive portrait of the son of Amenophis III and Tiye.

63 | Portrait of Queen Nefertiti

Quartzite; H. 36 cm; 18th Dynasty; No.6106; Ground floor, left, at entrance

This lovely head was discovered in 1932–33 by the English archaeologist John Pendlebury, in the south of the Amarna site, in a zone which had attracted attention by reason of the number of fragments of sculpture visible on its surface. The zone was only a few metres from a spot which had been excavated first by Petrie, and subsequently by a German expedition. The object was identified merely as 'the head of a princess', but despite the absence of any inscription it is certain that it is the beautiful Nefertiti, who is recognizable from several effigies, especially the famous painted limestone bust with a blue mortar head-dress, at Charlottenburg.

The head still bears the construction lines of an unfinished work. It was intended to be fixed on the body of a composite statue, by means of the long tenon which emerges from the neck. The back of the head is unpolished and scarcely even shaped, since it was destined to be hidden beneath a head-dress which could only have been a wig closely framing the face, and the ears were to be invisible.

Whether the sculptor was unable to finish his work, or whether he abandoned it at this point so as to show the procedure to others, it is certain that he did so deliberately. The eyes and eyebrows are simply traced in black and have not been inlaid as was probably planned. Intentional or not, this gives the queen the blurred yet intense expression of a person lost in thought.

By the position of the head, which is leaning slightly forward, the artist has succeeded wonderfully in expressing the inner tension of his model, who seems to be wholly engrossed in the contemplation of an ideal. The face is rendered sensual by its exquisite moulding, despite the expression of regal serenity which can only spring from calm certitude. It is the face of a person transported, of a woman fully committed to the new religious doctrines of her husband and sharing in his spiritual experience. There are many bas-reliefs to testify that Nefertiti nearly always took an active part in the cult of Aten, and some, discovered recently, would seem to show that she was more closely associated with the throne than the average royal wife.

64 | The steward Any in his chariot

Painted limestone; H. 27 cm; 18th Dynasty;
No.484; Ground floor 3, north side, case H

This stela was one of a set of six discovered in 1891 by Alexandre Barsanti, during the clearing of the tomb of a certain Any at Tell el-Amarna. The finding of such an ensemble all belonging to the same person (four of the stelae were still in place on one of the walls of the sepulchre) was particularly interesting because small private stelae, though common before, became very rare in the Amarna period when the exclusive cult of Aten eclipsed the old gods banished by the king. Such stelae were, in effect, modest testimonials of the popular veneration for the various Egyptian gods, but the scene on this example has no religious significance whatever. It merely depicts Any standing in a chariot in company with a charioteer, who holds the reins of two horses.

The few columns of text cut under the arch of the stela inform us that Any 'a true royal scribe... scribe of the offerings of the Lord of the Two Lands, steward', has just been the object of royal favour. This is confirmed by the picture. He is seen wearing a ceremonial white costume and a wig adorned with a cone of perfumed oil, and an unusual four-piece collar of heavy gold beads: this was the 'golden reward' bestowed by the king on those of his subjects who had distinguished themselves in some way.

The bas-reliefs of several contemporary tombs describe this ceremony, during which the king and queen, installed in a kind of loggia, proffer the gold necklaces which are the symbols of royal satisfaction.

Hence, this little stela is a kind of 'photo-souvenir', or snapshot, taken at the moment when Any is leaving the palace after being given his golden reward. It was probably 'Tjay, charioteer of the royal scribe Any', who had the stela carved; this is suggested by the short, three-line inscription in front of his head, and the fact that the artist has skilfully composed his picture so that the charioteer is not entirely masked by his master.

The cranium of Tjay and the shaping of Any's body are in the typical Amarna style, but the artist's real skill lies in his ability to seize upon and interpret life, without ever falling into excess: the pride of the successful man, the cunning of the servant who has succeeded in showing himself at his master's side, and the contained strength of the horses, who seem to mark time.

65 | The Amarna Royal Family making offerings to Aten

Alabaster; H. 1.05 m; 18th Dynasty; No.487; Ground floor, left of window

This carved alabaster block, with its sloping convex top, comes from the royal palace of Amarna. It belonged to the parapet of a flight of steps leading to the building's central chamber, where it was discovered by Petrie in 1891. The scene, which is in incised relief, is often singled out as a significant example of the revolutionary aesthetic which dominated the early stages of Akhenaten's religious reform. Beneath a solar globe, with rays that end in hands bringing life (in the form of the 'ankh') to their nostrils, Akhenaten and Nefertiti make their offerings to Aten, while a princess

(probably their eldest daughter Meritaten) plays the sistrum behind them. The three royal figures, who are similarly outlined according to the direction of the rays of the sun, are placed in a kind of triangle, the king being almost twice the size of the queen, who in turn is almost twice the size of her daughter.

The king stands beside two low altars with lotus flowers on them, and he proffers two vases to the god he believes unique and benevolent. He wears a pleated loincloth which accentuates, instead of hides, the exaggerated curves of his belly and pelvis, to which the full, symbolic forms of fecundity have been given. On his head sits the white crown, whose inordinate length curiously prolongs his drawn-out profile. The double cartouche containing the sun's canonical names is repeated six times on his chest.

The face is almost a caricature; the torso is too narrow, between the excessively broad shoulders and hips; the thighs are enormous and the limbs emaciated. In the king's figure, deformity is pushed to the point of paroxysm, as in the colossi of Karnak, and is repeated more or less faithfully in the similarly-posed silhouettes of Nefertiti and her daughter; the latter raises her sistrum in her right hand. The style dates this relief prior to the ninth or tenth year of the reign, during the first stages of the construction of Akhetaten (the horizon of Aten). This was the new capital which the king began building in the year 4, far from Thebes and the over-mighty priesthood of Amun, on an immense site which had never previously been dedicated to any god. Controversy will always surround the relative rôles of historic, political and religious considerations during the Amarna episode. The king's desire to neutralize the high priests of Amun is more than evident, for they had clearly become a state within a state. But there was also a need to add some kind of divinity to the Egyptian pantheon, who would be accessible to all the subjects of the empire, then at its zenith; was this idea more influential than the doctrines of Heliopolis, or the rôle of the king's parents, at whose court the Aten was already much favoured? The answers to these questions may vary, but one thing is certain; the Amarna 'heresy' was above all a personal adventure, which the mystical sovereign tried in vain to share with his people.
He himself directed the artists responsible for establishing the new aesthetic, a fact attested by an inscription at Aswan; and he personally wrote the great lyrical hymn to Aten, declaring himself to be the god's sole prophet:

'... Thou comest, O splendid one, to the sky's horizon, O living Aten, creator of life. When thou dost rise in the east, all countries are filled with thy perfection ... when thou goest down in the west, the earth is plunged in the darkness of death. When the shadows are dispelled by the darts of thy rays the Two Lands rejoice, awaken and arise; (the people) wash their bodies, put on their garments, and raise their arms to adore thee; all the land sets to work and the beasts rejoice in the pastures; the trees and plants put on their green; the birds fly from the nests, saluting thy ka with their wings ... Thou makest the boy-child to grow in the belly of his mother ... thou preparest Hapy (the floodwater) in the nether world and bringest him forth at thy will, to nourish the people ... Thou art in my heart and none other knows thee but thy son Neferkheprure, the chosen one of Re, whom thou hast permitted to understand thy ways and thy power ...'

66 | Inlay

Quartzite; H. 11 çm; 18th Dynasty; No.6207;
Ground floor 3, west side, case F

The Egyptian artist seems always to have had a taste for bright colours in mural art and statues. Many today have lost their tints which in former times were always painted. To the contrasts of colours, the Amarna artist added the refinement of contrasting materials. He invented composite statuary, with heads, hands and feet of jasper, quartzite or granite, fitted to bodies of white limestone. He adorned the walls of monuments with decorative motifs moulded in faience or multi-coloured pâte de verre! These were inlaid by a technique approximating to cloisonné, which had already been used in the Old Empire for non-vitrified, coloured pâtes. Likewise, in bas-reliefs and inscriptions he filled the carved details with quartzite, faience or pâte de verre (faces, hands and crowns).

Although broken and badly restored, this royal profile is one of the finest inlays found in 1922 by Woolley, during the excavations conducted by the Egypt Exploration Society at Tell el-Amarna. It originally came from a palace which once stood to the south of the town.

It is probably a profile of the king himself, as indicated by the elongated face, the shape of the mouth and the thick lips, and the exaggerated curve from neck to chin. The modelling of the face

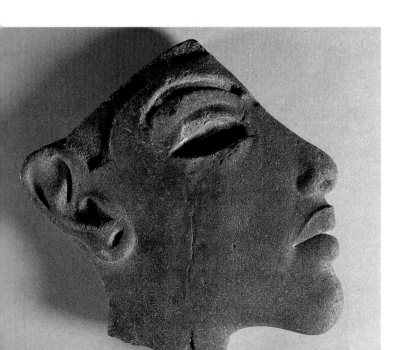

is very sensitive, particularly the mouth, the side of the nose, the contours of the eye and the fold of the eyelid.

Here the technique of inlay is pushed to its limits, for the eye and eyebrow were themselves inlaid, whereas on other similar profiles they are simply marked out with paint. In addition to this, the top of the brow is hollowed out to allow a crown made of some other matter to be fitted on the head.

67 | 'Shawabti' of the deputy Hat

Limestone, with coloured details; H. 20.5 cm; 18th Dynasty; First floor 43, one of the two central cases

Little is known of this fine yellow limestone statuette, other than the facts that it was bought in Cairo in 1908, that it was broken into two perfectly-fitting pieces, and that according to the *Journal d'Entrée* (No.39590) it comes from Thebes. Nonetheless, it deserves our consideration, because quite apart from its singular beauty, it has the added interest of belonging to the Amarna period. It would seem, in fact, that during this period, when Osirian beliefs and funerary practices were abandoned, 'shawabtis' were very rare, few indeed have survived. This is true at least of privately owned 'shawabtis', because curiously enough the royal tomb of the Darb el-Melek and a sculptor's workshop where they were made have yielded a number of funerary figurines of Akhenaten. These, with one exception, are all in fragments.

The single columns of text on the royal 'shawabtis' of Amarna generally give no more than the names of the king-prophet. By contrast, private funerary statuettes of the time may be recognized by their carved Atenist texts, several lines in length. When one reads these paeans, which extol the ideal of survival according to the cult of Aten, from whom all life flows, one wonders why the funeral furnishings still included 'shawabtis', so completely devoid are they of all Osirian references. Obviously, tradition remained very strong and sometimes the simultaneous presence of a hymn to the Sun Disc and of a few passages from the sixth chapter of the *Book of the Dead* (stripped, however, of any allusion to work in the next world) offers an indication that the new doctrine was ill-assimilated.

Although the figure carries the hoe and the mattock with the dignity of a monarch holding his sceptre, the text written on Hat's 'shawabti' says nothing of the chores of Osirian afterlife. It reveals more materialistic preoccupations, with a view to the more pleasant prospect held out by Aten:

'An offering which the king gives to the living
Disc which illuminates every land with its beauty,
so that he may send the sweet north wind, a long
life in the perfect west, a refreshing libation, wine
and milk on the table of offerings in his tomb, for
the 'ka' of the deputy Hat, living anew'.

Without neglecting the shape of the body, the
execution of the hands, the broad floral necklace,
or the long, grooved wig, the sculptor has lavished
his greatest skill upon the face, whose pleasing
features are heightened by several touches of
colour. A far cry, this, from the audacious beginnings of the aesthetic revolution; the statuette
probably dates from the first years of the reign of
Tutankhaton, and is an example of how the
excesses of Amarna art had been rejected. Indeed,
it was about this time that the young king changed
his name to Tutankhamun, to mark the return to
the orthodoxy of Amun.

68 | First anthropoid coffin of Tutankhamun *detail*

*Solid gold and inlay; total H. 1.875 m; 18th
Dynasty; No.T.219; First floor, east side, case 29*

On the morning of 4 November 1922, the first of
the sixteen steps leading to the inviolate tomb of
Tutankhamun was uncovered. Since that day,
abundant books and articles have related this
fabulous discovery, describing the unbelievable
treasures, or, less happily, the ridiculous myth of
the 'curse of the pharaohs'. The facts are now
well-known, so we shall limit ourselves to the most
important moments of the obstinate eight-year
quest conducted by Howard Carter and Herbert,
the Fifth Earl of Caernarfon, against the advice of
all the experts. In effect, after the fruitful excavations of Loret, in 1898, and Davis, (1902–12), it
was generally accepted that the Valley of the Kings
held no more surprises. This was the opinion of
Maspero, Director-General of the Antiquities
Service, who in June 1914 gave a concession to the
two Englishmen to dig in the area. Carter, by
contrast, was convinced that shards of pottery and
other objects bearing the name of Tutankhamun
discovered by Davis in 1907–08, were not the only

remains of the young king's tomb, but merely a
part of the equipment used during his mummification. According to Carter, the tomb had still not
been discovered; so, taking into account the various other excavations that had been made, he
decided to strip down to the rock a triangular zone
delineated by the tombs of Ramesses II,
Merenptah and Ramesses VI, not far from the
entrance to the valley. The real excavation work
began in the autumn of 1917, and almost immediately the remains of workmen's huts, thought
to have been built on the rock itself, were revealed
in front of Ramesses VI's massive tomb. The dig
continued all around for five years thereafter without result, and finally, on 3 November 1922, a few
weeks before the concession was to run out, the
despairing Carter ordered the huts demolished.
The next day, when he arrived at the site, he was
greeted by an unaccustomed silence: the longed-
for discovery had been made. The beginning of a
stairway cut into the rock was clearly visible where
the ancient workmen's cabins had stood. By the
time the twelfth step had been uncovered Carter
knew beyond doubt that his guess had been right:
the walled-up door which now appeared led, in
effect, to a royal tomb carrying the seal of the
necropolis. Four steps further down, Carter found
a tablet with the name of Tutankhamun. On 6
November, Lord Caernarfon, who was in England,
received news of the discovery; by the 23rd, he
was in Luxor with his daughter. In Carter's words,
this was the 'day of days, the most wonderful that
I have ever lived through'. We may well believe it,
and it is not hard to imagine his emotion when the
first tomb passage had been cleared of rocks and
he was able to pass a candle through the breach in
the wall that closed off the rest of the sepulchre.
As his eyes gradually became accustomed to the
gloom, little by little he began to pick out the
strange funerary couches, the statues, the chests,
and everywhere the glitter of gold. 'Can you see
anything?' asked the anxious Caernarfon; to which
Carter, almost dumb with astonishment, could
only respond with his famous phrase: 'Yes, wonderful things!'

The joy of the discovery was enhanced by relief,
for although the tomb had manifestly been visited
by robbers – holes had been made in the dividing
walls, then reblocked – nothing had been removed.
The first room, christened the 'Antechamber',
took seven weeks to empty; and it was only on 17
February 1923, that the archaeologist and his
sponsor were able to enter the funeral chamber,
after first coming up against what they thought

was a 'wall of gold', but which in fact proved to be the southern partition of the largest of four shrines of gilded wood protecting the stone sarcophagus and the three anthropoid coffins of the king. The remainder of the furnishings (according to the *Journal d'Entrée*, these amounted to 2099 separate objects) was piled up in an 'Annex' to the Antechamber which began to be emptied five years later, and in a 'Treasury' next to the room where the king lay. This room was closed off by a wooden door during the four years of patient study and restoration devoted to the eight envelopes of the royal mummy and their contents. After the dismantling of the golden vaulting fitted over the quartzite sarcophagus, the mummiform coffins (whose weight intrigued Carter) were opened during the 1925–26 season. He understood why these coffins were so heavy, when the second envelope was raised to reveal the final coffin containing Tutankhamun's mummy: it was found to be made of solid gold, like the famous mask that covered the head. Two sheets of gold, with an average thickness of three millimetres, had been hammered out to form the coffin's upper and lower parts, which were joined together by golden pins. Altogether the coffin weighed 110.4 kilograms. Gold was not used here for its rarity or value, but because in the eyes of the Egyptians it symbolized the incorruptible flesh of the gods whose ranks the king would join at his death. Like the other two coffins, the larger of which is made of gilded wood and the smaller of wood inlaid with gold plate, this one has the shape of the Osirian mummy adorned with the emblems of royalty: the 'nemes', with its cobra and vulture, the lapis beard denoting divinity, and the crochet and flabellum crossed on the chest. The unguents, which had been very heavily applied by the embalmers, had fused the first two coffins, the mummy and the mask into a single mass. They had to be heated in the tomb itself to a temperature of 500° with

primus stoves (the goldwork was protected with zinc sheets) before they could finally be separated. This over-use of unguents had had the effect of carbonizing the face of the mummy, and it is now hard to recognize the idealized features of the youthful god portrayed in the golden portraits of the mask and first sarcophagus.

People frequently allude to the fantastic treasures that were hidden in the tombs of the greatest pharaohs; some must in fact have been fabulously rich, but the real question is, *why* was there so much gold in Tutankhamun's? While his sepulchre is the only royal tomb in the Valley of the Kings to have survived intact, to deduce thereby that all the pharaohs must have been knee-deep in gold is to forget that the mummy of Amenophis II, by no means a minor pharaoh, was also discovered (by Loret) in its original coffin – which was made of wood. The same is true of the other royal coffins piled up in the cachette of Deir el-Bahari. The political and religious upheavals of the late 18th Dynasty perhaps partly explain the wealth of Tutankhamun's relatively small burial vault, for it is now almost certain that some of the pieces were not initially prepared for Tutankhamun.

At all events, none of them carries the smallest inscription that in any way threatens archaeologists, as has been so often affirmed. Caernarfon may have died a few months after the tomb was opened but it is conveniently forgotten that he had been ill for a long time previously, and this was the reason for his coming to Egypt. Carter died in 1939, at the age of 65, despite several premature announcements of his passing in the gutter press. A very slow-acting curse for a king who had only cause to congratulate himself on his posthumous destiny! After all, according to the ideal of the ancient Egyptians, he is today the most alive of all the pharaohs; his name is on millions of lips all over the planet.

69 | Amulets of Tutankhamun

Jasper, faience and gold; average H. 9 cm; 18th Dynasty; Nos.T.688, T.160, T.159, T.384, T.385; First floor 45, west side, case 66

If there was one prosperous industry in pharaonic Egypt, that industry was the manufacture of amulets. All Egyptians, whether nobles, scribes or peasants, believed in the magical properties of these innumerable figurines. While they lived, they wore them as pendants; and when they died, if they were rich, their mummies were covered with amulets according to the prescriptions of funerary ritual.

Amulets have many forms. They can portray imaginary divinities in the form of tiny statuettes. They can also be tools, parts of the human body, royal insignia, plants, animals or even hieroglyphs expressing abstract notions, and they vary from rough silhouettes to little masterpieces of delicate workmanship. They come in the form of gold, gemstones, faience and even wood, and they are so numerous that it would be nearly impossible to give a complete list of all the amulets favoured by the subjects of the pharaohs.

Despite his own divine status, the king himself sought their protection as proven by the many amulets found in the tomb of Tutankhamun.

On his body, they were made of very precious materials and constituted a kind of magical armour. Those discovered in the various caskets were chosen principally for their proven 'effectiveness', and hence were more of an everyday kind.

With the exception of the Isis knot, which is of jasper, all are in blue faience; only the 'djed' pillar is partially covered in gold. They are also considerably larger in size than ordinary amulets and four of them bear the king's first name, Nebkheprure.

The 'was' sceptre, a stick forked at one end and a stylized head at the other (probably the mythical beast of Seth) is a sign of strength and power.

The 'ankh', which is an element of costume, ensures eternal life; it is in the shape of the hieroglyph which signifies everything to do with the notion of life.

The 'tit' knot, or Isis knot, is in the form of a

tied belt buckle. This is clearly synonymous with protection, but not much is known of its exact significance. The material used is red jasper, the colour of the blood of Isis as confirmed in chapter 156 of the *Book of the Dead*, which specifies that the amulet must be hung around the dead man's neck by a cord of sycamore fibre.

The 'djed' pillar is the Osirian symbol of stability. It is not known exactly what this represents (perhaps a branchless tree-trunk) but it was probably assimilated with the backbone of Osiris, as described in chapter 155 of the *Book of the Dead*, which states that a dead person wearing a 'djed' pillar amulet round his neck will be 'especially blessed in the empire of the dead'.

Lastly, chapters 159 and 168 of the *Book of the Dead* indicate that the 'wadj' column should be cut out from amazonite, whose green colour recalls the elegant papyrus plant from which it borrows its shape. The 'wadj' guarantees incorruptibility of the body, vitality and eternal youth.

70 | Jewel casket

Gold and ivory; H. 14 cm; 18th Dynasty; No.T.89; First floor 25, west side, case 119

This little casket is unquestionably the most elegant of all those discovered in Tutankhamun's tomb, by reason of its purity of form, restrained decoration and beautiful materials.

The shape is simple, almost cubic, made up of plaques and pieces of ivory that have been carefully fitted together. The hinges and knobs, which enabled the casket to be closed with a piece of cord (of which some fragments remain), are in gold, and the lower extremity of each foot is lined with the same patinated metal. On the front and top of this small, precious piece of furniture, the only decoration is a part of the royal title, sculpted in shallow relief. The back is adorned with a floral colonette fixed to the centre of the panel. (The colonette has not been botanically identified but it was the heraldic plant of Upper Egypt.)

On the lid, beside the column of hieroglyphs where the names appear of the 'King of Upper and Lower Egypt, the Lord of the Two Lands, the Lord of crowns Nebkheprure, the son of Re, who loves him, Tutankhamun', a line of hieratic written in black ink shows what the original contents of the casket were: 'golden rings from the funeral procession'. In fact, the casket was found empty, but perhaps the rings referred to were those found by Carter, along with other miscellaneous objects, in another box. These had been inexplicably left behind by the grave-robbers, who had gathered them all together in a piece of knotted cloth. After the attempted robbery, they were put away by those in charge of the necropolis, who inspected the tomb and put it back in order, before once again closing it up – this time for thousands of years.

71 | Pectoral with 'wedjat' eye

Gold, lapis lazuli, turquoise and pâte de verre; H. of pendant 5.7 cm; 18th Dynasty; No.T.231; First floor 4, centre, case 32

To the impressive protection afforded by the eight successive envelopes covering the mummy of Tutankhamun, was added that of dozens of charms in the forms of pieces of jewellery. During the ritual embalming of the king's corpse, the embalmers placed no less than 143 of these items in predetermined places around the body. Accord-

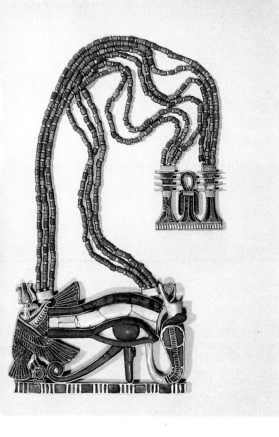

ing to Carter, this pectoral with its main feature of a 'wedjat' eye, was worn by the king during his lifetime. It was found on the royal breast under the twelfth layer of bandages, along with two other pendants representing a solar falcon and a winged scarab.

Because of its high reputation for effectiveness, the 'wedjat' eye was one of the most common Egyptian amulets. It represented the eye of Horus and was synonymous with good health, physical plenitude and prosperity. According to legend, the god lost his eye while battling with Seth to avenge his father, and the eye was subsequently retrieved by Thoth, who healed it and restored it to its owner. By tradition, it was pictured as a human eye rimmed with black, which became stylized with the addition of the curious stain that characterizes the cheek of the falcon.

72 | Statue of Anubis *detail*

Stuccoed wood, varnished and gilded; silver, gold, calcite, obsidian; H. of animal 57 cm; 18th Dynasty; No.T.447; First floor, No.45; case 54

On 17 February 1923, Carter, Lord Caernarfon and Pierre Lacau (then Director-General of the Antiquities Service) entered the largest catafalque of Tutankhamun's funerary vault for the first time. They were immediately confronted by this enigmatic statue of Anubis, which seemed to guard the entrance to the furthermost chamber of the tomb.

The black dog representing the god lay on a gilded casket in the form of a temple pylon, itself placed on a kind of portable stretcher. At the time of the discovery, the supple, sinewy body of the animal was still carefully covered with a piece of cloth dating from the year 7 of Akhenaten and only the head was showing. Beneath this protective covering was another layer of very fine gauze-like tissue, and a kind of shawl was knotted around the neck along with some plaited lotus and corn-flowers. Between the front feet lay the ivory palette of Princess Meritaten.

This statue, which is pegged to the sliding cover of the casket which serves as its base, is in stuccoed wood entirely covered in black resin except for the insides of the ears and the collar, which are gilded. The eyes are fashioned from gold, calcite and obsidian and the claws from silver.

Under its grooved edge, the gilded wooden casket bears hieroglyphic texts and a design of alternating groups of 'djed' pillars and 'tit' knots, two by two. It has several compartments and originally contained bunches of amulets which had been somewhat primitively wrapped in cloth, two alabaster bowls and various broad inlaid gold pectorals. However, these things had been disturbed by the thieves in their search for more precious stones.

What was the meaning of this statue shrine? and what was it used for? In hieroglyphic writing, the corresponding signs grouped in the same fashion make up a single title that introduces many others.

It may be translated as 'initiated into the secrets' (literally: 'he who is upon the secrets'). The sculpted image of the god lying on casket necessarily had this meaning: when carried in the funeral procession, then left in the tomb facing the royal catafalques, a sacred object of this kind would link the same idea with everything represented by the strictly funerary character of Anubis 'who is upon his mountain'. For Anubis has a multiple rôle in the world of the dead and in the necropolis itself, of which he is the lord, the guardian and the guide. As the inventor of mummification on behalf of Osiris (whose body had been dismembered by Seth), Anubis officiates over mummy wrappings; but, as 'he who presides in the divine pavilion' where the embalmers carry out their essential work, he is also the agent who brings the dead man before the tribunal of the gods, when the time comes for the weighing of souls.

73 | Painted wooden casket

Stuccoed and painted wood; H. of scene 15.3 cm; 18th Dynasty; No.T.324; First floor 25, case 20

This very beautiful chest, which unquestionably is one of the most remarkable of the Tutankhamun funerary furnishings, was placed on the floor of the antechamber against one of the two lifesize statues of the king that stood on either side of the access to the tomb-chamber. It was used as a repository for the royal sandals and indeed contained several pairs amid a jumbled pile of other objects, jewellery and clothing embroidered with beads and sequins.

The chest and its convex lid are richly adorned with paintings on stucco, which Carter, with some justice, compared to Persian miniatures. (His other comparison to Benozzo Gozzoli is perhaps less apt.) These paintings are executed with extraordinary skill and an attention to detail which bears up well under close examination with a microscope.

The design of the casket is made up of six scenes that are both parallel and symmetrically opposite to one another. The scenes are of the exploits in hunting and war of a king who may indeed have been a hunter (a number of his bows were found in the tomb) but surely died too young to have ever gone to war. On the surfaces of the convex lid, where he is called 'Wielder of the sword that crushes the Nine Bows', Tutankhamun is figured on one slope showering arrows on lions and lionesses. On the other, his targets are other wild animals such as antelopes, a pair of ostriches, a hyena and some wild asses. On the two sides of the chest, the king is portrayed in the same way, but animals have been replaced by Asiatics and Nubians respectively. The two ends are nearly identical: beside the two insets bearing his name, the king is portrayed as a human-faced sphinx who tramples a Nubian or an Asiatic, designated as 'the chieftans of Kush and of all foreign nations'. These are the classic themes of traditional Egyptian iconography extolling the king's implacable powers.

Whether confronted by fierce animals or in pursuit of the enemies of Egypt, the king is aided by the gods and remains imperturbable and hieratic above the mêlée. In the war-scenes, for in-

stance, there is no real combat, because the pharaoh himself is not involved in the fighting. He is playing a royal *jeu de massacre* with complete serenity; he is the incarnation of order and irresistible power.

Each of the four principal scenes is a kind of prototype of those found on temple walls from the 19th Dynasty onwards. Each is contained in a rectangular space carefully delineated by chequer board and stylized flowered frieze patterns. The king's chariot is figured at the centre of each panel, surmounted by a black line which is the hieroglyphic sign for the sky. The chariot faces either to the right (Asiatics and desert animals) or to the left (Nubians and lions).

Tutankhamun is featured standing upright in this vehicle; he controls the reins of his horses, at the same time drawing his bow. He is protected by two Nekhbet vultures holding a 'shen' sign and by a solar disc flanked by two 'uraei'. He wears a 'khepresh' head-dress, a loincloth and a corselet studded with jewels. One quiver full of arrows is slung across his back and another is propped beside him in the chariot, along with a case for

spare bows. The horses are sumptuously plumed and caparisoned; they rear above the first dead bodies over which the royal chariot is to pass.

The painter of the chest (unfortunately anonymous, in keeping with Egyptian tradition), has composed this scene with admirable skill and with the passage of time his colours have taken on a camaien aspect. The heaped-up, twisted bodies of wounded and dying Nubians are balanced by the ordered ranks of the royal entourage which includes fanbearers, carriers, archers and chariots; and the contorted faces of the enemies being despatched by the king's soldiers and dogs are in contrast with the calmly advancing Egyptians, who follow their pharaoh through a landscape filled with flowers.

A few short columns and a line of text say of Nebkheprure Tutankhamun that he is 'the perfect god, the image of the Sun rising over foreign lands, like Re when he appears, crushing the vile land of Kush, shooting his arrows against his enemies'.

74 | Model of a boat

Painted wood, linen; L. 1.18 m; 18th Dynasty;
No.T.459; First floor 15, case 50.

In Egypt, which is geographically dominated by the sovereign Nile, waterborne trade, transport or travel has always been the rule.

We are reminded of this fact by the veritable fleet of model ships and boats that were found piled up in the 'Treasury' of Tutankhamun, for use by the king on his voyage after the sun, for the ritual journeys to Abydos and Busiris (the holy cities of Osiris), or, more simply, for hunting and fishing in the game-filled marshes.

This model, which was found lying on a miniature granary on the south side of the room, is one of the rare examples of a boat with masts and sails, most of the others being elegant wherries with a single cabin or seat.

It was perhaps intended for some kind of posthumous pilgrimage, but the evidence suggests that it is a reproduction of the kind of ship used by the king during his lifetime, when he had to travel on the Nile.

The hull is simply shaped, like a raft of reeds or papyrus, with a tapering prow and wide, flattened stern like the tail of a fish. A large cabin with a stairway leading to its roof occupies the middle deck. This cabin is decorated with a painted chequerboard pattern, while the two 'naos' shaped fore and aft cabins are gilded with guard-rails adorned by lions and bulls, the symbolic images of royal power.

The mast stands athwart the central cabin and is rigged with a double yard and broad rectangular sail. (The sail is now very fragile.) On either side of the poop hang two long steering oars with gilded royal heads at their top ends.

75 | Scribe's palette

Ivory, gold, reed pens, coloured pigments;
L. 30.3 cm; 18th Dynasty; No.T.382; First floor,
west side, case 41

'Bring me the water pot and the palette, the pen-cases of Thoth, and the secrets pertaining to it. See, I am a scribe...' says a passage from Chapter 94 of the *Book of the Dead*. For an Egyptian, the possession after death of the palette of Thoth was to assimilate himself with the great god of Hermopolis. Thoth was not only the protector of scribes, but also of magicians, because his knowledge of the divine words (*ie*, the hieroglyphs and their creative power) endowed him with immense powers.

Hence Tutankhamun's funerary paraphernalia was bound to include a whole set of votive palettes and the full equipment of a scribe: two palettes for writing, a case for reed pens, and a curious ivory instrument probably used for smoothing sheets of papyrus. There was also a third palette which had belonged to Meritaten, daughter of Nefertiti; this was intended more for painting than for writing, since it contained white, yellow, red, green, blue and black colour capsules.

This palette is made from a simple piece of ivory with its ends sheathed in gold. Two round holes in the ivory still contain nuggets of blue and red ink (which have apparently been used) and seven reed pens packed into a narrow central cav-ity. On either side of this are carved the king's cartouches, proclaiming that he is beloved not only by Thoth, but also by Atum and Amon-Re. This is not the case with the other palette, which is entirely covered in gold and clearly dates from before the restoration of the cult of Amun because the king is still referred to as Tutankhaten.

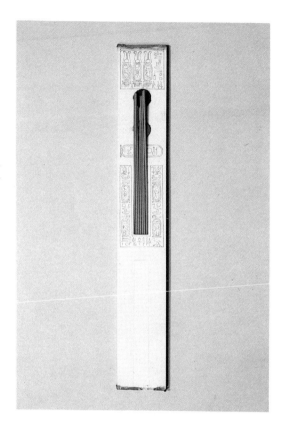

76 | Tutankhamun with his harpoon

Stuccoed wood, painted and gilded; H. 75 cm; 18th
Dynasty; No.T.994; First floor 35, case 44

The tomb of Tutankhamun contained 24 'naoi' of blackened wood, whose closed doors were carefully sealed by a short cord and a clay seal bearing the miniature stamp of the necropolis. Apart from two 'naoi' found on one of the three large funeral beds in the antichamber, they were all placed against the southern wall of the 'Treasury', and each contained one or several statuettes of gilded or resin-coated wood. Twenty seven of these represented various gods and seven the king himself.

The funerary rôle and significance of some of these statues has prompted much speculation. While the figurines of gods like Ptah, Atum or Sakhmet require no commentary, the presence of a god named Menkaret holding a mummy-shaped Tutankhamun high above his head is a mystery.

Tutankhamun with his harpoon

And why is the king pictured twice elsewhere standing on a leopard's back? Similar motifs on the walls of other royal tombs, like that of Sethos II, throw little light on these questions.

By contrast, the statuette shown here is of Tutankhamun standing on a papyrus raft, about to hurl a harpoon at an invisible animal, and we have no difficulty interpreting it. It is one of a pair which was found wrapped in cloth in one of the black vaults, along with another statue of the king and one of the god Ihy playing the sistrum.

The king wears a long pleated loincloth, sandals and a broad throat-piece; on his head is the red crown of Lower Egypt. He is not harpooning fish, like so many other individuals painted or carved on the walls of tombs from every epoch. Here, the statue alludes directly to an episode from the myth of Horus, which was graphically related centuries later on the walls of the Ptolemaic temple of Edfu, in the form of a sacred drama. According to this myth, Horus, disputing with his uncle the royal function first exercised on earth by Osiris, harpooned Seth, who had taken the form of a hippopotamus. Hence in this statuette Tutankhamun, as terrestrial incarnation of Horus, is about to hurl his weapon at a hippopotamus. The creature is not portrayed, for the obvious reason that it was the magical representation of evil. Like every other Egyptian sovereign, Tutankhamun had the responsibility of neutralizing the evil forces personified by the murderer of Osiris.

This beautiful figurine, one of the most well-modelled in the collection, is another clear indication of how the Amarna aesthetic has been moderated. This shows especially in the modelling of the body, emphasized by the shape of the loincloth which rides high over the hips but leaves the belly exposed. The sculptor has contrived to suggest movement with astonishing skill; the fact that the king appears to be striding forward gives the impression that the papyrus raft is also moving and the harpoon is about to be thrown. Indeed, the convergence between the weapon and the left arm, prolonged by the spur at the back of the crown, so clearly targets the invisible hippopotamus in the water in front of the raft, that it seems almost to be present.

The plinth is black and the papyrus raft is green, but the statuette itself is gilded all over, including the sandals, the details of the crown and the harpoon. All of these are made of bronze, as is the rope in the left hand, which retains its original colour. The eyes are inlaid with calcite and obsidian.

77 | Statuette of the god Amun

Schist (greywacke); H. 58 cm; end of 18th Dynasty; Ground floor 12, east side, case C

This lovely statuette, which is sadly incomplete and partially restored, was discovered at Karnak in 1905. It is carefully fashioned in green, fine-grained stone and represents the god Amun who, of all the Egyptian gods, probably had the most extraordinary destiny. Beginning as an obscure divinity of the Thebaid during the Old Kingdom, within a few hundred years he became the supreme figure in the Egyptian pantheon. Undoubtedly his very name, which means 'The Hidden One', contributed to his rise, since it lent itself very readily to all the assimilations and juxtapositions by which the syncretic Egyptian religion sought to approach the personality of an omnipresent but indefinable god. The priests of Thebes, who associated Amun with the ram and the Nile goose, skilfully took advantage of these possibilities when they had to develop a theology for the god that Ammenemes I ('Amun is pre-eminent'), the founder of the 12th Dynasty, had raised to the rank of imperial deity. Their response was to borrow from neighbouring cults as well as from the great doctrines of Memphis, Heliopolis and Hermopolis. The last of these enabled them to transform Amun into a god of prime importance, because one of the eight original deities of the Hermopolitan Ogdoad bore his name:

'O thou who wast the first to be, in the Earliest Time; O Amun that camest into existence in the beginning, no man knows from whence; no god was before thee, no god was thy companion, nor knew thy form; no mother could name thee, no father could beget thee and say: "Behold, this is my work". O god who didst fashion the very egg from which thou camest, O power of unknowable birth, O divine lord that arose spontaneously of thyself.'

Amun was also seen as a god of the air and of fertility, but his principal rôle was dynastic. He was, in fact, the 'king of the gods', sharing his glory with the goddess Mut, his wife, and their son, the moon god Khons. Amun's prestige was immense, as evidenced by his gigantic temple at

Part of an obelisk for Hatshepsut showing the god Amun

78 | The wife of the general Nakhtmin

Indurated limestone; H. 84 cm; end of 18th Dynasty; Ground floor 15, centre, case A

In spite of the deliberate mutilation inflicted on this statue of a woman in marble-like crystalline limestone, it nevertheless remains one of the most beautiful examples of Egyptian sculpture. Along with the superb head of a man exhibited in the same case, it was part of a group which was to 18th Dynasty sculpture in the round what the walls of the tomb of Ramose are to the art of bas-relief in the same period: unequalled masterpieces. The man was originally seated; his wife, smaller than he, stood to his left with her right arm around him.

The woman wears a shawl knotted under her right breast, and a clinging dress whose cunning, regular pleats accentuate and reveal her figure. The firm, well-formed breasts and the gentle curves of the hips are wonderfully graceful and sensual. On her head she wears a heavy, enveloping wig which frames the face between two bunches of carefully braided tresses; these are held in place at cheek level by a plain band, and the wig is crowned by a floral diadem of one lotus flower and two lotus buds. Their stems mark a slight depression across the top of the coiffure. She is also adorned with a broad collar and bracelets; in her left hand, she holds against her chest a 'menat' collar, which is a kind of liturgical musical instrument particularly associated with the cult of Hathor from the Middle Kingdom onwards.

The deliberate bludgeoning of the head has not effaced its beauty and nobility. The eyes were originally outlined in black, and the shape of the mouth heightened with red; this would have emphasized the wistful, dreamy expression, which, like the shape of the body, situates the statue in the years immediately following the Amarna period when its influence was still strong.

The origin of these two fragments is unknown, since they were bought by the museum in 1897. What remains of the inscription carved on their backs does not allow of any positive identification, only a few suppositions. The woman's name has vanished completely, but the man's is still legible despite the hammering it has received: he was called Nakhtmin and among other things he was a

Karnak which was steadily enlarged and embellished by all the pharaohs of the New Kingdom. The political power gradually accumulated by his priests was so great that some of them actually became kings towards the end of the 20th Dynasty.

In this statue, Amun is portrayed in traditional fashion as a god in human form, standing upright, his arms at his sides. His loincloth has a belt adorned with an Isis knot, and he wears bracelets, a broad collar, the divine beard and a corselet reduced to simple breast bands. He also wears his traditional low head-dress, which was originally topped by the two tall feathers of the gods of the air. These feathers must have been made of gold, which would explain their disappearance.

The rounded shape of the belly, which emphasizes the belt of the loincloth, bears traces of Amarna influence, while the gentle, smiling face has the same youthful charm as that of Tutankhamun. Hence, this statuette is probably one of the earliest examples we possess of the restoration of the cult of Amun after the Amarna interlude.

'royal scribe and general-in-chief'. Another Nakhtmin is known to us, who was responsible for the manufacture of five of Tutankhamun's great ushabtis; in addition to the titles of royal scribe and general, he was 'fanbearer at the king's right hand'. The Nakhtmin portrayed here probably also carried a fan, for we can see the remains of a broad curved feather to the right of his finely-wrought, undulating wig. Thus there is a good chance that they are one and the same person, who was probably of royal blood. Moreover, the left hand side of the text is broken off at the words 'King's son of...', which may signify that Nakhtmin was either a fully-fledged prince, if we add a cartouche after 'of', (in which case he would have been a younger son of Amenophis III) or else viceroy of Nubia. The title of 'King's Son of Kush' would in this case cover his purely administrative functions. For the moment, we have no way of choosing between the two possibilities.

The general Nakhtmin

79 | Ameneminet and his family worshipping the goddess Sakhmet

Limestone; H. 1.17 m; end of 18th Dynasty; Ground floor 10, to the right of the stairs

Although we tend automatically to associate the name of Saqqara with the Step Pyramid and the most beautiful of the great Old Kingdom mastabas, it should not be forgotten that this site was also the necropolis of Memphis from the time of the first dynasties right up till the Christian era. The recent discoveries of the tombs of King Horemheb and, in 1986, of Maya, Tutankhamun's treasurer, were really rediscoveries, in that clandestine excavations in the last century had already furnished certain European museums with magnificent reliefs and statues from them. At all events, they have served to remind us that Saqqara contains very fine New Kingdom sepulchres, dating from the end of the 18th Dynasty to the beginning of the 19th.

One of these rediscovered tombs is that of the 'overseer of craftsmen and head of gold-workers, Ameneminet'. It was originally unearthed in 1897–98 by Loret and partly dismantled, because it could not be completely cleared; which is how this wall-fragment came to the Museum, where it is only included in the temporary register.

Two superimposed scenes fill the decorated surface; one of these is sculpted in bold relief, and the other, below it, in intaglio. The upper register portrays Ameneminet, his wife and two of his sons in adoration of the goddess Sakhmet, who stands in a kind of chapel. Sakhmet is the paredra of Ptah, and watches over part of the Memphis necropolis; here she is represented as a woman with the mask of a lioness, bearing a solar disc on her head and grasping a 'wadj' sceptre and an 'ankh'. Ameneminet, who is offering her papyrus and lotus blossoms, is dressed in the fashion prevailing at the end of the dynasty (see No.96), in a rich pleated garment with billowing apron and an intricately braided wig. Tahesyt, his wife, who raises both hands in veneration, wears a dress which leaves no part of her anatomy to the imagination; her coiffure is topped by a cone of perfumed grease. Behind Tahesyt are the 'scribe of the treasury, Ptahmose' and the 'head of goldworkers, Amenemheb', who are probably the couple's two eldest sons. They await their turn to pay homage to the goddess; each has one hand raised toward

her, and carries offerings of papyrus and birds in the other.

The lower register is more of the same: two boys and two girls bringing plants, birds and fruit advance towards a heap of offerings dedicated to Sakhmet.

Similar scenes are innumerable and banal in Egyptian art, but not all are so remarkably well constructed and executed as this one, in which the bold innovation of Amarna is subtly blended with the rediscovered elegance of the reign of Amenophis III.

80 | Study for the ceiling of a tomb

Painted limestone; H. 15 cm; 19th–20th Dynasty; First floor 24, north side, desk No.12

Despite the forests of papyrus which covered the marshy zones of the Nile valley in antiquity, the noble writing material made with the fibrous pith of papyrus stalks was an expensive commodity. For his daily work, and sometimes for his own entertainment, the scribe tallying accounts, the artist making sketches, or the schoolboy going over

Pictorial ostracon showing the goddess Meresger

Pictorial ostracon showing a cat guarding geese

his homework used much cheaper materials, such as shards of pottery and limestone. 'Ostraca' of this kind (ostracon, the singular of the word, in Greek, means 'shell') were used abundantly from the time of the Old Kingdom up till the Arab epoch, and they have survived by the thousand.

Those ostraca of the New Kingdom which are written in hieratic prove to be very valuable records. They allow us to build up pictures of various sectors of economic activity (accounts of all kinds, lists of equipment, deliveries of products, staff quotas); and they provide literary works copied more or less completely in the writing schools (stories, lovesongs, proverbs, hymns). Figured ostraca offer sketches which sometimes seem to be drawn from life, along with satirical drawings, real or imaginary creatures, and the whole iconographic repertoire of royal or private tombs at the preparatory stage. Drawn as they are in black or touched up with colours, these genre scenes, pharaohs in battle and figures of gods often give us a better appreciation of how the Egyptian draftsman's sure touch was blended with freedom of line and an extraordinary sense of movement, than do his completed works.

This ostracon, which came to the Museum in 1903, represents a project for a ceiling pattern, like those which can be seen in many of the tombs of the Thebes necropolis. In fact, though the term may seem unsuitable, it is a panel, because the ceilings of tombs were nearly always divided into several square or rectangular areas by strips of text which were themselves ornamental. The pattern, which is still vividly coloured, is composed of stylized florets inside diagonally arranged squares. Geometrical motifs are the most common, often differing from one panel to the next (rosettes, spirals, zig-zags, stars, diamonds), but some of the more original examples have birds about to take flight, heads of oxen seen from the front, or pampres (vine-leaves) which are more or less stylized.

The various pieces of this statue, which were found in the Karnak trove in 1904, are not fragments of a broken statue but the six constituent elements of a 'constructed' work. The front part of the head, the torso and the arms, the two hands and the two legs were separately sculpted. They were then carefully assembled by a process borrowed from wooden statuary techniques under the Old Kingdom, which was described by Diodorus of Sicily (I,98):

'They (the Egyptians) do not conceive their statues as do the Greeks, according to the inner vision of their imagination; for, after they have arranged and cut the stone, they execute their work in such a way that all its parts fit together to the very last detail. This is why they divide the human body into $21\frac{1}{4}$ parts and regulate the symmetry of the work accordingly. Hence, after the workers have decided upon the height of the statue, each fashions the pieces he has chosen in his own workshop and the finished parts marry so closely with one another that it is quite astonishing.'

The king, who is identified by name by inscriptions carved on the supporting pillars of the legs, is portrayed standing upright with his arms hanging naturally at his sides. His clothes and wig have vanished, but enough tiny traces remain for us to conclude that Sethos was dressed in the traditional 'shendyt', in this case made of gold leaf. On the other hand, it is impossible to say which crown he wore, because all that is visible of it (around the ears) could just as easily have belonged to a 'nemes' as to a 'pschent', or indeed to any of the other types of royal headgear.

The modelling of the body and the very sensitive work on the face (unfortunately marred by the absence of the nose and the inlaid eyes) is more typical of 18th Dynasty art than of the Ramessid era. On the other hand, the relatively poor quality of the curved texts has led some experts to believe that the colossus had been usurped by the father of Ramesses II; the disappearance of the nose makes it hard to be categorical on this point. Nonetheless, despite the statue's poor state of conservation and the rather unfortunate restoration of the clothing, it is still a very fine piece which must have been most impressive when still in possession of its detachable crown, golden loincloth and the gold jewellery which originally covered the joints between the neck, body, forearms and hands.

82 | Handle of a mirror

Ivory; H. 15.1 cm; 19th Dynasty (?); No.1383; First floor, case H

The mirror, as an important toilet accessory, featured among the funerary furnishings of rich Egyptians from the Old Kingdom onwards.

However, mirrors of silvered glass did not appear in Egypt before the Christian epoch, with the result that the scores of mirrors possessed by the Cairo Museum are all made of reflecting plaques of metal attached to handles of various shapes and materials.

The oldest of these metal discs are in copper, but bronze and silver were also used, alone or in combination. Gold was apparently used for votive mirrors (none of these survive) but less precious metals could also be gilded or silvered with leaf or tincture.

Perfectly circular mirrors are very rare. Some are oval, and there is a single example in the form of a waterlily, with the waterlily's stalk serving as a handle. Otherwise, nearly all the mirrors we possess are in the 'solar' shape of a flattened circle, like that of the sun nearing the horizon. They are sometimes chased with a picture showing the presentation of the mirror to Hathor or Mut.

Whether the handles are made of acacia wood,

Mirror with Hathoric handle

ivory, gold, bronze or cloisonné metalwork, their varied and highly detailed forms in fact may be reduced to a limited number of types, with a clear predilection for figures from the amulet repertoire. These include knots for magical protection, 'wadj' columns conferring the vigour of the papyrus stem, and Hathoric colonettes. Although painted friezes inside Middle Kingdom sarcophagi (No.40) emphasize the 'solar' nature of the mirror by their handles, which have the form of supports for the divine symbol, in reality they seem to have been used very rarely.

On the other hand, figures in the form of statuettes are relatively common. These tend to take the form of naked girls with their arms pressed to their sides or raised to hold the disc above their heads. But other kinds do exist, and some of them are well-modelled like this little statue of the god Bes, from Thebes. Bes is a family god, a protector of women in childbirth. He is portrayed standing upright, with his arms hanging down awkwardly, in an attitude which is characteristically grotesque. The puckered face emerges from a lion's skin, and the body is deformed with pendulous breasts, twisted legs, and a tail which is an extension of the backbone. This curious mixture of man and animal is finely sculpted in ivory, now very fragile. It may originally have been enhanced with colour. The disc of the mirror was set into the figurine's broad head-dress, which lacks the usual plumes and here serves as a kind of capital.

83 | Bust of Ramesses II

Speckled black granite; H. 82 cm; 19th Dynasty; No.729; Ground floor 9, west side

In his *Guide de visiteur*, Maspero refers to this 'upper part of a royal statue' as dating from the 20th Dynasty and regrets that the beginning of the inscription on its back 'does not tell us which king's features are recorded by this lovely monument'. Although the inscription is limited to a description of the king as 'perfect god, many times victorious . . .' there can no longer be any doubt that this bust, which was discovered at Tanis, is that of a statue of Ramesses II.

From the statuettes (see No.86) to the great colossi, the known portraits of the greatest monarch of the 19th Dynasty are sufficiently numerous and characteristic to permit the necessary comparisons. Despite the difference in hair style, the Cairo bust probably most resembles the magnificent Ramesses II at the Turin Museum, a smaller replica of which is displayed in the same room. The bust wears the short, thick wig made fashionable by Tuthmosis IV (see No.52), while the

Turin Ramesses wears the 'khepresh'. In all other details of costume and attitude, the two are closely akin.

The king, who originally grasped the 'heqa' sceptre in a right hand raised to the centre of his chest, was undoubtedly seated, with his feet joined together and his left hand on his knee. He is dressed in a voluminous ceremonial tunic, delicately pleated to fan out from a knot which is visible almost directly beneath the right nipple. He also wears a broad throat piece, a bracelet displaying the 'wedjat' eye, and a diadem with the 'uraeus' which, along with the sceptre, recalls his rank.

Ramesses II, who died aged nearly 100, is portrayed here in the full flower of youth; despite the absence of the nose, the smiling features and full cheeks bear the authentic stamp of majesty.

84 | Construction tools

Wood and limestone. H. of level 31 cm; 19th Dynasty; collective No.2005; First floor 17, south side

The level, the plumbline and the set-square in this wall case originally came from Deir el-Medina, where lived the generations of workers who dug and decorated the deep tombs of the Valley of the Kings (and, as a secondary consideration, their own tombs beside their village). The level consists of three pieces of wood forming a right angle, with the small piece serving as a crossbar. The latter, which is horizontal when the angled ends of the two other pieces of wood are placed on a flat surface, carries a central mark to which the cord of the plumbline must be adjusted for perfect horizontality.

The plumbline consists of a straight piece of wood with two parallel pieces set into it. The cord, like that of the level, has an oval weight at its end and passes diagonally from the top of the vertical piece of wood to the end of the upper horizontal. Verticality was achieved when the cord touched the end of the lower horizontal.

The set square, whose wood is now warped, no longer delineates an exact right angle. It is inscribed with a funerary formula involving the god Ptah, protector of artisans and master of exactitude – as one might expect on a tool belonging to a builder. These three instruments are consummately simple and as such will probably disappoint some people, since they do not bear witness to any fabulous technique now lost forever in the sands of time. Though it is quite true that we cannot explain every aspect of Egyptian architecture, it is definitely not one of the world's unexplained enigmas. If one considers the worn-out rudimentary tools (metal chisel, wooden mallets) found in Egyptian quarries, there is good reason to be flabbergasted by some of the details of pyramid construction, by the sheer scale of the larger obelisks, and the perfect finish of a colossal monolith which must have weighed over 1500 tons. But for all that we should not imagine that the sculptors and architects of the pharaohs received assistance from extra-terrestrials using sophisticated instruments. The true marvel is that the Egyptians themselves should have achieved such spectacular results with their own human resources and the empirical use of nature's possibilities.

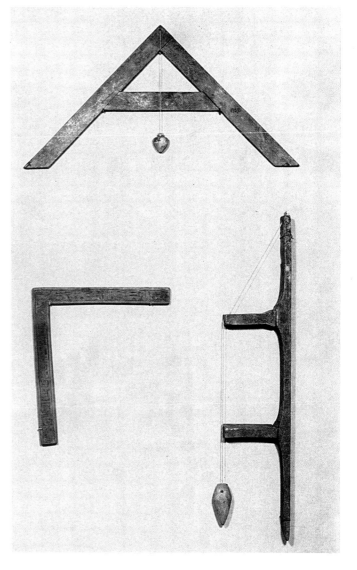

These possibilities, which are always available to be discovered, can sometimes be quite astonishing. For example, who would have imagined that the sliding coefficient of wet Nile mud is close to zero? Yet this was demonstrated at Karnak by Henri Chevrier in 1934. Basing his experiment on the famous scene from the tomb of Djehutihotep at el-Bersha, in which a colossal statue is hauled along by 172 men in four columns, Chevrier prepared a slide of fine clay; on this he placed a sledge loaded with two cubic metres of solid granite (about six tons), to which he harnessed fifty workers. The clay was wetted and the men told to pull; they all fell over immediately because the block of stone had slipped too quickly. Finally, it was discovered that no more than six men were required to move six tons of granite without undue effort!

Obviously, this does not explain everything, but perhaps it serves to bring certain colossal undertakings of the Egyptians down to a more human level.

85 | Sphinx of Ramesses II offering a vase of Amun

Crystalline sandstone; L. 37 cm; 19th Dynasty; Ground floor 15, case A

Of the various statues discovered in the Karnak trove, some were intact, but many more were found smashed and broken, like this little sphinx of Ramesses II. Fortunately, all its parts were assembled in 1905, with the exception of the large plinth in which it was originally set. This vanished base, which may have been sculpted from a different type of stone, probably bore a dedicatory inscription to Amun, since the king is seen proffering the sacred vase of the god. He is portrayed as a human-headed lion, and instead of front feet, he has hands which are slightly too large in proportion.

Despite certain well-rendered details, such as the muscles of the shoulders and the ridged vertebrae under the skin of the back, the body of the sphinx, with its stylized mane and broad collar, is treated in thoroughly conventional fashion.

By contrast, the king's face faithfully reproduces the easily-recognizable features of Ramesses II, who in this case wears the 'nemes' head-dress and a long straight beard. Even if his cartouches were not carved on the vase which the sphinx is presenting to Amun, the face can be identified conclusively as Ramesses, simply by the shape of the made-up eyes, the hooked nose and the small, smiling mouth, which may be found on so many other statues of this monarch.

The vase, whose spout has been broken away, has a lid shaped as the ram of Amun; similar vases exist with women's heads, for Mut, and falcon's heads, for Khons. Wall pictures, and texts show that these sacred utensils, which were 'of silver, gold, iron and copper' were carried in procession during the New Year Ceremonies which coincided more or less with the rise of the Nile floodwaters. The cortège of priests left the temple and made its way down to the river to draw the fertility-bringing water, which, according to one of the hymns to Amon-Re', came only by the will of the god.

This little sphinx of Ramesses II is not only a reminder of the ritual importance of water in daily worship, but also of the king's essential rôle in Egyptian life. The floods – which had to be neither too great, nor too little – depended upon him, and upon his ability to influence 'his father Amun' to provide the ideal 16 cubits of depth.

86 | Door of the burial chamber of Sennudjem

Painted and stuccoed wood; total H. 1.35 m; 19th Dynasty; No.2006; First floor 17, opposite east entrance

At the beginning of February 1886, during one of his annual inspection trips aboard the steamer belonging to the Antiquities Service, the 'Bulaq', Maspero was informed that an intact tomb had been discovered by some bedouins who had acquired a licence to excavate in the vicinity of their house.

The tomb in question was at Deir el-Medina, the ancient 'Place of Truth' where the artisans and artists of the royal sepulchres traditionally had their abode. It was indeed untouched, and today it bears the number 1 in the catalogue of private tombs of the Theban necropolis. The door which closed off the final vault was still in place, and its clay seals bearing the image of Anubis (which were unfortunately lost during the transfer of the funerary furnishings to the opposite bank of the Nile) were still attached to the bolt by a cord.

The hinges of the wooden door were held so perfectly in place by their limestone surround, that the stone lintel had to be broken in order to remove it undamaged. The boards making up the door were fixed by a frame of their own, whose elements are held together by tenons; on the outside, to the left, a block of wood with two bronze rings supported the sash bolt.

The stucco panel is decorated on two sides with painted scenes which are fully comparable to those which adorn the walls of the chamber; the colours are very vivid and well-preserved, with the yellow backgrounds that are characteristic of the 19th Dynasty.

On the exterior, only the central area, which is divided into two registers beneath the sky sign, is illustrated. The upper register, which is slightly larger than the lower, portrays the owner of the tomb worshipping Osiris, 'God of the Dead', and Maat, goddess of truth, justice, equilibrium and order. A text, written in short columns, tells us that the tomb contains the body of 'the servant in the Place of Truth Sennudjem', and that the two women with him, who hold long-necked vases, are his 'sister (meaning his wife), the lady of the house, Iyneferti', and behind her 'his daughter, whom he loves, Irunefer'. All three are dressed in fine linen garments – loincloth or long, pleated robes – and wigs of various lengths topped by cones of perfumed fat. Osiris, 'who presides in the west' is seated on a throne; on his head is the 'atef' crown, and he is sheathed in a mummiform garment which leaves only his hands free. He holds a 'was' sceptre of power and the insignia of royalty. Standing behind him and passing his left hand over his shoulder is Maat, (unnamed here), whom we recognize by the ostrich feather set in her headdress. Maat grasps an 'ankh' in her right hand.

A similar scene is shown in the lower register, but this time seven masculine figures are featured, who are worshipping Ptah–Sokar–Osiris, another god of the dead with a falcon's head, '... master of the sky, prince of eternity'; they 'prostrate themselves' before 'Isis the great, lady of heaven'. The text gives the names of the seven, who are the sons of Sennudjem: Khabekhent, the eldest, and his brothers, Pakhal, Rahotep, Khonsu, Ramose, Anhotep and Ranekhou, in pairs. Most of these

children were buried with their parents, since, in addition to a highly varied selection of funeral furnishings, the tomb was found to contain no less than twenty corpses, only nine of which were in sarcophagi.

The entire inside of the door is decorated. Above eleven columns of text, which are passages from Chapters 17 and 72 of the *Book of the Dead*, the upper third of the surface is taken up by a scene in which Sennudjem and his wife are seated under an awning with piles of offerings: vases, lettuces, loaves and vegetables. They are engrossed in a game of 'senet', a form of chequers or chess played on a board with 30 squares, the rules of which are now lost. Apparently, living people played it *à deux*, with pawns of two kinds and knucklebones; but in pictures from the *Book of the Dead*, the dead man has no visible opponent. We know that the stages of 'senet' were likened to the stages of the dead man's sojourn in the next world; and winning was equivalent to the soul's receiving a favourable judgement from the gods.

87 | The Israel stela

Dark grey granite; H. 3.18 m; 18th-19th Dynasty; No.599; Ground floor 13, east side

This historically important stela was discovered by Petrie in 1896, in the first courtyard of the temple built by Merenptah, 13th son and successor of Ramesses II, for his funeral cult. The raising of this temple involved the destruction of that of Amenophis III, a gigantic architectural ensemble nearby; nothing now remains of this save one or two foundations of walls or columns, and the celebrated colossi of Memnon which marked its entrance.

The stela itself comes from the latter temple, in which it had been erected by Amenophis III to commemorate a series of constructions in honour of Amun. What we assume is the other side (but which may seem to the visitor to be the back of the stela, because of the manner in which it is exhibited) carries a long inscription of thirty one lines, under a scene which takes up the top third of the monument. Nearly all the text and illustration was hammered off during the Amarna era, but

remained sufficiently visible to be re-engraved by Sethos I 'in honour of his father Amon-Re, king of all the gods'. This information is given in the short vertical inscription between the symmetrical scenes of the arch, where Amenophis III is portrayed in a 'pschent' and 'nemes', offering wine and libations to Amun.

After a complete list of the king's titles, the first 25 lines of the text describe the splendours of his funerary temple – the floor was 'paved with silver', the walls and gates 'plated with electrum' – and enumerate the construction work undertaken by Amenophis at the temples of Luxor and Karnak, and Soleb in Nubia. The end of the inscription is confined to the remarks made by the god, who as a mark of satisfaction 'does wonders' for the pharaoh and his son and lays the whole world at his feet, north, south, east, and west.

On the other side, the dark granite is not so highly finished, but the surface is occupied by much the same motif, as in all the great royal stelae. Beneath a solar disc, the arch is decorated with two scenes; wearing ceremonial costume and the 'blue crown', and carrying royal sceptres, Merenptah, flanked to the left by Mut and to the right by Khons, stands before Amun, who proffers

the 'khepesh', a kind of scimitar symbolizing victorious military power.

Above this is the text from which is derived the monument's name – 'The Israel Stela'. A duplicate of this was found at Karnak, on one of the walls of the 'Cour de la Cachette'; and in fact the name is undeserved, since out of the 28 lines, 25 celebrate Merenptah's triumphant victory over the Libyans, who had threatened Egypt in the fifth year of his reign.

The name of Israel does not appear until the penultimate line, in a reference to the conquered peoples of Palestine. It is hard to say whether an actual military campaign is being discussed, or whether the sequence of phraseology is taken from some redundant official text: 'Israel is laid waste, her seed exists no more!' Nonetheless, it is understandable that the stela should have been given this name at the time of its discovery, because this mention of Israel is unique in Egyptian text, whilst the name of Egypt (Misraïm, in Hebrew) occurs nearly seven hundred times in the Bible. Moreover, Merenptah was then considered to be the pharaoh of the Exodus, whereas today we tend to think that he reigned a few years earlier.

88 | Satirical papyrus *detail*

Papyrus and mineral-based colours; H. 13 cm; 20th Dynasty; First floor 29, north side, case 9

The *Journal d'Entrée* is somewhat vague about the registration number and provenace of this papyrus; it would seem that it was acquired at Tuna el-Gebel, and probably dates from the 20th Dynasty.

A number of illustrated ostraca and several papyri have survived which, like this one, bear scenes of parody where men are replaced by animals – monkey-musicians, a cat guarding geese, a lion playing the lyre. (The best known are now at Turin.) This brand of humour, worthy of Aesop, the Tale of Reynard the Fox, or La Fontaine, mocks human weaknesses and parodies class situations by making animals adopt the behaviour and gestures of people. It seems to have been especially popular with the Egyptians, who

added their own twist of rôle reversals in an upside-down world. Thus we find pictures of hereditary enemies such as the lion and the ibex playing 'senet' together, or animals who usually attack domestic herds given the responsibility of guarding them.

This papyrus, which is sadly damaged, is of the latter kind. It perhaps reflects the social upheavals of the end of the 20th Dynasty, and expresses regret for violent changes, which saw the rich dispossessed and men with no property at all suddenly acquiring consequence.

It is interesting to compare the scene on the left hand side of the fragment with the similar one on Princess Kawit's sarcophagus (No.32). In both cases, the subject is a lady at her toilette, with two servants, one of whom offers her a drink while the other dresses her hair. Only here the lady is a mouse; dressed in a long, fine dress, she sits on a raised chair, with legs resting on a stool. In one

forepaw, she holds to her pointed snout a cup which has just been filled by the cat facing her; in the other she may have held a mirror to observe the work of the hairdresser cat, who is about to add another tress to her heavy, ungainly wig. To the rear of these three figures stand a nurse-cat carrying a swaddled baby mouse with Walt Disney-type round ears and a servant cat with a fan and a jar.

On the right hand side, the remainder of the papyrus shows a group of foxes who are serving water to an ox, whose head seems to emerge from a stall. Nothing remains of any illustration on the left.

89 | Statue of Ramesses III as a standard bearer

Dark grey granite; H. 1.40 m; 20th Dynasty; No.674; Ground floor 15, west side

The last great pharaoh of the New Kingdom died the victim of a palace conspiracy after triumphantly repelling attacks from Libya and an invasion by the legendary 'Sea People'. He is here portrayed carrying the 'august standard of Amun', as he must have done in life when he took part in religious ceremonies.

The exemplary piety of Ramesses III is recorded in the Great Harris Papyrus, which lists the many donations he made to the principal temples of Egypt. The king is portrayed advancing, holding against his left arm the sacred staff of Amun, surmounted by a ram's head. He is dressed in a finely pleated ceremonial loincloth with a starched apron covered in rich metalwork; this consists of five 'uraei' hanging from a cat's head. He wears a secular wig, adorned with the royal 'uraeus' and arranged over a kind of tight bonnet; the sides of the wig cover the ears and fall low to the powerfully-muscled torso, at the same time framing and accentuating the regular oval shape of the fine-featured youthful face.

Despite the absence of the lower part of the statue, which is perhaps still at the bottom of the Karnak trove, the monument still has very fine proportions which are more elegant than other works of the same period. It is powerful yet massive, like the statue-pillars of the great funerary complex of Medinet Habu, the design for which was copied by the king from that of Ramesses II.

Ramesses III is identified by his two cartouches carved on the forepart of his shoulders, with the first name reiterated on the buckle of his belt. The nearly complete list of his titles is inscribed down the staff. Of the five titles regularly used by the Egyptian pharaohs since the Middle Kingdom (the word 'pharaoh' having never been used as such), four only remain here: the 'Horus' title, only borne by the kings of the first two dynasties; the 'Two Ladies' title, which ensured the protection of the two tutelary goddesses of the South and the North; the title of king of Upper and Lower Egypt, which is inscribed in a cartouche and is in fact the first name of enthronement; and the title 'Son of Re' which began as a simple epithet and later became the actual 'name' of the sovereign. To complete this list, the title of 'Golden Horus' would have to be inserted in the third position, thus identifying the king with Horus, the conqueror of Seth.

Ramesses III was titled as follows: 'The Horus: strong bull, great of kingship; the Two Ladies: of Great jubilees, like Tatenen, the Golden Horus: whose years are many, like Atum; the king of Upper and Lower Egypt; Usermaatre-meryamun, Son of Re, lord of crowns: Ramesses, ruler of Heliopolis.'

90 | Ostracon with plan of a royal tomb

Painted limestone; H. 83.5 cm; 20th Dynasty; No.4371; First floor 24, east entrance of room

It may seem curious that a civilization which constructed so many edifices should have left so few architectural plans or drawings. Nonetheless, the only documents of this type known to us are an ostracon of the 3rd Dynasty bearing design calculations for an archway; a rough plan for a vault; the cross-section of a column; a study for a naos; a tablet of stuccoed wood with outlines and measurements for a building on the banks of the Nile or beside a canal; a design for a royal tomb on papyrus; and, finally, the large limestone ostracon shown here.

The ostracon was broken into four pieces which still fit together fairly well. It was discovered by Daressy at Biban el-Muluk in 1889, during the excavation of the tomb of Ramesses IX, and seems to be a rough working drawing of the same; probably it was used by the overseer and then thrown away.

The walls of the cave-sepulchre are shown by a double red line with white in between; the doors are drawn flat and painted yellow.

Apart from the inscription by the access stairway, the names and measurements of the rooms, written in hieratic in black ink, have almost entirely vanished. Fortunately, the Turin Papyrus, which includes a large segment of the plan for the tomb of Ramesses IV, has supplied the missing information. Thus we know that the corridors and 26-step stairway with a ramp down its centre were called 'passageways of the god', and that the god in question was Re, the sun. At the bottom of the stairs, on either side of the first corridor, are niches known as 'the shrines in which repose the gods of the East' . . . (on the right) '. . . and West' (on the left).

After two other corridors, the tomb widens and we enter a first room known as the 'hall of waiting', where the dead man had to wait a while in patience during the funeral rites. Then came the 'chariot hall' normally with four pillars, where this element of the royal funerary furnishings was left. Between the pillars, two lines trace the incline to the tomb-chamber itself, named 'the house of gold in which he (the king) reposes'. At its centre, a white rectangle marks the position of the royal sarcophagus. In the Turin plan, the tomb possesses other rooms beyond this for 'ushabtis', statues of gods and precious objects, and the actual sarcophagus of Ramesses IV, in the form of a cartouche, is shown surrounded by several successive envelopes. It was these shrines, rather than the jewels which would have covered the king, that led to the idea of the 'house of gold'; for they would have been panelled with gilded wood as in the tomb of Tutankhamun.

The visitor may dream of the fabulous treasures of the great royal sepulchres, now gone foreover.

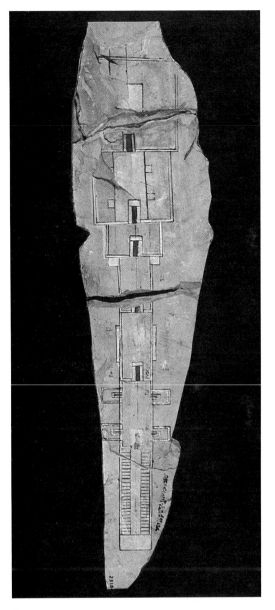

Nevertheless, it is by no means certain that all the tombs were as sumptuous as that of the young king. Only the empty rock-cut rooms remain; their special names, and the scenes covering their walls, show that in the eyes of the Egyptians their succession signified the sun's voyage through the night. That voyage ended in the sarcophagus room, where the king lay resting, waiting to be reborn, like the morning sun.

91 | Small funerary stela

Painted and stuccoed wood; H. 28 cm; 22nd
Dynasty; No.3365; First floor 22, case C

The Museum possesses several dozen smaller wooden stelae of this kind. They are painted and often gilded, with dates ranging from the 21st to the 30th Dynasty. As a rule, they belonged to members of the clergy, who are seen depicted facing a divinity, usually Re-Harakhty. For this reason, Mariette baptised them 'Harmakhis stelae'.

This example comes from the region of Thebes (some say from Deir el-Bahri, others from Qurna). It is divided into two registers of unequal size,

which have retained the freshness of their colours. The largest section of the stela is taken up by a rather commonplace portrait of the dead woman – a lady named Djedamuniufankh – worshipping Re-Horakhty, who faces her across a table loaded with offerings. The scene is contained within a space defined by the symbols of the universe: the curved sky is supported by two 'was' sceptres resting on the ground, and a winged solar disc surmounts the five short columns of a funerary formula which is supposed to ensure that the lady will receive offerings and provisions.

Beneath this tableau, the lower part of the monument bears 'a small composition worthy of note', which was probably Mariette's reason for sending the stela to Paris for the 1867 Universal Exhibition. This is, in fact, a very rare picture of the necropolis; to the left stands the tomb, preceded by a pylon surmounted by two pyramidions. These are built on the edge of cultivated land, on the first undulations of the desert. At centre, a kneeling woman is seen in the traditional attitude of grief, with one hand raised above her head. To the right, a table of offerings is set up beside a pool, in the shade of a sycamore and two date-palms. This is the funerary garden mentioned in several texts; the dead person wishes his soul to return to this garden in the form of a bird, where it will walk beside the pool, perch in the branches of the trees, or refresh itself in the cool shade of the sycamore.

92 | Cover of mirror box

Ivory and sycamore wood; L. 28 cm; 21st Dynasty; No.3794A; First floor, east door

To protect the delicate reflecting surfaces of mirrors (see No. 81), the Egyptians used semi-circular cases made either of coloured basketry or of animal skins. They also used boxes which could be extremely precious as decorative objects, worthy of a place in a king's funeral furnishings. This example was found, according to the *Journal d'Entrée* '... in June 1886, during the stripping (of the mummy), on the breast of queen Hont-taui'. This queen was Duathathor-Henttawi, wife of the priest-king Pinudjem I; her remains were found in the midst of various royal mummies which her husband had saved from pillage and stored at Deir el-Bahri, in a hiding place that was only discovered in 1881, by Maspero.

The case, which is made of pieces of sycamore stuccoed on the inside and veneered with ivory on the outside, was so designed as to fit the two elements of the mirror exactly, with a circular part for the disc and a rectangular extension for the handle. The cover, which was opened by turning horizontally on a pivot, matched this form exactly; and it is this cover, with its elegant carved and painted ivory design, which is the principal interest of the piece. It is composed of a central motif, judiciously surrounded by secondary motifs, the ensemble being edged with a geometrical frieze pattern. The rectangular panel corresponding to the mirror handle extends almost to the centre of the circular part; in its lower half is engraved a large bouquet with birds hanging from it and in the upper half, occupying the centre of the cover, is the graceful figure of a naked girl garlanded with lotus-blossom. This girl is of royal blood, to judge by the heavy tress hanging beside her wig; and her only adornments are a broad necklace and bracelets on her arms, wrists and ankles. She holds an ornamental bunch of flowers and proffers one of those decorated horns which are represented in

several Theban paintings as containing precious oils and perfumes from Syria. Above a frieze of alternating stylized fruits and flowers, the remainder of the circular area carries a symmetrical décor in which two birds are seen landing near their nests, on either side of a clump of papyrus. Below the fruit and flower frieze, the design is completed by almost entirely geometrical lotus petals. The colours, which have acquired a fine patina over the ages spent lying in mummy wrappings, now possess a monochrome quality. This adds, if anything, to the refinement and naturalism of the scenes depicted, which would not have been unworthy of an Amarna artist.

93 | Inner coffin of Psusennes I

Silver and gold; L. 1.85 m; 21st Dynasty; No.6289; First floor 11, centre

Many people who come to the Museum are so dazzled by the sumptuous wealth of Tutankhamun that they fail to notice a door close to the king's largest funerary shrine, which leads to three small rooms. In doing this, they overlook certain treasures which are fully deserving of interest. The first room contains the antique funerary furnishings of Queen Hetepheres, wife of Snofru and mother of Cheops, discovered by the American Reisner at the foot of the Great Pyramid; and the other two contain the royal funeral trappings uncovered at Tanis by the Frenchman, Pierre Montet.

This last discovery, in spite of its importance, did not create a sensation comparable to that of Carter and Caernarfon. It took place in 1939–40, at a time when the newspapers had no need of archaeological news to make their daily headlines.

Tanis was an important delta town which was capital of Egypt for a certain period after the fall of the New Kingdom. Today, it is no more than a huge 'kom', $3\frac{1}{2}$ kilometres long, which culminates 35 metres above sea-level. The great temple of Amun has vanished and no single important building remains standing, but the impressive broken colossi and sections of obelisks that may still be seen lying in ruins testify to what the city must have been during the epoch of the Ramessid kings. In the last century, excavations by Jean Jacques Rifaud, Mariette and Petrie brought to light a number of monuments, well before Montet began his series of digs. In the end, these led to the discovery of several royal burial chambers, which, in Montet's words '... bore practically no resemblance to the Old and Middle Kingdom pyramids, nor to the sepulchres of the Valley of the Kings.' These were the tombs of Psusennes I, Osorkon II and Shoshenq III, priest-kings of the 21st and 22nd Dynasties.

The graves of the latter two had been violated, but that of Psusennes was still intact. In addition to the king's own funerary furnishings, it contained those of one of his generals, Wendjebauendjedet; those of one of his immediate successors, King Amenemope, buried in a tomb-chamber originally assigned to a certain Queen Mutnodjmet; and, finally, those of an obscure King Heqakheperre Shoshenq, previously unknown to Egyptologists.

The massive, constricted edifices of these royal tombs had been set (without any visible superstructures) within the precincts of the temple of Amun, thus inaugurating a royal custom which we know from Herodotus (II,169) was still being used at Sais as late as the 26th Dynasty.

The mummy of Psusennes was protected by several layers of wrappings, a pink granite sarcophagus, an anthropoid sarcophagus, and, finally, a covering and mask of gold. It should be emphasized that, despite the opulence of the rest of the tomb, the two stone outer coffins were usurped from elsewhere. The first, whose lid is adorned with a magnificent depiction of Nut in relief, (Ground floor room 33, No.6337) comes from a cenotaph of Merenptah, the successor of Ramesses II, and the second originally belonged to a noble of the same era.

The silver coffin, whose casket and lid were held in place by rivets and tenons, exactly fitted into the black granite sarcophagus. The king is portrayed on the lid, a smile on his face, his body tightly

Funerary mask of Psusennes I

bound in bandages, the arms crossed on the chest, and the royal sceptres gripped in the hands. He wears the 'nemes', with a 'uraeus' of solid gold, the divine beard is attached to his chin by cords which extend to his ears, and around his neck is a broad collar of floral beads. This is not inlaid with stones or pâte de verre, merely carved into the 'white metal' like the rest of the finely-executed feathered decoration, which includes three birds with the heads of a vulture, a ram and a falcon with wings spreading across the chest. Two columns of text, extending down to the feet, contain two direct appeals from the dead king to 'his mother Nut', that 'she may spread her wings over him', and render him 'like those who are indestructible and indefatigable', *ie*, like the two pole stars, which never go out of sight.

'Isis the great, divine mother, Lady of the West' and 'Nephthys, divine sister, Lady of funerary offerings', are shown in lamentation at the feet of the dead man, on the raised part of the lid.

The coffin case had suffered badly from the humidity of the tomb and had to be carefully restored. Nonetheless, all its perishable elements (wood, tissue, leather and ivory) have disappeared. The lower part of it bears an image of Nut spreading her wings, and the sides are a continuation of the feathered design of the lid. A line of text running around the edge of the lid reproduces a prayer of Psusennes and the comforting words of Nut.

94 | Golden tableware from the Royal Tombs of Tanis

Gold; H. of ewer 19.8 cm; 21st Dynasty; First floor east, case 11

The unknown Shoshenq, buried in the antechamber of the tomb of Psusennes in his strange, silver falcon-mummy sarcophagus, had no tableware for his use after death. By contrast, Psusennes, Wendjebauendjedet and Amenemope yielded about thirty different sacred vases in precious metal: bowls, plates, stands, a pot with a spout, paterae, goblets and carafes which demonstrate both the refined taste and the extraordinary craftsmanship of contemporary artisans.

The three objects shown here have a simplicity and elegance of form which the New Kingdom seems sometimes to have lost under a plethora of decoration.

The little, round, straight-necked bowl, with 24 flutings around its waist, is slightly less than 8 cm high. Four cartouches are engraved on its collar. On the right are the name and first name of Psusennes, whose Egyptian form, Pasbakhaenniut, means 'the star which rises for the city'. On the left is the name of his mother, Queen Henttawy, after her title of 'mother of Khons', which indicates that she has produced an heir to the throne.

The flat bowl is 16 cm in diameter and has 16 flutings centred on a rosette with 16 petals. This also belonged to Psusennes, as attested by one of the two inscriptions carved under its lip. The other inscription mentions one of the king's daughters 'the divine mother of Khons the child, the royal daughter Isetemkheb'.

The ewer bears the name of the 'perfect god Amenemope-miamoun, beloved of Osiris lord of Abydos'. The body of this libation vase is soldered to the foot, while its spout is held in place by three rivets and the flat lip is fitted into the neck.

96 | Statuette usurped by Shoshenq, son of Osorkon I

*Green breccia marble, veined with white; H. 48 cm;
late 18th and 22nd Dynasty; Ground floor 20,
case C*

According to the text on the back of this statue –
which is unquestionably one of the loveliest to
have emerged from the Kamak cachette – it must
be dated in the 22nd Dynasty, since it is described
as representing 'the first prophet of Amon-Re,
king of the gods, the generalissimo and prince
Shoshenq, the justified one, son of the lord of the
Two Lands, Osorkon (I) meryamon . . .'

At first glance, the experienced eye will recognize that this is impossible, and that the
statuette has been usurped; everything about it is
characteristic of the end of the 18th Dynasty; the
costume, the proportions, the features, even the
evident distinction of the individual portrayed.
Moreover, the idea of a great priest of Amun
grasping the sacred ox-horned emblem of Hathor
is unthinkable.

Thus this statue portrayed a priest of Hathor
who probably lived under Tutankhamun, since the
features are much like those of the young king.
This priest, whose name we shall never know, is
dressed in a long tunic with pleated and starched
sleeves and apron. A sash is wound around the
hips. The regular tresses of his abundant wig fall
clear of the pierced lobes of his ears and he carries
the emblem of Hathor in his left hand and a sort
of folded handkerchief in his right.

The artist who restored the statuette during the
Libyan period contrived to repair it by carefully
dovetailing a new sleeve to replace a broken piece.
He also carved a fresh inscription on the back of
the support pillar, the image of Amun on the
chest, and that of Osiris on the apron, having first
effaced the pleats of the garment. Less successful
was his attempt to recarve the lost left hand, which
is now much too short and completely shapeless.

It may seem strange to the modern mind that
no attempt was made to remodel the face, but this
would be to apply our own form of logic. If one
wrote one's name on a statue, that made it as
completely one's own as if it had been specially
sculpted; for the Egyptian, it was not even necessary to erase the name of the previous owner. This
is borne out by the existence of several other royal
monuments which bear as many as three titles in
the place of the original protocol.

97 | Statuette of Osorkon III

Fine-grained limestone with traces of polychrome;
H. 18 cm; 23rd Dynasty; Ground floor 20, case C

This fine statuette was found in several pieces in
the 'favissa' of Karnak, in 1904 and 1905. It remains incomplete, but its fluidity of modelling and
delicacy of sculpture fully merit our attention.

The subject is a pharaoh pushing a boat dedicated to Amon-Re. Of this divine vessel, only the
stern and the steering oars remain, but the cracks
in the stone amply suggest the king's movement by
their very shape.

The king is on his knees, with his left leg bent
forward and his right stretched back. The pose is
very plastic, and would seem respectful in the
extreme were it not for the raised head and the
level gaze. He wears a pleated 'shendyt' held up by
an ornamented belt, and on his head is the 'khat',
a kind of wig-cover comparable to the 'nemes', but
more rounded and lacking the side-flaps falling to

the shoulders. These two elements of the royal
costume were originally covered with gold leaf
applied to a base which has taken on a carmine,
almost mauve hue.

On the front of the base begins a double inscription which develops symmetrically around its
edge. The beautiful, carefully carved hieroglyphs
tell us that the monarch portrayed here was the
'lord of the accomplishments of rites in Ipet-Sut
(Karnak) . . . the king of Upper and Lower Egypt
Usermaatre Setepenamun . . . the son of Re, born
of his (own) belly, Osorkon meryamon, son of Isis,
beloved of Amon-Re king of the primordial gods'.
Thus we are contemplating Osorkon III, a king of
the 23rd Dynasty, who is only distinguished from
Osorkon II, a king of the 22nd Dynasty with
exactly the same names, by the description 'son of
Isis'. (Osorkon II was 'son of Bastet'.)

When one recalls that, as a consequence of the
Libyan anarchy of the Third Intermediate Period,
the dynasties to which these two kings belonged

were partly parallel, with one reigning over the Delta and the Valley up to Herakleopolis, and the other over the rest of the country, one can well imagine the problems such extremely similar names can present to historians.

The statuette was probably a royal ex-voto, either commemorating the gift of a portable boat for the processions of the divine reliquary, or the launching of a great river barge for the annual voyages of Amon-Re to his southern harem (at the temple of Luxor). Since the vessel itself cannot be described we merely note that the text in the base mentions the two ships upon which the sun travels: the 'mandjet', which daily sails across the sky and the 'mesketet', which navigates the nocturnal underground.

98 | Statue of a princess
detail

Dark grey granite; H. 83.5 cm; 22nd–23rd Dynasty; No.843; Ground floor 24, right of entrance

Although they are funerary in character, the texts which almost completely cover the seat and plinth of this statue, which was found in the 'favissa' of Karnak in 1904, make it a useful document for the historian. In conjunction with inscriptions on other similar monuments, they enable us to reconstruct geneaologies, pinpoint successions and establish chronologies.

Thus we know that the lady of high rank portrayed here was 'the august Shebensopdet, daughter of the first prophet of Amon-Re, king of the gods, the general Nimlot of Herakleopolis', and that the latter was himself 'the royal son of the Lord of the Two Lands ... Osorkon (II)'. Moreover, the double inscription on either side of the lady's feet, on the flat part of the base, tells us that the statue was made for 'his sister, whom he loves' by her husband 'the prophet of Amun of Karnak and prophet of Montu, lord of Thebes ... Hor', who also bears other titles, some honorary ('sole friend') and some corresponding to real functions ('scribe of the documents of the Great House').

Shebensopdet is seated in a slightly rigid hieratic pose which is nonetheless very pleasing. Her chair is cube-shaped, with a low back; her hands rest on her knees, the right palm downward and the left holding a lotus flower. She wears a long tunic with flared sleeves and a finely grooved wig, reaching almost to her breasts. The images of Isis, Osiris and Nephthys are carved on the front of her tunic, along with the ram of Herishef (Arsaphes), lord of Herakleopolis. Herakleopolis was the cradle of the 22nd Dynasty and the town of which Shebensopdet's father was the most prominent personage, before being appointed head of the priesthood of Amun by Osorkon II.

99 | Cube-statue of Hor, prophet of Montu

Schist (greywacke); H. 51 cm; 25th Dynasty; Ground floor 25, case D

Among the original types of Egyptian statuary (stelephorous, naophorous, standard-bearers, etc) the cube-statue is certainly one of the most characteristic. When they first appeared in the Middle Kingdom, these statues took the form of perfectly cube-shaped blocks of stone with heads emerging and limbs seemingly flat against them. Evidently these compact forms were adopted because they were unlikely to be damaged by accident, and they enjoyed a considerable vogue until the Later Period.

This example was found in perfect condition in 1904, in the Karnak trove. It represents a certain Hor, a prophet of Montu; a column of text carved on the stand between the subject's feet relates that the effigy was made at the request of the 'elder son of his elder son', who, like his grandfather, was named Hor.

Hor appears to be gathered in on himself, as if to resist the ravages of time. He is seated, with his thighs drawn up to his chest and his crossed arms resting on his knees. He wears a loincloth and a carefully braided wig, and he stares straight ahead. The serene expression of the highly idealized face is that of a man who is convinced of his own immortality; and this gift was bestowed on Hor by the piety of his grandson, who, by dedicating a statue in his image in the temple, enabled him to remain for all time near to the god, and thus to receive his share of the divine offerings. This is made quite clear at the beginning of the funerary formula carved on the front of his loincloth, prior to the enumeration, customary at the time, of the titles and ancestry of 'the prophet of Montu lord of Thebes, who served for one month in the first rank, relative of the king, Hor the justified, Ankhkhons... etc'.

The modelling of the body, whose curves mask the massive, squat aspect of the ensemble, and the attention paid to detail and to the carving of the texts, along with the perfect finish of the stone, would all seem to prove that what is known as the 'Saite renaissance' in fact began with the Psammetic kings.

100 | Head of King Taharqa

Black granite; H. 41.5 cm; 25th Dynasty; No.1185;
Ground floor 25, centre

This black stone head, which is probably the most beautiful piece of 25th Dynasty royal sculpture in existence, was originally bought at Luxor. Hence the larger-than-life statue to which it belonged must have stood in one of the temples of Thebes, and perhaps in the largest temple of all, that of Amun, at Karnak. Taharqa, like the other kings of the 25th Dynasty (which was called 'Kushite' by the Egyptians and 'Ethiopian' by the Greeks) gave

proof of a special attachment to Amun. This was because the principal deity of Thebes was also that of distant Napata, upstream from the fourth cataract of the Nile, whence Pi(ankh)i, the founder of the dynasty, had come to impose his writ from the Sudan to Egypt. The great god of Thebes had a large temple at the foot of the Gebel Barkal, the holy mountain of Napata. In 1916, Reisner found a colossus of Taharqa on this site; this statue, which is now at the Khartum Museum, is interesting because it gives us some idea of the original figure of which the Cairo head was once a part. Despite their difference in size, the two statues must have been very much alike. Both depicted the king walking forward, wearing the 'shendyt', and a head-dress which was neither that of Amun, nor the 'pschent', as has been suggested, but the crown of the god Onuris, ie a hemispherical skullcap topped by a low cylindrical mortar and four straight feathers.

This head-dress, the unpolished parts of which were originally plated with gold, was adorned with the two 'uraei' which the Kushite sovereigns affected as a symbol of their double suzerainty over the Sudan and Egypt. These were carefully hammered off, like the uraei in the bas-reliefs of the temples, after the successful military campaign waged in Nubia by Psammetichus II had led to the installation of the 26th Dynasty.

Despite a certain idealization of the 'African' features of the Nubian monarch, and despite its mutilated condition, the Cairo head offers a more personalized portrait than that of the Khartum statue, where the face seems more conventional and less vigorous.

On the back of the head, the remains of a supporting column preserve a part of the coronation title of the king whom the Assyrians were to overcome, shortly before the fall of their own empire.

101 | Statuette of Montemhet

Green breccia marble and black granite; total H. 40 cm; 25th Dynasty; No.893; Ground floor 20, case C

By comparison with the other, better-known portraits of the celebrated 'fourth prophet of Amun and prince of the city', this perfectly preserved little monument shows to what point the iconography of a single individual could juxtapose idealization and realism, during the Late Period.

The famous black stone bust discovered in 1897 by Margaret Benson at the temple of Mut (No.1184, Ground floor, south side) is a fine portrait, full of life and almost too realistic in execution. By contrast, this statuette, which came from the Karnak cachette, obviously depicts a younger man; but even when the difference of age is considered, it is hard to recognize the same person in these perfectly executed, but far less personal features.

Montemhet is portrayed in a kneeling position,

privilege of kings, and a broad, lined wig, thrown back over his shoulders. A special Hathorian pendant, the emblem of the great Egyptian judge, hangs from three strings of olive-shaped beads around his neck. Below the winged solar disc which occupies the stela's rounded top is a 13 line text. This consists of Montemhet's prayer to Amun, in which he requests the god (among other things) to 'banish sickness from his body . . . to grant him a perfect burial-place in the necropolis of his city . . . (and) to allow his name to endure as long as the stars in the sky'. On the back of the statuette is an invocation to the god of the dead man's city, known to Egyptologists as the 'Saite formula'. The statue is built into its original plinth of black granite.

In addition to his two most commonly-used titles, the address to Amun gives that of 'governor of Upper Egypt'. Along with his title of 'prince of the city', this must have been the most real to Montemhet, a skilful politician who began his career under Taharqa, contrived to retain his office under the Assyrians by obtaining the nomination of Esarhaddon, and continued in the same position well into the reign of Psammetichus I, after the change of dynasty.

The fact that so prominent a personage was only ranked as 'fourth prophet of Amun' shows that in the time of the '(female) Divine Adoratrices', the masculine priests of Amun had lost the essence of their power.

sitting on his heels, with his hands resting on the curved top of a stela which he holds upright in front of him. He wears the 'shendyt', which during the Late Period was no longer the exclusive

102 | Statue of Amenirdis the Elder

Black granite; H. 1.09 m; 25th Dynasty; Ground floor 30, south side

This statue is somewhat overwhelmed by a thick pillar at its back, to which it probably owes its almost intact survival. The stone was reutilized in the construction of a Coptic dwelling, and the sculpted side was buried face down in the earth so that the remainder could be used as a doorstep. Thus, it was discovered in 1937, close to the temple of Luxor, to the east of the great courtyard of Amenophis III.

The monument lacks only its feet and its base.

A four-column text on the back indicates that the portrait is that of the 'Hand of the god, Amenirdis'. This title, which alludes to the creative but solitary act of the primordial god in the ancient cosmogony, is one of those borne during the Libyan, Kushite and Saite periods by the princesses described as 'wives of the god' or 'Divine Adoratrices of Amun'.

At the outset of the New Kingdom, with Amun solidly in place as the predominant dynastic deity, the 'great royal wife' was also the 'wife of the god'. But when the monarchy established itself in the Delta at the time of the 21st Dynasty, this religious function devolved to a princess who was sworn to celibacy and obliged to ensure her succession by adopting a child. This custom was exploited for political ends by contemporary monarchs, who, finding themselves contained in the north, saw an opportunity to gain control of the Thebaid by imposing a princess of their own line as 'daughter' of the reigning 'Adoratrice'. In this way Pi(ankh)i forces Shepenwepet I, daughter of Osorkon III, to adopt his sister Amenirdis; and a few decades later Psammetichus I, the founder of the 26th Dynasty, imposed his daughter Nitocris on Shepenwepet II, thereby supplanting Amenardis the Younger.

Surrounded by a harem, the Divine Adoratrice fulfilled her rôle as wife of the god. She united herself to the divine body, charmed Amun by her beauty and soothed his heart with her playing of the sistrum. But, in assuming the most obvious prerogatives of royalty (titles, celebration of the cult) she also exercised a political power which grew so much that she actually supplanted the high priest of Amun and usurped his functions.

The inscription on the back of this statue, which represents the sister of the conqueror Pi(ankh)i in her trappings as a divine wife, (long, clinging dress, Hathorian crown, floral sceptre), indicates that it was made by her daughter, the wife of the god Shepenwepet 'so that her name would endure in the house of Amun for all eternity'.

103 Statue of Petamenope as a scribe

Yellow quartzite; H. 74 cm; 26th Dynasty; Ground floor 24, north side

No fewer than eight statues of Petamenope have survived all told. Although this individual does not seem to have had any particularly important titles, he was sufficiently rich to have been buried in a veritable funerary palace, the largest in the entire Theban necropolis. This statue, which portrays him in the attentive pose of a scribe about to set pen to paper, is the most beautiful and the best-preserved of the four which emerged from the Karnak trove. It is also one of the most extraordinary testimonials we possess as to the archaic sentiment which appears in many areas during the Saite era, with a declining civilization attempting to rediscover its origins and what it felt to be its golden age.

The Saite sculptors, abandoning the overrefinement of the New Kingdom, sought inspiration in the art of the pyramid era and even of the Middle Kingdom. They imitated the simplicity

and pure lines of their forebears, but usually failed to achieve the same vigorous quality.

Dressed in a simple loincloth which clearly has nothing to do with contemporary fashions, the wigless Petamenope is seated with his legs crossed. Over his loincloth, and spread from one leg to another, is a partially unrolled papyrus; the left hand holds the roll, and the right, which rests on the sheet, is assumed to be grasping a reed pen. One or two funerary formulae on the front and edge of the statue's base indicate the subject's titles, his name and the name of his mother; the title of 'chief ritualist'; which occurs most frequently, is repeated on the rolled-out part of the papyrus.

Although they are separated by two thousand years of history, it is hard to avoid the comparison between this Saite scribe and the famous 'scribe accroupi' at the Louvre. The position, the clothes, the hair and even the base of the statue are similar. But it is also easy to see the points at which the two pieces diverge: perfectly furnished quartzite, as opposed to the painted limestone which allowed the artist to lighten the volume of the ensemble by detaching the arms from the body; impersonal modelling of Petamenope's body, rather than the realistic treatment of a torso going to fat; and finally, the serious face and vague stare, in contrast to the other statue's almost smiling features, enlivened by inlaid eyes.

Contemporary 'archaic' statues, which usually come from temples rather than tombs, are nearly all sculpted in hard, fine-grained stone. This material favours painstaking execution coupled with a perfect finish, but lends a kind of coldness which derives from its overtones of imitation.

104 | Statue of the goddess Thoeris

*Green schist (greywacke); H. 96 cm; 26th Dynasty;
No.791; Ground floor 24, south side*

If there is one statue in the Cairo Museum to
which Mariette's Lower Epoch descriptions '...
incredible finish' or 'almost too perfect execution'
may be applied, it is this statue of Thoeris with its
highly polished stone and dark, metallic glint. The
inscription on its base reveals that a certain
Pabasa, majordomo of the Divine Adoratrice
Nitocris, daughter of Psammetichus I, dedicated
this figure to the goddess. It originally came from
Karnak, where it was found to the north of the
Great Temple in a perfectly-sealed sandstone
'naos'. This obviously explains its exceptional state
of preservation.

The monstrous female pachyderm, who at the
outset belonged to the class of demons, not divinities, is portrayed standing upright, with two
clawed hands resting on two magic knots, the
symbols of protection. The head of the hippopotamus, with half-open jaws revealing tongue and
teeth, is topped by a three-part wig and low cap,
with a crocodile skin hanging down the back. This
skin accentuates the curious compactness of the
enormous body, which is both feminine and
animal, as it stands on its lion's legs.

The hanging breast and fecund, rounded belly
remind us that the protection of this goddess was
usually invoked at childbirth; known under various
names which describe the different aspects of her
personality, Thoeris (a hellenised form of the
Egyptian Ta-weret 'the great') is sometimes assimilated with Hathor or Isis in her rôle of wet-
nurse. Many amulets attest that her protection was
sought at every stage of life:

'I am Reret (the sow); she who attacks with her
voice and devours, when she approaches, he who
speaks loudly...

I am Thoeris in her might, who fights for her
possessions...

I am Ipet, who dwells in the Horizon ... the
mistress of whom men go in fear...'

These inscriptions appear on the back of a
statuette in the Louvre.

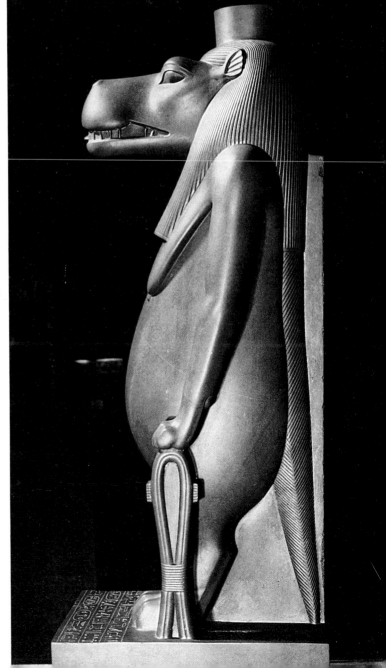

105 | Statuette of the god Horus

Bronze with gold inlay; H. 22.5 cm; 26th Dynasty; First floor 19, centre

The art of Egyptian bronzesmiths was not confined to the manufacture of the innumerable Late Period statuettes, literally thousands of which are owned by the Cairo Museum. On occasion, they produced pure masterpieces of royalty, especially in the Libyan period; but one would have to go to the Louvre to see the beautiful Karomama, brought from Egypt by Champollion himself, or to the Greek National Museum in Athens to see the full, slightly heavy contours of the Lady Takushit.

There are no pieces to compare with these in Cairo; nevertheless, although it is rather small, this statuette of a falcon found at Sais in 1893, can enable us to form an idea of the results achieved by the bronzefounders of Ancient Egypt.

The falcon-image of Horus stands on a rectangular plinth, solidly on its feet, with folded wings and tail trailing. The bird originally wore a slender 'pschent', of which only the base of the red crown and a part of the 'uraeus' remain. Having been cast according to the cire-perdue process, in a mould from which the molten metal expels the initial form molded in wax, the bronze idol was subsequently damascened; *ie*, threads of gold were hammered into the bronze to outline the plumage of the wings and back, to accentuate the characteristic markings of the cheek, and to adorn the breast with a tiered collar and heart amulet.

On the front of the stand, a short inscription informs us that this statuette was ordered by a certain Imhotep, son of Padineith and the lady Iah.

106 | Statuette of the god Ptah

Bronze; H. 25 cm; 26th Dynasty; No.4480; First floor 19, centre

This little bronze figurine represents the god Ptah. The great demiurge of Memphis is portrayed in human form with the body tightly arrayed in a mummiform sheath, from which only the hands emerge to grasp a 'was'-sceptre against the chest. A close-fitting cap covers the skull and there is a long square beard and a collar. The details of this traditional image of Ptah vary from one statuette to another; the beard can be curved instead of straight, the cap can be worn with the feathered head-dress borrowed from Tatenen 'the land that emerges', the oldest god in the pantheon of Memphis. Also, the sceptre can be composite, incorporating the 'djed' pillar and the 'ankh' with the 'was'; the clothing can be more complicated; and, finally the bevelled plinth on which the god stands can disappear altogether if he is represented in a sitting position.

No one knows exactly what the name of Ptah means – it can be associated with two word roots, signifying 'opening' and 'sculpting' – but his personality needs no introduction. The ancients credited Ptah with the invention of technical skills, and the Greeks identified him with Hephaistos. The historical importance of Memphis brought him to the fore as one of the patron deities of royalty and jubilee festivals. Assimilating the personalities of Sokaris and Osiris, Ptah also became a funerary god; but above all, he occupied a special place among the creators, because according to the theological system of Memphis he was the author of creation by the word, *ie*, the conception in the heart, the seat of all thought, of the words formulated by his tongue. This cosmogony was perhaps the most intellectual of any developed in Egypt; the others restricted themselves to explaining the beginning of the world by way of the yearly spectacle of the land reborn in the wake of the retreating Nile floodwaters. For nearly all Egyptian cosmogonies, everything began with the 'Nun', the primordial ocean from which emerged a muddy hillock on which the world was later constructed (starting with an egg brought by Thoth to Hermopolis or Atum's solitary labours at Heliopolis . . .). From this point onwards, stories of the creation varied from city to city, each of which tended to give the principal rôle to its own particular deity, just as each original village had once done for its local god.

Little by little, Ptah formed a family, with the lioness Sakhmet for a wife and Nefertum, the perfumed lotus, as his son; from the 18th Dynasty onwards, he was associated with the bull Apis, whose cult went back to the very earliest dynasties and who had previously remained independent. The ox-god, who in his earthly form lived in a sacred stable within the precincts of the Great Temple of Ptah, was considered as a manifestation, a herald of the god; at his death, the bull was ceremonially buried in the underground chambers of the Serapeum at Saqqara, and a search was carried out all over Egypt for the young calf which, born of a cow that had been impregnated by a lightning bolt from the sky, might carry the markings that would confirm him as the new Apis. There were 29 of these markings, according to Aelian; perhaps corresponding to the 29 days of the lunar cycle. The most important were described by Herodotus (III,29): 'The bull who receives the name of Apis has the following characteristics: he is black, with a white triangle on his brow, a mark in the shape of an eagle on his back,

the hairs of his tail doubled, and a scarab mark under his tongue . . .'. It was Mariette's discovery in 1851 of the huge collective grave of the Apis bulls which ushered in the era of great archaeological excavation in Egypt, and which yielded a host of important historical records.

A short inscription, carved on the stand of this statuette of Ptah, assures us that the god will grant life to a certain 'Horemkheb, son of Horwedja, who brought Shepenese into the world'.

107 | Colossus of Amenhotep, son of Hapu

Red granite; H. 2.15 m; Saite epoch (?); No.3;
Ground floor 48, north east corner

This colossal statue, which, along with other monuments of the same size, welcomes the visitor at the entrance to the Cairo Museum, was discovered in 1892 just south of the valley of the sphinxes and a few yards from the first pylon of the Temple of Karnak.

What remains of the text carved on the plinth and the loincloth tells us that the subject is 'the royal scribe and scribe of recruits Amenhotep, son of Hapu'. In other words, he was the celebrated architect and minister of Amenophis III, who built many of the great monuments of Thebes under the lavish reign of that monarch; in particular, the royal funerary temple, of which nothing remains save the colossi of Memnon which guarded the entrance.

In gratitude for his services, the king granted Amenhotep the signal favour of a funerary temple distinct from his tomb; which, though violated long ago, still remains to be discovered by archaeologists in the Qurnet Murai sector. By a decree (of which the British Museum possesses a copy) Amenophis personally assumed the organization of the funerary cult of his devoted 'chief architect'; and the measure certainly contributed mightily to the perpetuation of his memory. Indeed, coupled with his own reputation, this honour led to the realization of Amenhotep's singular destiny, which was to become one of the rare men of Ancient Egypt to be deified.

Apart from certain kings who, for special reasons, were accorded a particular cult after their deaths, but who anyway were of divine birth, a very few common men were counted among the gods, either because they were drowned in the Nile, or because their learning and intelligence had enabled them to accomplish extraordinary works.

Amenhotep belonged to this last category, as did the illustrious inventor of stone construction in the far-off times of King Djoser, the great Imhotep, known to the Greeks as Imouthes and identified by them with Asklepios. These two individuals had to wait many years before they were deified. Because of his statues in the Temple of Karnak, Amenhotep was at first so much in demand as an intermediary between Amun and his worshippers, that some of the inscriptions carved on his effigies were almost rubbed away by the caresses of human hands. Later, he was revered as a sage and prophet, before becoming the healing god Amenothes in the reign of Ptolemy II Philadelphus.

In this capacity, he was incorporated in the later sanctuaries of Karnak, Deir el-Medina, Deir el-Bahri and Tod, as Imouthes-Asklepios 'Healer, beneficent god, who sleeps neither by day nor by night, the better to attend to the voices of his supplicants'.

The most important shrine of the cult, which included an oracle and a sanatorium, was that of Deir el-Bahri. It was dedicated to the triad formed by the two deified men, and Hygie, the personification of health and daughter of Asklepios. The sanctuary was built at the beginning of the Ptolemaic era at the level of the upper terrace of the ruined temple of queen Hatshepsut, where a third underground chamber was later dug as an extension to those of the 18th Dynasty.

It is not known how Amenothes, who gradually superseded his associates, contrived to cure his devotees. However, if we are to believe the evidence of a certain Polyaratos in 260 BC, his

interventions were highly effective:

'I was the victim of a very serious and dangerous malady, which lasted for eight years . . . I sought the advice of doctors, but they could not restore me to health. But I was told by many that the miracles wrought by Amenothes were very numerous, that he was compassionate, and that many men sick unto death had been healed by his offices . . . being myself sick unto death I hastened in supplication to the temple of Amenothes, and Amenothes helped me, curing me in the eyes of men; when I had recovered my health, I sought to honour Amenothes and the other gods of his cult and his altars, by writing down a description of their miraculous works on behalf of those who come to the sanctuary of Amenothes, suffering under any affliction . . .'

On the front of the plinth of this statue, which dates from the Saite epoch (or the last indigenous dynasties), is a line in Greek added at the time of the Roman Caesars. This attests that the memory of Amenhotep endured in the minds of men; nor did it disappear with the coming of Christianity, for men in Upper Egypt bore the name at least until the sixth century AD.

108 | Late royal head

Black granite; H. 46 cm; 29th Dynasty (?); Ground floor, east side, case C

Under its number 28512, the *Journal d'Entrée* indicates that this beautiful black granite head (which carries no attribution, unfortunately) was purchased at Tmai el-Amdid in 1888. Thus it probably comes from the antique Mendes, capital of the 14th nome of Lower Egypt, where a ram deity was worshipped. The smiling, enigmatic face has a definite family resemblance to the royal portraits of the Saite epoch. It portrays a king wearing the 'khepresh' or 'blue crown', the so-called 'war helmet' affected frequently even by the peace-loving Akhenaten.

In reality, the helmet must have been of leather decorated with faience beads (see No.62). Here it

looks to be carried on a more flexible cap which fits closely over the skull, and it is adorned with a 'uraeus', the body of which describes a double figure of eight behind the rearing hood of the cobra. This detail constitutes an element for dating the piece, because it is found from the 26th to the 29th Dynasty, but disappears in the 30th.

By comparison with similar heads whose subjects are beyond doubt, this one exhibits certain peculiarities: for example, even though the head-dresses are alike, the eyebrows are more clearly-defined than in the portrait of Apries, and the eyes more almond-shaped than those of Amasis. The provenance of the head is also an important ele-

ment in the process of identifying it. Mendes was the place of origin of the kings of the 29th Dynasty, which was the last indigenous dynasty, and it is tempting to think that this is a portrait of one of them. Rather than one of the two Nepherites or Psammuthis, it is probably Hakoris (390–378 BC) who, although a usurper, nonetheless made himself the dynasty's greatest pharaoh, in the twenty-odd years of his reign. The Kansas City Museum possesses a little kneeling bronze of this king, who was astute enough to conclude an alliance with Athens in order to resist the advancing Persians. Identified by the first name of Khnemmaatre, which is carved on the belt of his loincloth, the Kansas City statuette wears the same 'blue crown' with the same royal cobra coiled in the same double figure of eight.

109 | Naos of Saft el-Hinna
detail

Black granite; H. of each register, 27 cm; 30th Dynasty; No.790; Ground floor 24, centre

Egyptologists admit two meanings for the Greek word 'naos', both of which are related to Egyptian archaeology. It can mean the inmost room of a religious building, the 'holy of holies', which looks like a chapel with its own roof, though within the temple proper. More often, however, the word 'naos' describes the shrine in the chapel, which harboured the statue of a deity under a convex or pyramid-shaped top. This essential element of the Egyptian temple, sometimes made of wood under the New Kingdom, was invariably cut from a single block of stone during the Late Period. The majority of the Museum's fifty 'naoi' date from this period; eleven of these, which originally came from large towns, go back to the reigns of the two Nectanebos, whose main activity in the 30th Dynasty was the restoration of the temples that had been damaged or neglected during the civil wars and the Assyrian and Persian invasions.

This large black granite 'naos' falls into the latter category. Its remains were discovered in several stages, first by local farmers in 1865, and then by Naville at Saft el-Hinna in 1885, on the ancient site of Pi-Sopdu, not far from Zagazig on one side and the entrance to the Wadi Tumilat on the other. The three-line dedicatory inscription, which extends all round the base, makes it clear that this enormous shrine, with its gold-encrusted copper doors, was installed by king Kheperkare Nakhtnebef (Nectanebo I) in the temple of 'his father Sopdu, lord of the East'. The originality of this monument (which must originally have had a roof in the form of a pyramidion like that of the 'naos' of Nectanebo II, which is still in place in the sanctuary of the temple of Idfu), lies in the sumptuous decoration of its surfaces. These are divided into low registers, six on the outside and five on the inside. They constituted a veritable catalogue of several hundred small figures carefully lined up beneath long rows of sky-signs, including divine emblems, cult paraphernalia and deities before which the king is seen prostrating himself or making offerings.

The god Sopdu was an Asian importation. Here he is represented in various more or less composite forms, but most often as a falcon because Horus was his principal affiliate. Hence, when the priests opened the doors of the 'naos' each morning to celebrate the divine cult on behalf of the pharaoh, it is likely that the effigy that met their eyes was that of a falcon. The Egyptian temple, aptly defined by Sauneron as 'one of the points of emer-

gence of the divine', was strictly speaking the 'abode of the god'. Thus the Egyptians considered that a portion of the deity, incarnate in the statue, could be actually said to inhabit it; and the function of the cult was to protect this essence and provide it with all the vital necessities. The statue would be washed, dressed, perfumed, incensed, given things to eat and drink as a part of the daily offices of the priests, which they carried out as they recited the words of the rituals. The priests were thus 'servants of the god' in the most domestic sense; but despite the prosaic nature of these thrice-daily tasks, they were considered to be of prime importance for all humanity. In exchange for the services rendered to him, the god maintained the equilibrium of a created world that was continually being tested and threatened. It was only this kind of cosmic exchange process, carried out in the highly functional edifice that was the temple, which stood between the organized universe and chaos. It ensured that when each night was past, the sun would once again burst forth from the darkness, as it had done since the First Occasion.

110 | Sarcophagus cover of the dwarf Teos

Grey granite; H. 1.80 m; 20th Dynasty; No.1294; Ground floor, north side

From the Saite era onwards, in addition to wrappings of various weights, cloth bindings, etc, the wealthy dead were frequently endowed with heavy stone sarcophagi (anthropoid or otherwise) which might weigh upwards of twenty or thirty tons. These sarcophagi were cut from the hardest granite and might be totally covered in texts and

illustrations from the great funeral books of the royal cave-sepulchres, or else simply marked with the names and titles of the deceased.

The coffin of the dwarf Teos, or Takhos (Djedher in Egyptian), was of this type (only the lid is shown here). This coffin was brought up in 1911, by Quibell, from a tomb-shaft at Saqqara. The shaft contained several similar coffins, and it had already been entered by Mariette in the last century.

The decoration of this coffin lid is quite exceptional because on its flat surface the usual religious scenes have been replaced by a kind of portrait of the dead man; and furthermore he is represented naked. His unusual physique is realistically depicted by a very delicately-executed intaglio relief. On either side of the portrait are sloped surfaces, each with six columns of text reproducing certain chapters from the *Book of the Dead*. Above the head, two lines inform us that the owner of the sarcophagus, who was 'at the side of Osiris, who rules in the West, the great god, lord of Ro-Setau' (*ie*, the region through which the dead must travel on their way to the next world) was 'a dwarf who danced in the Serapeum on the day of the funeral of Apis, the great god, king of the gods', that his name was Djedher (Teos, or Takhos in Greek) and that he was the son of Petekhons and the Lady Tenethapi.

Nearly two thousand years earlier, towards the end of the 6th Dynasty, Harkhuf, the great explorer of Africa, had brought back a pygmy for the 'dances of the god', and his size had delighted the young king Pepy II. It was perhaps because the simian shapes of their bodies were reminiscent of the capering dog-headed divinity who welcomed the sunrise with his cries, that dwarfs were thus employed as sacred dancers. At all events, they are portrayed as such in numerous pieces of metalwork and on the bas-reliefs of mastabas.

On the inside of the coffin lid, Nut, the goddess of the sky who holds the sun aloft in her arms, is seen surrounded by the twelve hours of the night; these are depicted as squatting figures with stars on their heads.

The bottom of the casket is covered by a large illustration of the goddess of the West, and on the sides (both interior and exterior) are religious scenes and texts. A line of text runs all around the coffin, in a band just under the lip; here Teos expresses through prayer his gratitude to a certain Tjaiherpato, a great official in the reign of Nectanebo II, the last of the indigenous pharaohs, for having wished that the dancer should be buried beside him; for it goes without saying that Teos could never have afforded so magnificent a sepulchre on his own. The sarcophagus of this eminent person, which puts a precise date on that of the dwarf, was indeed found in the same burial chamber.

111 | Archaising bas-relief *detail*

Fine limestone; H. 30 cm; 30th Dynasty; No.6020; Ground floor 24, left, at entrance

Because of their proportions and the torus that usually surmounts them, sculpted architectural elements of this type are frequently mistaken for lintels. While all the examples possessed by the Museum are of much the same size and much longer than they are high, their thinness rules out this possibility. On the contrary, the archaeological evidence would tend to show that they were meant to serve as friezes on the outside walls of a variety of tombs that appeared in the Delta (Athribis, Bubastis, Buto) during the Saite epoch. These tombs were simple sepulchres with the chapel serving as a vault to keep soil humidity away from the mummies they contained; the reliefs were probably attached to the upper sections of the walls, which explains both their thinness and the torus.

This bas-relief, one of the most beautiful, came into the Museum in 1920 after being discovered by chance by some 'sebakhin' at Tell el-Farain, *ie*, on the site of Buto, the ancient capital of the Northern Kingdom and the domain of Wadjet, the cobra goddess. The composition of the scene is standard: a procession of eleven bearers of offerings (the photograph shows only the first of these) advancing towards the dead man, who is pictured on the far left hand corner. The latter is seated on a low-backed chair, whose animal-feet are placed on little supports. He wears a loincloth and a short

wig and holds a long staff in one hand whilst the other is laid flat on his thigh. A column of finely-sculpted hieroglyphs in front of him state that his name was Horhetep and that he occupied two priestly functions which are hard to define; but at any rate the first of them, which was linked to Buto, had certainly existed since the Old Kingdom. The bearer of offerings, who seems to be wigless, has a kind of sash around his hips; he leads a small calf by a rope and carries three geese and a bowl of lotus blossoms.

At first sight, the general impression is one of perfection; this relief is clearly the product of extraordinary skill. But when one looks closer, one perceives that despite the meticulousness of the work and quality of certain details, the modelling is undeniably heavy. The somewhat languid charm of this kind of Egyptian art, which is sometimes called 'neo-Memphite', by reason of its blatant intent to imitate the bas-reliefs of the Old Kingdom mastabas, is far removed from the living vigour of its model.

112 | Coffin of Petosiris
detail

Wood, inlaid with pâte de verre; L. 1.95 m; early ptolemaic era; No.6035; Ground floor 49, centre

The Antiquities Service owed its discovery of the tomb of Petosiris in 1919–20 to an inhabitant of El-Ashmunein, who came seeking a licence to excavate a 'temple' he had found on the mountainside. The 'temple' proved to be a sepulchre built for the father and elder brother of Petosiris, high priest of Thoth before the conquest of Egypt by Alexander, and later enlarged to receive the bodies of himself and his family.

The tomb is sited at Tuna el-Gebel, the necropolis of ancient Hermopolis. It does indeed look like a small Ptolemaic temple, with its portal, columns and pillared vault; and it is interesting for more than one reason. The various bas-reliefs covering the walls bear witness to an astonishingly successful (though short-lived) attempt to associate Egyptian and Greek art, while the inscriptions beside the usual funerary texts reveal the fully-fledged philosophical and religious thought which gave Petosiris the reputation of a scholar in the eyes of his contemporaries.

The task of excavating the tomb fell to Gustave Lefebvre, who later wrote a magnificent book about it. When he reached the underground chambers, it became clear that Petosiris' imposing sarcophagus, like the others in the vault, had been violated, for there was a hole in the casket at head height. Thus it appeared impossible to verify whether or not the priest of Thoth had indeed received the burial promised to him by Tjehiau, his second daughter, in an inscription carved on the façade of the tomb:

'After thy death, Thoth will grant thee a fine embalming by Anubis, and thy body shall come to this tomb encased in a fourfold coffin: one of juniper wood, one of pine, one of sycamore and one of stone. These shall form thine abode this day; they shall be carved with thy name and inlaid with precious stones of every kind.'

For form's sake, Lefebvre removed the heavy stone sarcophagus lid – the mummy was indeed long gone, but the wooden coffins still remained. There were two (not three, as promised in the text) in different states of preservation. The first, which was made of sycamore wood covered in yellow stucco, was almost entirely rotted away; the second, by contrast, was of dark pine and proved to be intact, with colours 'worthy of a king's casket'. The mummiform lid, under a sky-sign in lapis lazuli, bears five long columns of hieroglyphs whose colours are heightened by a nearly black background. These colours are not, as one might expect, produced by inlays of 'all kinds of precious stones'. They consist of elements of coloured glass, used conventionally to imitate turquoise, lapis lazuli, carnelian, jasper, ivory or emerald. Each

hieroglyph is a tiny masterpiece in itself. The same virtuoso technique may have been used to decorate the sarcophagi of Petosiris' family; at all events, that of Djedthothiufankh, his elder brother, was definitely adorned in this way, as proved by a fragment of his coffin lid now in the Turin Museum.

The text, which gives one of Petosiris' titles – 'Great one of the Five, master of the works' – is an incomplete copy of Chapter 42 of the *Book of the Dead*, in which the physical parts of the deceased are identified with those of the gods:

'My hair is the hair of Nun;
My face is the face of Re;
My eyes are the eyes of Hathor;
My ears are the ears of Wepwawet;
My nose is the nose of Khentkhas;
My lips are the lips of Anubis;
My teeth are the teeth of Selkis ...'

This is clearly a traditional text invoking magic, which is far removed from the moral tone of some of the other inscriptions in the tomb:

'... It is a good road, the road of God's faithful; he is blessed, whose heart leads him to it. I shall tell what has befallen me, I shall apprise thee of the will of God, I shall assure thine entry into the knowledge of his spirit.

If I have come to this place, to the city of eternity, it is because I have done good upon earth, and because my heart has rejoiced in the ways of God, from the day of my birth unto this day ... I have sought justice, and I have hated iniquity ... I have not consorted with those who knew not the spirit of God...'

113 | Healing statue of Djedher-the-Saviour

Black granite; H. 65 cm (statue) + 31 cm (base); end of 4th century BC; No.4752; First floor 19, corridor

When Daressy published the texts of this statue for the first time in 1918, immediately after its accidental discovery at Tell Atrib (the modern Benha, known to the Greeks as Athribis), he was right to prophesy that it would 'be bound to acquire a certain celebrity in the field of Egyptology'. Indeed, the piece does occupy a special place in the statuary of the Egyptians, because it represents not merely a living, breathing person, but also a veritable instrument of magic. This statue is a saviour placed at the disposal of his contemporaries by the person it portrays, with a view to curing all forms of animal bites through the magical powers of its texts and illustrations.

A second example of this monument once existed, as is proved by a plinth now in America. It consists of two parts, each distinguished by the nature of their inscriptions; the base which bears a biographical text, and the statue proper, which is entirely covered with magical formulae (except for the face, the hands and the feet).

The inscriptions etched on the sides and edges of the base reveal that the statue is a portrait of Djedher, who was chief guardian of the gates of the temple of Athribis, in the time of Philip Arrhidaeus, half-brother of Alexander the Great. Among other duties, he was responsible for the care of the sacred falcons and their eventual mummification, to which purpose he had built an edifice with twelve chapels.

The carefully-wrought statue depicts Djedher seated on a flat cushion, in the block-statue pose, with his legs drawn up to his chest and his crossed arms resting on his knees above a 'cippus' of Horus. This 'cippus', by representing the young god trampling crocodiles underfoot and subduing other dangerous creatures (scorpion, lion, oryx, snakes) beneath the grinning mask of the prophylactic Bes, was a powerful charm for the Egyptians against the bites and wounds caused by such animals. The mere presence of a 'stela of Horus on the crocodiles' in a house was considered effective, but it seems to have operated mainly by physical contact, recitation, or washing. These stelae came in all sizes and materials, portable or otherwise.

The purpose of placing Djedher in the middle of a shallow basin, communicating with a deeper one in front, was to permit just such contact, which of course did not require any ability to read. All people had to do was to pour water on to the statue, then collect it again once it had run over the various carved formulae, thereby becoming charged with their magical properties. In general, these properties consisted of the actual words uttered on various occasions by the divinities pictured beside the formulae, when themselves threatened by dangerous creatures. The water would subsequently be drunk, or used as a lotion.

It would seem that Djedher was indeed considered by the ancients to deserve the title 'saviour' incorporated into his name. The worn aspect of the carved signs and figures in the basin facing his effigy proves that people came often to draw his magically protective and curative water.

114 | Sculptor's model

Limestone; H. 9.8 cm; Ptolemaic period; First floor 24, west side, case W5

Specialists differ as to the exact rôle of these objects, which are usually called 'sculptor's models', but can also be 'experiments' or 'studies'. Some see them as no more than teaching equipment used

for training artists, whilst others think they have a votive character, and were placed in temples or chapels by the faithful. It would seem that the truth lies somewhere in between; although many are indubitably religious in nature, others have come down to us still rough-hewn, with cross-hatching, toolmarks or thickness gauges still evident. These are definitely the work of apprentice sculptors, or models for use in teaching.

Most of the models we possess are in limestone, rather than plaster. They come in the form of plaques with one or several pictures in bas-relief, or as little sculptures in the round, conventional enough despite their delicacy of execution. From the 26th Dynasty to the Ptolemaic period, their repertoire is limited to representations of gods, kings, animals, hieroglyphs or parts of the human body; the latter category, along with royal busts, usually being executed in the round.

This little goose, carved in a limestone slab, was given to the Museum by King Fouad in 1936. It has been restored but the bird itself is still intact. With a fine eye for detail, the artist has depicted the bird on the point of laying an egg, and he has contrived most beautifully to show the difference between the boldly chiselled wing feathers and the fluffy down of the breast and abdomen.

115 | Ptolemy V Epiphanes bringing offerings to the Buchis bull

Painted and gilded limestone; H. 73 cm; Ptolemaic period; Collective No.6159; Ground floor 34, south side

This stela is probably the loveliest of all those yielded by the underground corridors of the Bucheum of Hermonthis (south-east of Luxor, known today as Armant) where, from the time of Nectanebo II to that of Diocletian, the Buchis bulls sacred to the god Montu were ritually interred.

The necropolis was discovered in 1929–30, in the course of excavations conducted by Mond for the Egypt Exploration Society. It is comparable, despite its lamentable state of repair and the fact

that it was in use for a much shorter period, to the great Serapeum of the Apis.

The archaeological harvest at Armant was less abundant than that of Saqqara, but nonetheless produced a number of valuable records, among them this stela, which dates from the 25th year of Ptolemy V (181 BC).

The arch of the stela is filled by symmetrical decoration dominated by a winged solar disc. Below this stands Ptolemy V, the Hellenistic sovereign responsible for the tri-lingual decree recorded on the famous Rosetta Stone, which enabled modern man to break the code of the hieroglyphs. He is pictured offering the sign of the green field to the Buchis and to Montu in his animal form. The bull, which was originally gilded

all over, carries the customary head-dress of Montu between his horns. This consists of a solar disc, and two 'uraei'; he is qualified as 'living soul' and 'herald of Re'.

At the bottom of the stela is a five-line text which gives very precise dates; among other things, it tells us that the Buchis which died in the 25th year of Ptolemy V and Cleopatra I was born in the year 11, and that its lifetime spanned 14 years, 10 months and 24 days. As it happens, this last affirmation is false; one has only to make the calculation oneself to discover that the bull in question only lived 13 years, 10 months and 24 days. Nevertheless, documents of this kind (there were hundreds at the Serapeum) are invaluable for establishing chronologies, especially when they can be cross-checked with known dates.

116 | Statuette of a satyr with wineskin

Terracotta with traces of paint; H. 8.5 cm; Ptolemaic period; No.6102; First floor 39, north side, case N4

'I have never excavated for Greek or Roman monuments. Hence the very small number of objects belonging to this category in the Museum collection'. The words are Mariette's, in the preface to his *Notice des Principaux Monuments Exposés ... à Boulaq.* They are a clear admission of his lack of interest in works which were not the product of pure pharaonic art.

All the same, this beautiful terracotta statuette from the area around Rosetta, north-west of the Delta, must have found grace in his eyes, since he not only had it purchased for the Bulaq Museum, but also sent it to the Paris Universal Exhibition in 1878.

Mariette's first idea was that the statuette was of Aeolus; then, more simply, he concluded that it must be a wind spirit. This in fact is what immediately comes to mind, because it is obvious that air is supposed to be coming out of the bag held by the figure. But if one looks closer, one soon understands that the figure is a satyr: his pointed ears, mantle of skins and tail leave no doubt of it.

In that case, why is he holding a bag full of air? After all, one would expect a satyr's wineskin to be full of wine! and the expression of surprise and mortification on his face shows that he, too, was hoping to find wine. It has been suggested that this is an illustration of some lost Alexandrian fable or epigram. This may be so, but whatever the object's significance may be, it is of exceptionally high quality. By contrast with the usual practice in Egypt, where terracotta work tended to be crude and shaped in one mould only, the various elements of this statuette must have required several different moulds. The pieces were then stuck together with barbotine retouched with a chisel, and provided with a vent-hole to allow air to escape during the subsequent firing process.

If the Alexandria Museum did not possess the head of an identical statuette, which probably means that the origins of both were local, one might suppose that this fine piece was foreign made. At all events, the precise, generous treatment is reminiscent of work from the late fourth and early third centuries before Christ.

Whether the satyr originated in Greece or in Egypt, one can only admire the skill of the artist in making the wind seem so vividly present. The satyr's mantle billows out like a sail; and the strength he is bringing to bear is cunningly rendered by the vigorous muscles, the fingers clenched around the neck of the wineskin and the swollen veins of the arms.

117 | Statuette of Somtus-Herakles

Bronze; H. 26 cm; Ptolemaic period; No.6111; First floor 39, west side, case 3, coming from room 40

The archaeological provenance of this Hellenistic bronze is unknown; it was given to the Museum by King Farouk in 1937. It is marked in the *Journal d'Entrée* under the number 67928, with the brief comment that it is the 'statue of a king'. At first glance this is what it seems to be, since the figure wears a royal 'nemes'. But the fact that it also holds one finger to its mouth, a gesture common to all late bronzes portraying god-children, means that it must be one of these.

Another possibility is that it is a Harpocrates; this Greek name exactly transcribes the Egyptian expression for 'Horus the child', the son of god *par excellence* who was also the model on which all the other so-called god-children were based. However, if we examine it carefully, the most probable solution is that this statuette (now incomplete) portrays the god Somtus-Herakles, *ie*, a pure product of Egyptian syncretism. It is known that this peculiarly Egyptian tendency to syncretize became very frequent in the Late Period; brought about by the ancient division of the country, it consisted in the substitution of hybrid, but progressively more universal deities for the old local gods. Syncretism was the Egyptian way of comprehending the personality of an omnipresent, unpredictable divine being, by juxtaposing it with the names and characteristics of older gods whose attributes had once been more distinct.

But let us return to the statuette itself. On the 'nemes', beside the right ear, is the hook for the

special lock of hair worn by 'sons of gods' and princes, and on the top of the head-dress the presence of a small hole indicates that a crown originally rested upon it. A comparison with bronzes of the last indigenous dynasties shows that this was the 'Hemhem' crown, a highly complex affair consisting of ram's horns surmounted by a triple 'atef' with feathers and uraei on either side and topped by three solar discs. It is worn by Horus; by the king identified with him (eg, Tutankhamun, in the scene on the back of his throne); and also by the god Somtus, whose name is the Greek form of an Egyptian expression meaning 'the Uniter of the Two Lands'. Somtous is a form of Harpocrates indentified with Arsaphes (Herishef in Egyptian) the ram-god of Herakleopolis Magna sometimes referred to as 'the Child'.

During the Graeco-Roman epoch, the young Horus as vanquisher of Seth was identified with Herakles, another destroyer of monsters. Coins from Herakleopolis portray this divinity as a man who sucks his finger but also carries a club. Hence this statuette could practically be completed in supposition, since it is clear from other portrayals that the left hand held at hip height grasped a club, with the heavy end near the shoulder. This is how the Herakleopolitan deity is figured on the non-visible side of a liturgical tunic found at Saqqara, which dates from the end of the Ptolemaic or the beginning of the Roman period (this item is exhibited in the corridor leading to First floor room 29).

Thus this statuette of Somtus-Herakles is a strange example of the contact between two religions and aesthetic outlooks, which, despite many attempts to do so, never succeeded in merging coherently. The stiffness of the pharaonic 'nemes', the slack curves of the body and the typically Greek dislocation of the hips, accentuating the folds of the garment, exude a strong 'just back from Egypt' feeling.

The treatment of the face, and the prominent, almost popping eyeballs characteristic of the portraiture of kings like Ptolemy II and Ptolemy V, enables us to date this statuette in the second century BC; and the odds are that it originally came from Herakleopolis.

118 | Portrait of a young woman

Encaustic-painted wood; H. 31 cm; late First-early second century AD; No.4310 (collective); First floor 14, south side

It was an early seventeenth-century Roman aristocrat, Pietro Della Valle, who brought from Egypt the first known examples of Roman period funerary paintings. These are now referred to as 'Faiyum Portraits'. While most of them did actually come from the Faiyum, the ones exported by Della Valle, which were still attached to mummies, originated from Saqqara; and similar portraits have been found more or less everywhere in the Nile Valley, from Tanis to Aswan.

The Hawara excavations of Petrie, followed by those of Albert Jean Gayet of Antinopolis, yielded an extensive crop of funerary portraits between 1890 and 1910. Their numbers today are estimated at more than 700, in collections all over the world.

These portraits may be viewed as the final phase of development of the Egyptian funeral mark; but they did not supplant it, because cartonnage or stucco masks continued in use despite their advent. They also represent a significant record of easel painting in the Roman era, which is nowhere so abundant or so well-preserved as in Egypt, though it flourished throughout the Empire. Moreover, in Egypt, it is well-defined both in space and in time.

The techniques seem to have varied very little. A few portraits, the oldest of all, are painted on canvas, but nearly all the rest were executed on wooden boards which were then attached to the mummies by the skilful manipulation of bandages, or by the cartonnage stucco.

After first applying a preparatory coat to the wood, the artist used either the encaustic method (*ie* mixing colours with melted wax and applying them in small dabs before they dry), or simple distemper on a white background. In some cases, both techniques were used simultaneously.

The kind of portrait shown here continued in use till the second quarter of the third century AD, though its heyday was between the mid-first and mid-second centuries. Comparisons of elements such as hairstyles and jewellery for women, and the presence or absence of beards for men, enable the paintings to be fairly accurately dated.

The provenance of this fine portrait of a young woman is unknown, as is the date of its entry into the Museum collection. It is painted in encaustic on a small board. A fragment of the support is missing, and it is fissured in several places along the grain of the wood. In the middle of the octagonal frame originally defined by the bandages (fibres from these can still be seen adhering to the painting), the face, turned slightly to the right, is seen almost front view against a faded background which was once a dark blue-grey. A mass of tight black ringlets covers the head, almost completely hiding the ears, from which hang gold earrings,

each with a pair of pearl pendants. The dress lays the neck bare, revealing a thick gold necklace, to which a ring or crescent is attached.

The expression is serious, almost gloomy, as is often the case. The young woman has the same gentle but concentrated and almost surprised look which occurs with varying degrees of intensity in all these portraits. Particular stress was always laid on the eyes, which are often troubled and sometimes disproportionately large.

119 | Portrait of Alexander Severus

White marble; H. 24 cm; early third century AD; Ground floor 34, east side, case B

Anyone who visits Egypt may find it curious that Roman ruins there are so rare and so modest in scale. In most other countries conquered by the Romans, the opposite is the case. The reason, however, is simple: in order to be accepted in a country which had become their personal property rather than a province of the empire, the Roman emperors were obliged to behave like pharaohs. In spite of their heaviness, the monuments they erected continued perfectly in the Egyptian tradition. But in the bas-reliefs of the epoch the kings we see wearing the heavy paraphernalia of antique royalty or ritually massacring the enemies of Egypt are none other than Nero, Hadrian or Caracalla.

In the domain of statuary, apart from a few unsuccessful attempts to combine styles, Egypt produced works which were purely Roman in type and character, notably portraiture.

This carefully finished white marble head originally came from Luxor. It represents a young bearded man. The neck is broken off at the base, below the chin, and the nose and ears are damaged, but the resemblance with the busts of Alexander Severus at the Louvre, at Florence and at the Vatican leaves no doubt that this is the prince who became emperor in AD 222 after the assassination of Elagabalus by the praetorian guard.

The somewhat lofty gentleness of the boyish face, smiling but languid, is well suited to a portrait of this emperor; who, though he lacked the cruel and debauched nature of his cousins, was also devoid of a forthright personality.

As the son, grandson and great-nephew of the famous Syrian empresses who dominated the Severan dynasty but also enabled it to continue, Alexander Severus first allowed his grandmother Julia Maesa, then his mother Julia Mammaea, to hold the reins of power. He was finally assassinated in AD 235, along with his mother, by an army exasperated with his weakness in the face of the barbarian invasions across the Rhine.

120 | 'Spirit statue' of the Nubian prince Maleten

Sandstone, with traces of paint; H. 75 cm; first century BC–third century BC; Ground floor 40, west side, case H

This strange and massive object resulted from the excavations of the Eckley B. Coxe Expedition to Nubia (University of Pennsylvania) in 1907. It was found at Karanog, a site in Egyptian Nubia which is now submerged beneath the waters of Lake Nasser, in the princely tomb numbered G.187. Subsequently, it was brought back to Cairo with a few other statues by MacIver. According to Maspero, it represents a 'spirit statue'. But while the dead man is portrayed as a man-falcon, he non-

etheless fully retains his human aspect and appears to be trailing his feathered wings and tail like a ceremonial cape. Hence, this is a re-interpretation of the bird spirit of the ancient Egyptian funerary cult, whose only human characteristic was his head.

The man stands stiffly on a base which is fashioned from the same block of stone as he. He wears a three-layered, long-sleeved tunic and sandals of Egyptian design. His head is covered by a short wig or cap, and he is shown 'in majesty', accoutred in the symbols of his rank: diadem, bracelets, sceptre and staff. These were originally held in his arms, which are pressed against his sides and crooked at the elbow. He also wears a heavy pectoral of large beads, with a clasp on the left shoulder made of three cartouches with no names inscribed on them. An effigy of Amun, the dynastic god of Napata, hangs from a chain that passes across the pectoral.

A square hole in the top of the skull shows that the statue must once have been crowned with a solar disc, an echo of those sometimes seen on the heads of bird-spirits dating from the pharaonic epoch.

After a domination of Egypt that lasted a hundred years, the so-called 'Ethiopian' dynasty from Napata was forced southward first by the Assyrians, then by Psammetichus II in the early sixth century BC. At this point in time, Meroe became the capital of a kingdom which developed its own more and more separate civilization, preserving certain pharaonic traditions but oriented in the main toward Africa. The language of this kingdom, which has yet to be deciphered, and its art, though frequently marred by a barbarian taste for over-much adornment, attest to its considerable originality.

Although Karanog is in the far north of the Meroitic kingdom, African traits (in the shape of the features and the massive construction of the body) are predominant in this 'spirit-statue'. This African quality led to its being exhibited in 1966 at Dakar, during the First World Festival of Negro Arts; and it was subsequently shown (in the same year) at the Paris 'Art Négre' exhibition at the Grand Palais.

Chronological references

It is important not to forget the very arbitrary nature of the dates assigned to the events of Egyptian history: although the dates of the last millenium before the birth of Christ are known to be relatively exact, as we go further back it becomes increasingly difficult to be precise. The main thing is to have a framework within which the great periods of the Pharaohs' history can be placed in relation to one another, after the long period of uncertainty of prehistoric times.

Thinite Period: 3000–2780

I and II dynasty, after the unification of the country by Narmer, probably the Menes of Manetho.

Old Kingdom: 2780–2280

III dynasty: Djoser (Step Pyramid).
IV dynasty (2620–2560): Snofru, Cheops, Chephren, Mycerinus (pyramids of Giza).
V dynasty (2560–2420): Userkaf, Sahure, Neferirkare, Niuserre, Wenis.
VI dynasty (2420–2280): Teti, Pepy I, Merenre, Pepy II.

First Intermediate Period: 2280–2052

VII–VIII dynasty: period of anarchy about which very little is known. IX–X Herakleopolitan dynasties, contemporary with the beginning of the XI Theban dynasty.

Middle Kingdom: 2052–1780

XI dynasty (2052–2000): Mentuhotep.
XII dynasty (2000–1780): Ammenemes and Sesostris.

Second Intermediate Period: 1780–1580

XIII–XVII dynasty: more than fifty kings among which were the Hyksos invaders in the North (XV–XVI dynasty) and the kings of the Theban dynasty (Kamose, Ahmose) who reconquered the country.

New Kingdom: 1580–1085

XVIII dynasty (1580–1314): Amenophis and Tuthmosis, Hatshepsut, Akhenaten and the Amarna period, Tutankhamun, Horemheb.
XIX dynasty (1314–1200): Sethos I, Ramesses II, Merenptah.
XX dynasty (1200–1085): Ramesses III, Ramesses XI.

Third Intermediate Period: 1085–715

XXI dynasty (1085–950): Smendes and Psusennes at Tanis; priest kings at Thebes (Herihor, Pinudjem).
Three Libyan dynasties, parallel to a certain extent:
XXII dynasty of Bubastis (Sheshonq, Osorkon, Takelot); XXIII dynasty of Tanis (Pedubaste); XXIV dynasty of Sais (Bocchoris).

Low Period: 715–332

XXV 'Ethiopian' dynasty: Pi(ankh)i, Shabaka, Taharqa.
XXVI Saite dynasty (663–525): Psammetichus, Necho, Apries, Amasis.
XXVII dynasty (525–404): first period of Persian domination (Cambysses, Darius, Xerxes).
XXVIII–XXX dynasty: last indigenous dynasties of Sais, Mendes and Sebennytos (Nectanebo).

Greek Period: 332–30

Macedonian dynasty followed by Ptolemaic Dynasty (304–30): Ptolemies, Cleopatra VII.

Roman Period (30 BC – end 4th century AD)

followed by

Byzantine Period (395–638)

up to the

Arab Conquest (641)

Glossary

Akh, one of the components of the personality of any individual.

Amulets, small symbolic figures endowed with protective powers, worn both by the living and the dead.

Amun, Theban divinity who became dynastic god from the Middle Kingdom.

Anubis, funerary god personified by a black dog, *see* page 118.

Apis, sacred bull worshipped in Memphis where it was regarded as a manifestation of Ptah.

Atef, *see* crowns.

Aten, solary disc promoted to the position of unique god by Akhenaten.

Atum, one of the forms of the sun god Heliopolis, representing the sun at the end of its course.

Ba, one of the elements of man's personality corresponding more or less to the notion of soul.

Bastet, cat goddess worshipped at Bubastis in the Delta.

Bes, domestic spirit, protector of women giving birth.

Buchis, sacred bull of Armant assimilated to Montu.

Canopic jars, vases in which the viscera were preserved under the protection of the Four Sons of Horus.

Cartouche, elongated loop surrounding the last two names of Pharaoh.

Cenotaph, imitation tomb which does not contain the body of the deceased.

Crowns, Egyptian crowns are numerous and varied. They are the privilege of kings and gods. The simplest types are illustrated by the royal crowns: red and white crowns symbolizing respectively the kings from the North and the South; the *pschent* or double crown which combines both; the blue crown or khepresh incorrectly referred to as 'war helmet' and which only became common from the XVIII dynasty. The pleated *atef* crown, very similar to the white royal crown, belongs to the god Osiris. All the other crowns can be studied in relation to these simple types if they are broken down, or by adding various elements: diadem, double feather, *uraeus*, solar disc, ram horns. The *hem-hem* crown is for example composed of three *atefs* laid on ram horns and decorated with *uraeus* and solar discs. These composite head-dresses are sometimes very complex and their symbolic meaning escapes us more or less totally.

Duamutef, spirit with a dog's head, *see* the Four Sons of **Horus**.

Ennead, group of nine gods. The most important, known as 'Great Ennead', was that of Heliopolis.

False door, architectural element of the tomb through which the deceased can remain in contact with the world of the living.

Flabellum, large ceremonial fan.

Flagellum, *see* sceptres.

Geb, god of the ground, husband of Nut.

Hapi, spirit with the head of a baboon, *see* the Four Sons of **Horus**.

Hapy, personification of the high waters of the Nile which bring fertility to Egypt.

Hathor, goddess with a very complex personality personifying among other things love, dance, joy, and generally represented in the form of a cow or a young woman with a cow's head.

Heb-sed, royal jubilee festival celebrated in theory after thirty years' reign.

Hemhem, *see* crowns.

Herishef, ram god of Herakleopolis.

Horus, name used by the Egyptians for many different gods, the main one remaining Horus, son of Isis and Osiris.

Horus, Four Sons of, spirits who protect the viscera and ensure that it will function eternally. They were considered to be the four children begotten by Horus on his own mother. These were Imset (human-headed), Hapi (baboon-headed), Duamutef (dog-headed), and Qebehsenuf (falcon-headed): they were protected respectively by Isis, Nephthys, Neith and Selkis.

Hyksos, Greek version of an Egyptian expression referring to the Asian tribes which dominated Egypt between the Middle and the New Kingdoms.

Imhotep, architect and minister of King Djoser, worshipped as a healer god during the Late Period.

Imset, spirit with a man's head, *see* Four Sons of **Horus**.

Isis, one of the most popular Egyptian deities, sister and wife of Osiris and mother of Horus.

Jubilee, *see* Heb-sed.

Ka, manifestation of the energy of life which, like *akh* and *ba* is one of the elements of the human personality.

Khepesh, sort of scimitar, symbol of royal valour in battle.

Khepresh, *see* crowns.

Khepri, Heliopolitan god represented as a beetle personifying the changing sun.

Khnum, demiurge represented as a ram modelling his creatures on a potter's wheel.

Khons, lunar god often represented as a man with a falcon's head, regarded as the son of Amun and Mut.

Maat, goddess, protectress of the equilibrium of the universe, incarnating truth and justice.

Mammisi, word created by Champollion to refer to the buildings, within the temple walls, where were celebrated the mysteries of the birth of the sun gods.

Mastaba, Arabic word meaning 'bench' used by Egyptologists to refer to a private tomb of the Old Kingdom.

Min, god of fertility represented in ithyphallic form in Coptos and Akhmin.

Mnevis, sacred bull of Heliopolis incarnating the god Re.

Montu, ancient war god of Thebes where he was gradually supplanted by Amun.

Mut, vulture goddess of Thebes, wife of Amun and mother of Khons.

Naos, 'saint of saints' or tabernacle of the temple, *see* p. 164.

Neith, ancient war goddess from Sais assimilated by Athena by the Greeks.

Nekhbet, vulture goddess of El-Kab, protectress of High Egypt.

Nemes, royal head-dress composed of ribbed and pleated material wrapped around the head. It is identifiable particularly by the two pointed folds which it forms on each side of the forehead, with two pleats falling on each shoulder, and terminating in a ringed pleat at the back.

Nephthys, sister of Seth, Osiris and Isis who plays a discreet part in the legend of Osiris.

Nine Bows, the nine races, traditional enemies of Egypt and dominated by the king.

Nome, Greek word designating the administrative divisions of Egypt (twenty-two provinces for Upper Egypt and twenty for Lower Egypt during the Late period).

Nut, goddess of the canopy of the heavens, wife of Geb.

Ogdoad, group of eight primitive gods personifying the elements of the original chaos.

Osiris, god of the dead who has assimilated the personality of ancient funerary gods (Khentamenti, Sokaris...). Husband of Isis and posthumous father of Horus, he is said to have reigned among men.

Ostracon (pl. ostraca), chip of limestone or fragment of pottery often used as writing material as papyrus was expensive.

Protocol, five names of the Pharaoh as he ascends the throne, *see* p. 140

Pschent, *see* crowns.

Psychostasis, term which refers to the famous scene representing the weighing of the deceased's heart and not the actual 'weighing of the soul' as in Greek literature.

Ptah, god of Memphis where he was regarded as creator of the world and inventor of technology, one of the patrons of royalty and in charge of jubilee festivals.

Qebehsenuf, spirit with a falcon's head, *see* the Four Sons of **Horus**.

Re, supreme sun god, worshipped in Heliopolis from the earliest times, one of the most powerful personalities of the Egyptian pantheon.

Sakhmet, belligerent goddess represented as a lioness, wife of Ptah and mother of Nefertum.

Sceptres, term used to refer to batons of various sizes held by the kings and the gods. The most well-known are the sceptre-*was*, with a canine head, usually the attribute of male gods, and the *wadj*-sceptre (or papyrus rod) which is the attribute of goddesses. Those belonging to Osiris are the *heqa*-sceptre, hooked and derived from a shepherd's crook, and the flagellum, incorrectly referred to as 'fly whisk', which he holds across his chest, and later became the attribute of the deceased identified to this god.

Serdab, Arabic word used to refer to the walled corridors of mastabas where the statues of the deceased were stored.

Serekh, stylized frontage and map of a royal palace, bearing the 'name of Horus', first of the five royal names.

Seth, god from the oases, associated with the notion of evil because of his part in the legend of Osiris.

Shawabti, small mummy-shaped funerary figure, *see* p. 97.

Shen round cartouche symbolizing everything that

is encircled by the sun during its daily course.

Shendyt, pleated royal loin cloth.

Shu, god of the air and space who, with Tefnut, forms the first divine couple.

Sma-twy, Egyptian expression meaning 'reunite the two countries'. Decorative design symbolizing this reunion found on the sides of royal thrones.

Sobek, crocodile god worshipped in many parts of Egypt and particularly in Fayoum.

Sopdu, falcon god, patron of the oriental marches of the Delta.

Tatenen, ancient demiurge from Mephis personifying the first pieces of land to emerge from the chaos.

Ta-weret, hippopotamus goddess whose name means 'the great'; she protects the mother and child.

Thoth, lunar god represented in the form of an ibis, worshipped particularly in Hermopolis; inventor of the art of writing. He was the patron of scribes.

Royal titulature, *see* protcol.

Uraeus, Greek version of an Egyptian referring to the serpent found on the foreheads of gods and kings.

Ushabti *see* shawabti.

Wadjet, guardian goddess of Lower Egypt, represented as a cobra.

Table of concordance between various object numbers

Number in book	Exhibit number	*Journal d'Entrée*	Temporary register	*Catalogue Général*	Special inventory	Location in museum
1		34210		64863		P. 53
2		66628				P. 54
3		27434		14238		R. 43
4	4000–40003	35054		52008–11		R. 43
5		88123				P. 42
6	6255	65422				P. 42
	6256	65415				
7	6281	71298				R. 43
8	3056	32161				R. 43
9	3072			1		R. 43
10	6008	49158				R. 46
11		68921				P. 42 corridor
12	88			1426		R. 31
13	223			3–4		R. 32
14				1744		R. 32
15	4244			36143		P. 43
16	138	10062		14		R. 42
17	149	40679				R. 47
18	140			34		R. 42
19		56601				R. 47
20		39534				R. 36
21		30273		35		R. 42
22	6267	66626			14580	R. 48
23	79			1534		R. 41
24		44173				R. 42
25	175	34568		1413		R. 42
26	230–31	33034–35				R. 42
27	161	30796		60		P. 32
28				1536		R. 46
29	6080	46724				P. 27
30		66329				R. 23
31		56274				P. 34
32	623	47397				P. 48
33		36809				R. 21
34	4010	32158		14717–52701		P. 3
35				20561		R. 21
36	6116	46694		52702		P. 3
37	4221	21366				P. 43
38		43928				R. 22
39	340	31619		486		R. 22

Number in book	Exhibit number	_Journal d'Entrée_	Temporary register	_Catalogue Général_	Special inventory	Location in museum
40	3104	32868		28083		P. 37
41		44419				P. 34
42	506	20001		395		R. 16
43	3970	30876		52003		P. 3
44	280	30948		259		P. 32 corridor
45	3888	4663		28501		P. 47
46	4031	4624		52671		P. 3
47	415	36335		34002	11607	R. 12
48	6139	53113			11440	R. 11
49	428	43507 A				R. 12
50	6058 E	91396–7 & 9				P. 49
51	6228	63672				P. 49
52		36336		42080		R. 12
53	3822 A–E			24095	4218	P. 17
54		37534		42083	11568	R. 12
55	4257	38257				P. 43
56				51025	146	P. 13
57	4940	37525	2/12/26/17			P. 50
58		30172		5003		R. 11
59		38642				P. 34
60	5323	31382		4475 (not published)		P. 34
61	6257				11720	R. 12
62		67921–A			13223	R. 3
63	6206	59286				R. 3
64	484	29748		34177	13432	R. 3
65	487		30/10/26/12			R. 3
66	6207	47173			13228	R. 3
67		39590				P. 43
68	T. 219	60671				P. 4
69	T. 688	61789				P. 45
	T. 160	61791				
	T. 159	61833				
	T. 384	61783				
	T. 385	61859				
70	T. 89	61449				P. 25
71	T. 231	61901				P. 4
72	T. 447	61444				P. 45
73	T. 324	61467				P. 35
74	T. 459	61328				P. 15
75	T. 382	62081				P. 4
76	T. 994	60710				P. 35
77		38049			13812	R. 12
78		31629–30		779 A–B	13583	R. 15
79			5/7/24/15			R. 10
80		36407				P. 24
81	724	36722		42139		R. 14
82	1383			44047		P. 34

Number in book	Exhibit number	*Journal d'Entrée*	Temporary register	*Catalogue Général*	Special inventory	Location in museum
83	729			616		R. 9
84	2005			1935		P. 17
				1936 (not published)	4214–17	
				1938		
				1939		
85		38060		42146	13580	R. 15
86	2006	27303				P. 17
87	599	31408		34025		R. 13
88		31199 (?)			393	P. 29
89	674	36682		42150		R. 15
90	4371			25184		P. 24
91	3365		25/12/24/20		9427	P. 22
92	3794 A	26278		44101		P. 12 corridor
93	6289	85912				P. 11
94		85896–7				P. 2
95		86098		4396–4401		P. 24 corridor
96		36988		42194	13643	R. 20
97	37426		42197			R. 20
98		37383		42228		R. 24
99		37150			893	R. 25
100	1185			560		R. 25
101		37852		42237		R. 20
102		67871				R. 30
103		37341				R. 24
104	791			39145		R. 24
105		30335				P. 19
106	4480	22081		38447		P. 19
107	3	37206		1199		R. 48
108		28512		838		R. 34
109	790			70021		R. 24
110	1294	47398 A		29307		R. 49
111	6020	46591				R. 24
112	6036	46592				R. 49
113	4752	46341				P. 19 corridor
114		67910				P. 24
115	6159	54313				R. 34
116	6102			26752 (not published)		P. 39
117	6111	67928				P. 39
118	4310			33244		P. 14
119				27480	1014	P. 34
120		40232			1204	P. 40

Index

Aahmes 86
Abasha Pasha 10
Abbas Hilmi II 14
Abd el-Qurna, Sheik 102
Aboukir 148
Abusir 51
Abydos 23, 24, 43, 72, 73, 78, 86, 87, 93, 120
Académie des Inscriptions et Belles Lettres 10, 13, 14, 86
Aegyptiaca 34
Aelian 161
Aeolus 174
Aesculapius 34
Ahhotep 11, 12, 13, 85
—coffin cover of 83
Ahmose 84, 86
—stela of 86–87
Ahmose-Nofretiri 87
Aida 13, 38
Akh 181
Akhenaten 100, 109, 111, 117, 163
—head of 104–107
Alexander Severus 178
Alexander the Great 169, 171
Alexandria 10, 16
Alexandra Museum 174
Amarna 103, 107, 108, 110, 111, 122, 124, 127, 136, 144, 149
—Royal Family 109–110
Amasis 163
Amenemheb 127
Ameneminet and family 126–127
Amenemope 144, 147
Amenhotep, colossus of 162–163
Amenirdis the Elder, statue of 156–157
Amenirdis the Younger 157
Amenophis 100
Amenophis II 92, 93, 114
Amenophis III 93, 96, 98, 100, 102, 104, 107, 126, 127, 136, 138, 156, 162
—statuette of 95
Amenophis IV *See* Akhenaten
Amenothes 163
Ammenemes 75
Ammenemes I 123
Ammenemes III 82
—bust of 79
—pectoral of 80
Amon-Re 92, 121, 134, 138, 150, 151, 152
Amosis 86
amulets 181
Amun 64, 68, 88, 95, 109, 121, 124,

136, 138, 139, 150, 152, 156, 163, 179, 181
—statuette of 123–124
—temple of 68, 92, 144, 154
—vase of 134
Amun-Djoser-Akhet 90
Anastasi, Consul 9
Anhotep 136
Anubis 57, 136, 171, 181
—statue of 117
Any in his chariot 108
Apis 161, 167, 172, 181
Apries 163
archaeological sites 17
Armais 46
Armant 172
Arsaphes 153, 176
Arthribis 52
Art Négre Exhibition, Paris 179
Asasif 66
Ashmolean Museum 24, 29
Asklepios 162
Assyrians 179
Aswan 15, 177
Asyut 78
atef 181
Aten 104, 108, 109, 111, 181
—temple of 102
Athena 65
Athribis 167, 171
Atum 68, 78, 121, 161, 181

ba 181
Baraize 89
Barbarians 178
Barsanti, Alexandre 59, 108
Bastet 181
basin, stone 28–29
bas-relief, archaising 167–168
Bellefonds, Louis Linants de 10
Benha 52, 171
Benson, Margaret 155
Berlin 51
Berlin Museum 83
Bes 131, 171, 181
Biban el-Muluk 141
Bonaparte 9
Bonnefoy 11
Book of the Dead 78, 93, 97, 98, 111, 115, 136, 167, 169
Borchardt, Ludwig 31, 51, 61
Boston Museum 46
bowl, blue faience 90–91
bracelets 24–25
British Museum 162
Brunton, Guy 74
Bruyère 90
Bubastis 167
Bucheum of Hermonthis 172
Buchis bull 172–174, 181
Bulaq 11, 12, 13, 14

Busiris 73, 120
Buto 167

Caernarfon, Lord 112, 117, 144
Caesar, Julius 98
Cairo Porter 60
Canopic jars 181
Canopus 148
Capart 60
cat sarcophagus 99
Caracalla 178
carpenter's tools, models of 90
Carter, Howard 112, 116, 117, 118, 144
cartouche 181
cenotaph 181
Champollion, Jean François 9, 160
Charlottenburg Museum, West Berlin 96,107
Cheops 40, 144
Cheops, statue of 43
Chephren 13
Chephren, statue of 45–46
Chevrier, Henri 133
Cleopatra I 174
Coffin Texts 78
Coxe, Eckley B. 179
crown 181

Dakar 179
Daninos 38
Darb el-Melek 111
Daressy 64, 102, 141, 171
Dashur 50, 61, 80, 82
Davis, Theodore 98, 112
Deir el-Bahri 84, 90, 114, 142, 143, 163
—temple of 64, 66, 67, 88
Deir el-Medina 89, 90, 135, 163
Della Valle, Pietro 177
Description de l'Egypte 9
Deutschen Orient-Gesellschaft 51
Devéria 85
Dieter, Arnold 90
Diocletian 172
Diodorus of Sicily 130
Dira abou el-Naga 84
Djedamuniufankh 142
Djedthothiufankh 169
Djedher 167
Djedher-the-Saviour, statue of 171
Djehutihotep, tomb of 133
Djer 24
Djoser 28, 29, 35, 36, 45, 162
—statue of 32–34, 32
Domains of Sahure, Procession of 51–52
Dourgan, Marcel 14
Dromos 10
Drovetti, Consul 9
Duamutef 149, 181

Duathathor-Henttawi 143
Durham Museum 102

Ecole Civile 10
Egyptian Exploration Fund 67, 86
Egypt Exploration Society 110, 172
el-Beled, Sheikh 13
—statue of 48–50
Elagabalus 178
El-Ashmunein 168
El-Bersha 77, 133
El-Lahun 74
Emery, W. B. 29
Ennead 181
Eugénie, Empress 13, 86
Exodus 138
Ezbekiyya 10
Ezbet el-Walda 26

Faiyum 79
—portraits 177
falcon, head of 70
false door 181
Farouk, King 26, 175
Festival of Negro Arts 179
firman 9, 10
Firth, Cecil Mallaby 32, 50
flabellum 181
flagellum 181
Florence 178
Floris, Matteo 11
Fluviale, Compagnie 11
Fouad, King 172

Gayet, Albert Jean 177
Geb 181
Gebel Barkal 154
Gebelein 65
Gerzean period 22
Gilukhepa 96
Giza 12, 14, 14, 53
—pyramid of 45, 46
Gozzoli, Benozzo 118
Great Pyramid 144
Great Sphinx 53
Grébaut, E. 14, 31, 57
Greek National Museum,
    Athens 160
Green 59
Gregory XIII, Pope 90

Hadrian 178
Hakoris 164
Hall 67
Hapi 149, 181
Hapu 162
Hapy 100, 181
Harkhuf 167
Haroeris 98
harpist, statuette of 78
Harpocrates 175, 176

Harvard University 46
Hat, shawabti of 111
Hathor 67, 91, 124, 130, 150, 156,
    159, 171, 181
—temple of 96
Hatiay 102
Hatshepsut 89, 96, 123, 163
—sphinx of 88
—temple of 88
Hawara 177
Heb-sed 35, 181
Heliopolis 32, 40, 109, 123, 140, 161
Helwan 26
Hemaka 15
hemhem 181
Henttawy 147
Hephaistos 161
Heqakheperre Shoshenq 144
Herakleopolis 152, 153, 176
Herakles 176
Herbert, Fifth Earl of Caernarfon See
    Caernarfon, Lord
Herishef 153, 176, 181
Hermopolis 121, 123, 161, 169
Herodotus 45, 79, 100, 144, 161
Hesat 78
Hesesi 56
Hesyre 37
—wooden panel of 35–37
Hetepdif 31
Hetepheres 15, 144
—palanquin 61
Hetepsekhemwy 31
Hierakonpolis 24, 29, 59, 70, 93
hippopotamus figurine 74
Hont-taui 143
Hor 149
—cube statue of 153
—ka of 82
Horemheb 126
Horemkhauf 70
Horhetep 168
Horus 68, 100, 117, 122, 140, 149,
    164, 171, 175, 181
—statuette of 160
Hygie 163
Hyksos 61, 85, 181

Idfu 24, 70
—temple of 122, 164
Ihy 122
Imhotep 32, 34, 160, 181
Imouthes 34, 162
Imouthes-Asklepios 163
Imset 149, 182
Imset, Cuamutef 100
Institut Français d'Archéologie
    Orientale 64
Inyotef 62, 84
—stela of 72
Ipet 159

Ipet-Sut 151
Ipi 61, 62
Irni, stela of 26
Irunefer 136
Isetemkheb 147
Isis 70, 94, 98, 99, 115, 136, 147,
    149, 153, 159, 182
Isma'iliya 16
Ismail Pasha 11
Israel stela 136–138
Itjtawy 70
Itji 58
Iyneferti 136

jars, canopic 148–49
Journal Officiel 9

ka 182
Kaaper 48
Kaemhesit, family of 56
Kaemrehu 55
—mastaba of 54–55
Kamose 84, 86
Kansas City Museum 164
Karanog 179
Karnak 15, 68, 75, 92, 95, 98, 109,
    123, 124, 130, 133, 134, 138, 140,
    150, 151, 152, 153, 154, 155, 157,
    159, 162
—water clock 98
Karomama 160
Karoy 96
Kawit, sarcophagus of 67, 138
Kha, lamp of 100
Kha-ba-Sahure 52
Khabekhent 136
Khaemhet 104
Khamerernebty, King and Queen 46
Khartum Museum 155
Khasekhem 59
—statue of 29, 30, 70
Khasekhemwy 29, 59
Khentkhas 171
Kheperkare 68, 164
khepesh 182
khepresh 182
Khepri 78, 182
Kheruef 104
Khnemmaatre 164
Khnum 182
Khons 123, 134, 138, 147, 182
Khonsu 136
knives 21
Kom el-Ahmar 70
Kom es-Sultan 43

Labyrinth 79
Lacau, Pierre 117
Lady of Sais 64
Lauer, Jean-Phillipe 28, 29, 35, 50
Lefebvre, Gustave 169

Legrain 68, 98
Lenormant, Charles 10
Lepsius, Richard 93
Lesseps, Ferdinand de 10
Leyden 102
Licht 70
Liverpool Museum 102
Loret, V. 14, 93, 103, 112, 114, 126
Louvre 11, 48, 73, 96, 107, 158, 159, 160, 178
Luxor 15, 64, 84, 138, 152, 154, 172
Luynes, Duc de 45

Maat 136, 182
Maatkara 88
MacIver 179
Madamud 76
Maesa, Julia 178
Maherpra 93
Maidum 38
Maidum Geese 40, 42
Maleten, Prince of Nubia 179
Mallawi 16
Mammaea, Julia 178
Mammisi 182
mamour 11
Manetho 34
Mariette, Auguste 10, 16, 35, 45, 48, 72, 83, 85, 142, 144, 159, 161, 167, 174
Maspero, Sir Gaston 14, 39, 61, 68, 82, 112, 131, 135, 143, 179
mastaba 182
Maunier 84
Maxmillian, Archduke 10
Maya 126
Medinet Habu 140
Meir 60
Meketre 62, 64
Memnon, colossi of 136, 162
Memphis 10, 31, 68, 99, 100, 123, 126, 160
Mendes 163
Menkaret 121
Menkheprure 93
Menkheperre See Tuthmosis III
Mentuhotep I 62, 67, 88
—bas-relief of 64
Merenptah 112, 136, 138, 144
Merenre 59
—statue of 59
Mereruka 55, 56
Meresger 128
Meritaten 109, 117, 121
Meroe 179
Meryt 73
Metropolitan Museum of Art, New York 62, 66, 70, 98
Mimaut, Jean François 9
Min 182
Ministry of Public Education 10

mirror handle 130
mirror box cover 143–144
Misraïm 138
Mit Faris 79
Mit Rahina 31
Mnevis 182
model, sculptor's 172
Mohammed Ali 9
Mond 64, 172
Montemhet, statuette of 155–156
Montet, Pierre 144
Montu 64, 152, 172, 182
Morgan, Jacques de 14, 52, 80, 82
Musée du Petit Palais, Paris 102
Mut 123, 130, 134, 138, 182
—temple of 155
Mutnodjmet 144
Mycerinus 48
—triad 46

Naga el-Deir 78
Naharina 96
Nakhtmin, wife of 124–126
Nakhtnebef 164
naos 182
Napata 154, 179
Napoleon III 11
Napoleon, Prince 11
Naqada II period 22, 23
Narmer 24
Nasser, Lake 179
Naville 67, 164
Nebhepetre Mentuhotep 64
Nebkheprure 115
Nectanebo I 164
Nectanebo II 164, 167, 172
Neferirkare 53, 59
Neferkheprure 110
Nefertiti 107, 109, 121
—portrait of 107
Nefertum 161
Nefermaat 40
Neith 149, 182
Nekhbet 81, 119, 182
Nekhen 70
nemes 182
Nepherite 164
Nephthys 146, 149, 153, 182
Nero 178
Netjerikhet 32, 35, 36
Niankhpepy-the-Black, statue of 60
Nimaatre 81, 82
nine bows 182
Ninetjer 31
Nitocris 157, 159
Niuserre 48
—pyramid of 55
Nofret 15, 40
Nofret, statue of 38
nome 182

Notice des Principaux Monuments Exposés…à Boulaq 174
Nout 98
Nubheteptikhered 82
Nubia 179
Nun 161, 171
Nut 100, 144, 167, 182

Ogdoad 182
ointment jar 102
Onuris 155
Osiris 35, 72, 78, 93, 94, 98, 99, 111, 114, 118, 120, 122, 136, 147, 149, 150, 153, 161, 167, 182
—temple of 43
Osorkon I 150
Osorkon II 144, 151, 152
Osorkon III 157
—statuette of 151–152
ostracon 127, 182
—plan of royal tomb 140–141
Ottoman Empire 9

Pabasa 159
Pakhal 136
Palermo Stone 58
palette, Libyan 23
palette, Narmer 23, 29
papyrus, satirical 138–139
—Great Harris 139
—Turin 141
Paris Exhibition 13
Pasbakhaenniut 147
pendants, fly-shaped 85–86
Pendlebury, John 107
Pennsylvania, University of 179
Pepy I 29, 70
—statue of 58–59
Pepy II 167
Perert 98
Petamenope, statue of as a scribe 157–158
Petekhons 167
Petosiris, coffin of 168–171
Petrie, Sir W. M. Flinders 24, 40, 43, 45, 74, 96, 107, 109, 136, 144, 177
Philadelphia Exhibition 13
Philip Arrhidaeus 171
Pi(ankh)i 154, 157
Pinudjem I 143
Pi-Sopdu 164
Pliny 46
Polyaratos 163
prophet of Montu See Hor
princess, statue of 132–133
protocol 182
Psammetichus I 156, 157, 159
Psammetichus II 155, 179
Psammuthi 164
pschent 182
Psusennes I 147

—inner coffin of 144–146
psychostasis 182
Ptah 34, 68, 100, 104, 121, 126, 133, 182
—statuette of 160–161
Ptahhotep 55
Ptah-Sokar-Osiris 136
Ptahmose 127
Ptolemy 68
Ptolemy II Philadelphus 163, 176
Ptolemy V Epiphanes 172, 174, 176
Puech 14
Pyramid Texts 78

Qasr el-Nil 14
Qebehsenuf 149, 182
Qena 21, 85
Quibell, James Edward 21, 28, 29, 35, 56, 59, 70, 98, 167
Qurna 142
Qurnet Murai 162

Ra 73, 78, 98
Ra Horakhty 99
Rahotep 15, 40, 136
—statue of 38
Ramesses II 72, 89, 112, 130, 136, 140, 144
—bust of 131–132
—sphinx of 134
Ramesses III 98, 139–140
Ramesses IV 141
Ramesses VI 112
Ramesses IX 141
Ramesses XI 98
Ramessid era 92
Ramose 104, 124, 136
Raneb 31
Ranekhou 136
Rawer, panel of 53–54
Re 110, 119, 141, 171, 182
Re-Harakhty 142
Reisner, G. 46, 78, 144, 154
Reret 159
Rifaud, Jean Jacques 144
Ro-Setau 167
Rosetta Stone 172
Royal Canon of Turin 82
royal head 163–164
royal tomb, plan of 140
Royal Tombs of Tanis 147

Sabatier, Raymond 11
Saft el-Hinna, naos of 164–165
Sahure 51, 52
Said Pasha 11, 85
Sais 144, 160
Saite epoch 163, 167
Saite era 34, 50, 157, 166
Saite formula 156
Saite renaissance 153

Sakhmet 121, 126, 161, 182
Salt, Consul 9
Saqqara 10, 26, 29, 32, 35, 48, 50, 52, 55, 56, 57, 61, 103, 126, 161, 167, 172, 176, 177
Sarcophagus Texts 77
satyr, statuette of 174
Sauneron 164
sceptre 182
Schiaparelli, Ernesto 100
sculptor's models 172
Sekhemrekhutawy 82
Selim Hassan 53
Selkis 149, 171
Senenmut 88
Sennudjem, burial chamber door of 135
Sepi, sarcophagus of 77
Seqenenre 84
Serabit el-Khadim 96
Serapeum 10
serdab 182
Serefka 43
serekh 182
Sesostris 75
Sesostris I 64, 68
Sesostris II, uraeus of 73
Sesostris III 72, 80
—head of 76
Seth 98, 117, 118, 122, 140, 176, 182
Sethos I 72, 138
—colossus of 128
Sethos II 122
Settgast, Jürgen 90
shawabti 182
Shebensopdet 152
Sheikh Farag 78
Shemu 98
shen 182
shendyt 183
Shepenwepet I 157
Shepenwepet II 157
Sheshi 57, 58
Shoshenq 147
Shoshenq, statuette usurped by 150
Shoshenq III 144
Shu 183
Siamun 102
Sikaherka, statue of 75
Sinai 96
Sitamun 72
Sithathor 73
sma-twy 183
Smith, William Stevenson 40
Snofru 50, 144
—pyramid of 38
Sobek 79, 183
Sokaris 55, 161
Soleb 138
Somtus-Herakles, statuette of 175–176

Sopdu 164, 183
Sphinx 46
spirit statue 179
Steindorff, Georg 24
stela, false door 56
—funerary 142
—Harmakhis 142
—Israel 136–138
Step Pyramid 28, 32, 57, 126
—faience panel from 34–35
Strabo 10
Suez Canal 11, 13
Syria 144

Taharqa 156
—head of 154–155
Tahesyt 127
Takhos 167
Takushit 160
Tanis 15, 79, 98, 131, 144, 149, 177
—Royal Tombs, tableware from 147
Tatenen 83, 160, 183
Ta-weret 159, 183
Tell Atrib 171
Tell el-Armana 107, 108, 110
Tell el-Farain 167
Tenethapi 167
Teos, sarcophagus cover of 166–167
Teti, pyramid of 56
Tetisheri 86, 87
Tewfik 14
Thebes 64, 68, 86, 88, 104, 109, 111, 123, 128, 131, 136, 142, 144, 149, 154, 157, 162
The Book of Coming forth by Day 93
Thoeris, statue of 159
Thoth 94, 98, 99, 116, 121, 169, 183
Ti 55
Tiaa 92
Tiye 98, 107
—statuette of 96
Tjaiherpato 167
Tjay, statue of 103–104
Tjehenu 24
Tjehiau 169
Tjuyu 98
Tmai el-Amdid 163
Tod 64, 163
tools, construction 132–133
triad, Mycerinus 46
Tuna el-Gebel 169
Turin Museum 100, 131, 169
Tutankhamun 15, 16, 74, 98, 124, 126, 141, 144, 149, 150, 176
—amulets of 115, 116
—anthropoid coffin of 112–114
—jewel casket of 116
—model boat of 120
—pectoral of 116
—scribe's palette of 121
—with harpoon 121

—wooden casket of 118–119
Tutankhaton *See* Tutankhamun
Tuthmosis, Prince 100
Tuthmosis I 86
Tuthmosis III 68, 86, 88, 93
—statue of 89
Tuthmosis IV 92, 93, 95, 131

Universal Exhibition, London 11
Universal Exhibition, Paris 12, 86, 143, 174
uraeus 73, 182

Userkaf 50

Valley of the Kings 84, 93, 98, 100, 112, 132, 144
Valley Temple 46
vase, antelope 22
vases, stone 27–28
Vassali, L. 40
Vatican 178
Vienna Exhibition 13

Wadi Tumilat 164

Wadjet 167, 183
Wendjebauendjedet 147
Wepwawet 171
Winlock, Herbert

young woman, portrait of 177–178
Youssef Zia Effendi 10
Yuya 96
—shawabti of 97–98

Zagazig 16, 164
Zaki Saad 26

Aubin Imprimeur
LIGUGÉ, POITIERS

Achevé d'imprimer en octobre 1987
Nº d'édition 6936/2304 / Nº d'impression P 25423
Dépôt légal, 5762-novembre 1987
Imprimé en France (Printed in France)
ISBN 2.01.012297.6